IMAGES
of America

STREETCARS OF CHATHAM COUNTY

PHOTOGRAPHS FROM THE COLLECTION OF THE GEORGIA HISTORICAL SOCIETY

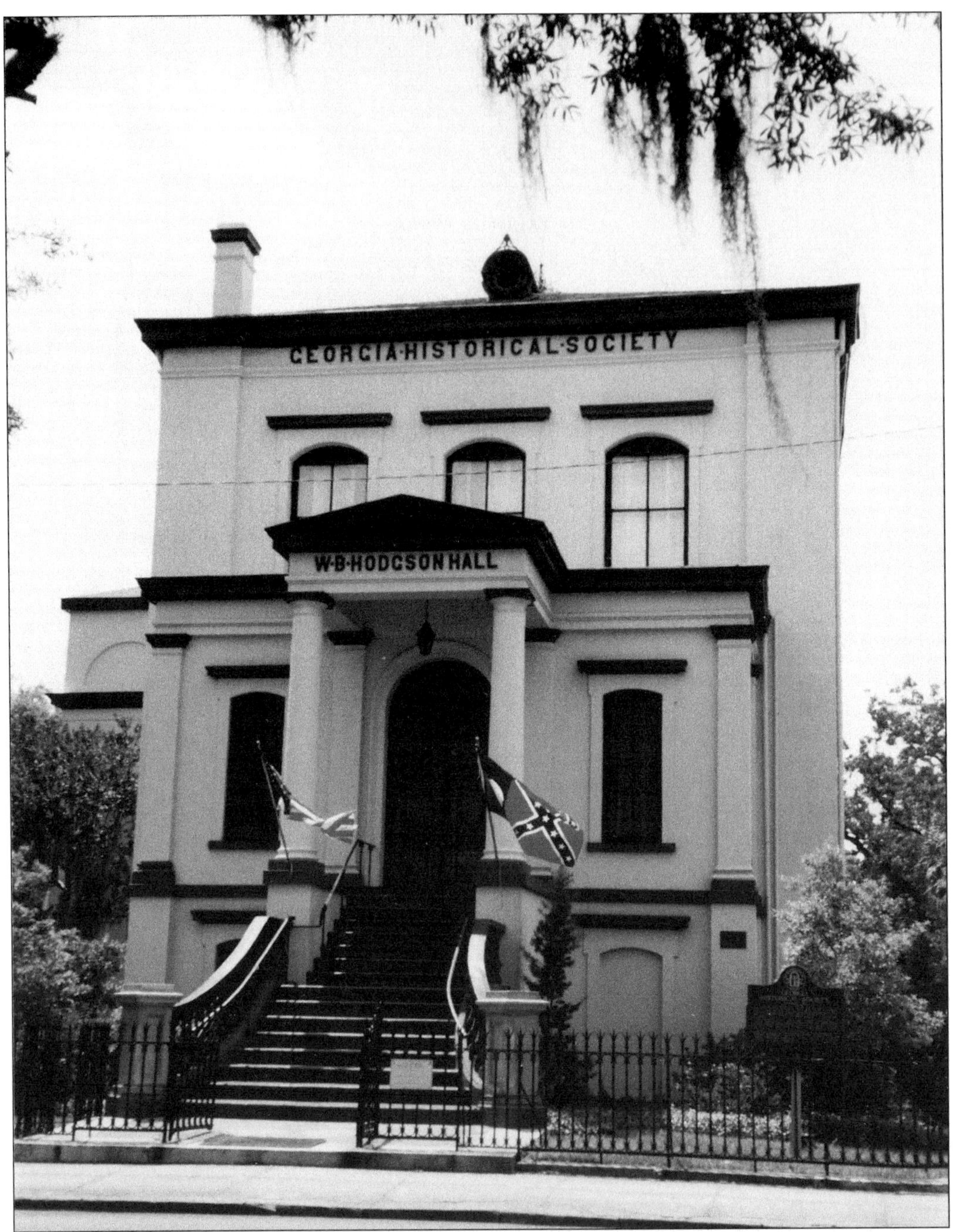

The Georgia Historical Society is headquartered in Hodgson Hall in Savannah. Hodgson Hall, named for William B. Hodgson, became the third home of the Society in September of 1875. The building was officially dedicated on February 14, 1876, and has been the Society's statewide headquarters ever since. Housed within Hodgson Hall is one of the finest library collections of archives, manuscripts, photographs, books, and maps relating to the state of Georgia. The library is free and open to the public. Hodgson Hall is located at 501 Whitaker Street, Savannah, GA, 31499.

IMAGES
of America

STREETCARS OF CHATHAM COUNTY

PHOTOGRAPHS FROM THE COLLECTION OF THE GEORGIA HISTORICAL SOCIETY

Mary Beth D'Alonzo

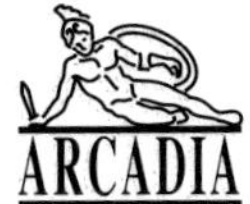

ISBN 0-7385-0179-4

Published by Arcadia Publishing,
an imprint of Tempus Publishing, Inc.
2 Cumberland Street
Charleston, SC 29401

Printed in Great Britain.

Library of Congress Catalog Card Number: 99-63304

For all general information contact Arcadia Publishing at:
Telephone 843-853-2070
Fax 843-853-0044
E-Mail arcadia@charleston.net

For customer service and orders:
Toll-Free 1-888-313-BOOK

Visit us on the internet at http://www.arcadiaimages.com

Contents

Acknowledgments 6

Introduction 7

1. The Early Lines: 1869 to 1888 9

2. Suburban Destinations 31

3. Electrification: 1889 to 1902 55

4. Local Stops 75

5. The Electric Companies 107

Index 127

ACKNOWLEDGMENTS

The impetus for this book was my concern for animals and their habitats. Human encroachment into seemingly empty land has devastating effects upon its natural inhabitants. To better understand today's construction practices, I decided to examine the history of Chatham County's expansion. Cheryl Brauner knew of old streetcar tracks near Bonaventure Cemetery and suggested that I look into their history. I realized this would be a good means to study the movement of Savannah's population. I am thankful to Cheryl for all her ideas, her help proofreading, and her constant input and encouragement

All photographs and images used in this book came from the collections of the Georgia Historical Society (GHS), and most of my research was done in GHS's library and archives. I am grateful to a number of people for their assistance with this book. For allowing me time to accomplish much of the research, I thank Frank Wheeler. For their help editing, I thank Jessica Burke, Frank Wheeler, Kim Ball, Janice D'Alonzo, and Anne D'Alonzo. For help while researching, I again thank Kim and Jessica as well as Coby Linton. For her technical and professional expertise, I thank Mandi Johnson. I am also grateful for Jessica's input and ideas, which helped me clarify some of my thoughts. In addition, I would like to acknowledge Sam.

INTRODUCTION

The streetcars of Chatham County began operation in 1869. A letter to the editor in the July 26, 1865, *Savannah Daily Herald* asked the question, "Why can't we have a street railroad on some of our principle streets?. . . Let some influential men take hold of this at once." In Savannah, as in so many towns, land development and the creation and expansion of public transportation were inextricably related. Those individuals who owned much of the land surrounding Savannah had a vested interest in exposing to the public the attractions of their lands in the hope of improving their own businesses. Often, it was these people who were instrumental in establishing the various systems of transportation. To increase patronage of the streetcar lines, many types of activities were planned, and amenities were built.

For their part, those who were unable to afford their own means of transportation welcomed the opportunity to travel outside Savannah for the purpose of residency, employment, recreation, and health. Frequently stated purposes for creating a system of transportation included access to lower rents and more jobs for the working class, bigger and better homes for the upper class, and the creation of vacation spots with mass appeal. Streetcars were billed as being beneficial to the population at large.

The people involved with streetcars, through ownership or patronage, helped determine the directions in which the cars traveled. One way of discovering more about a community is to examine everyday destinations and activities. Home, work, and vacation locations provide glimpses into the life of the individual and the community at large.

The first mule or horse-drawn streetcars of Savannah left the city for its suburban hinterlands. In December of 1866, The Savannah, Skidaway, and Seaboard Railroad Company was incorporated to run lines to Thunderbolt, Isle of Hope, Montgomery, Beaulieu, and White Bluff. In March of 1868, enough stock in the company had been purchased to begin building the line. Later that year, the company received permission to run lines over streets within Savannah. The *Savannah Morning News* gave regular updates on the progress of construction and on January 29, 1869, stated, "Our street railroad is now an established fact."

Through the years, many companies were formed to provide service to various parts of Chatham County. The early cars were pulled by mules or horses, or powered by steam. Beginning in 1890, horses and steam engines were slowly replaced by overhead electric wires.

Through mergers and acquisitions, the number of companies was gradually reduced. George Parsons, a businessman from Kennebunk, Maine, began buying the small independent lines. By 1901, most of Chatham County's streetcar lines were consolidated into what was referred to as the Parsons System of Street and Suburban Railways. In 1902, he sold this system to Savannah Electric Company. Electric streetcars lasted another 44 years before being phased out by gasoline powered buses. The last electric streetcar in Savannah ran on August 25, 1946. The pages that follow trace in greater detail the development of Chatham County's streetcar companies and lines.

One

THE EARLY LINES: 1869–1888

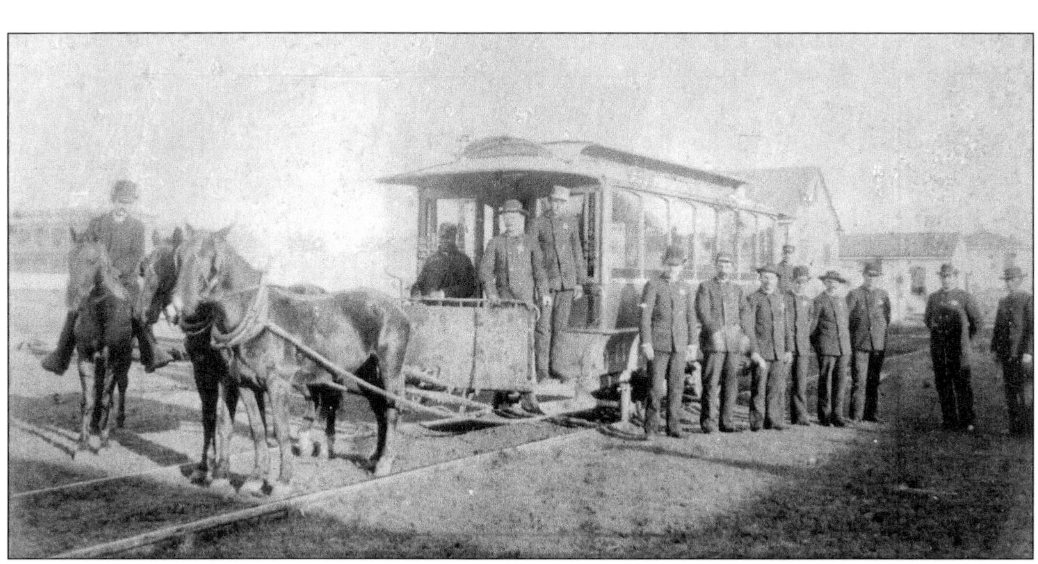

On December 20, 1866, the General Assembly of the State of Georgia granted a charter of incorporation to the Savannah, Skidaway, and Seaboard Railroad Company (S.S. & S.). On July 22, 1868, Mayor Edward C. Anderson and the alderman of Savannah passed an ordinance granting the company the exclusive right-of-way over all city streets for a period of ten years.

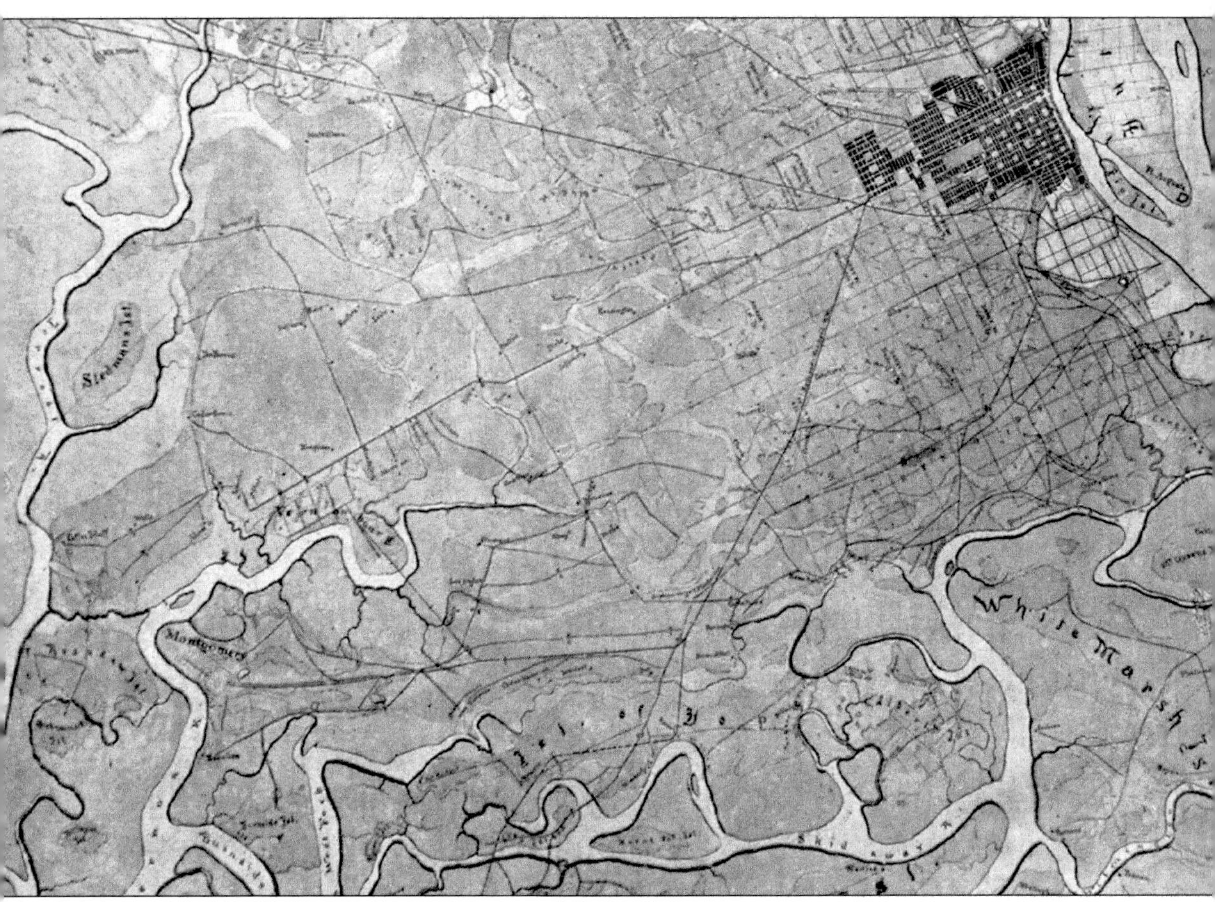

Pictured here is an early map of Chatham County. The first streetcar lines were planned to run to the outlying areas that gradually became resorts as well as suburban communities. Lines ran to Thunderbolt and Isle of Hope. Branch lines ran to White Bluff and Montgomery. Stops were made at Catholic and Bonaventure Cemeteries, Sand Fly, Bethesda, and Beaulieu.

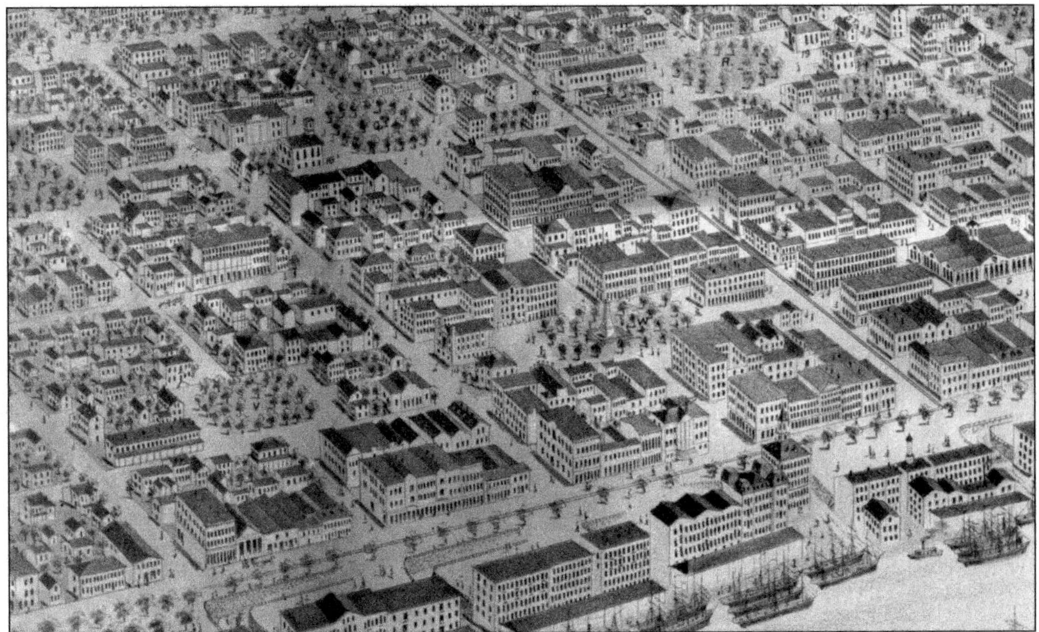

Ground was broken for the S.S. & S. Depot on July 15, 1868, near the toll gate on White Bluff Road (near what is now Thirty-seventh Street) on land given to the company by David R. Dillon. Preparatory work on the main line to Isle of Hope and two branches (one to Montgomery and another across the Vernon River to White Bluff) was finished in December. Rails were laid, starting at Bay and Drayton Streets running to Whitaker Street and then toward the depot. Two horse-drawn cars with a seating capacity of 12 each were put on the track in January 1869. Construction allowed them to proceed as far south as Charlton Street. By springtime, cars were running to Isle of Hope. This 1891 print, *Bird's Eye View of Savannah, Georgia,* by Augustus Koch, shows tracks laid on Bay and Whitaker Streets.

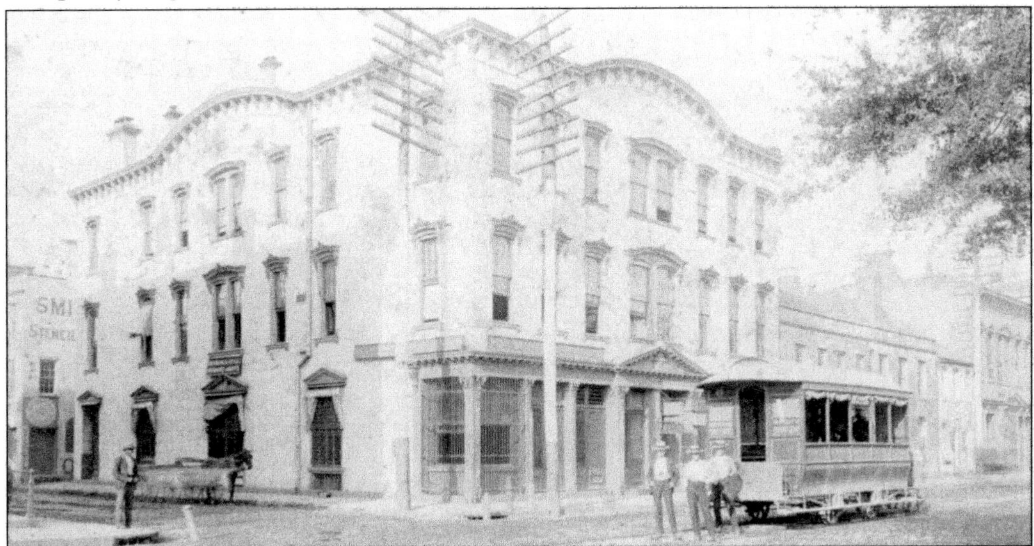

In November, cars were also running along Bay and West Broad Streets between the City Exchange and the Central of Georgia Railroad Buildings. This is a later view along Bay Street of a horse-drawn car.

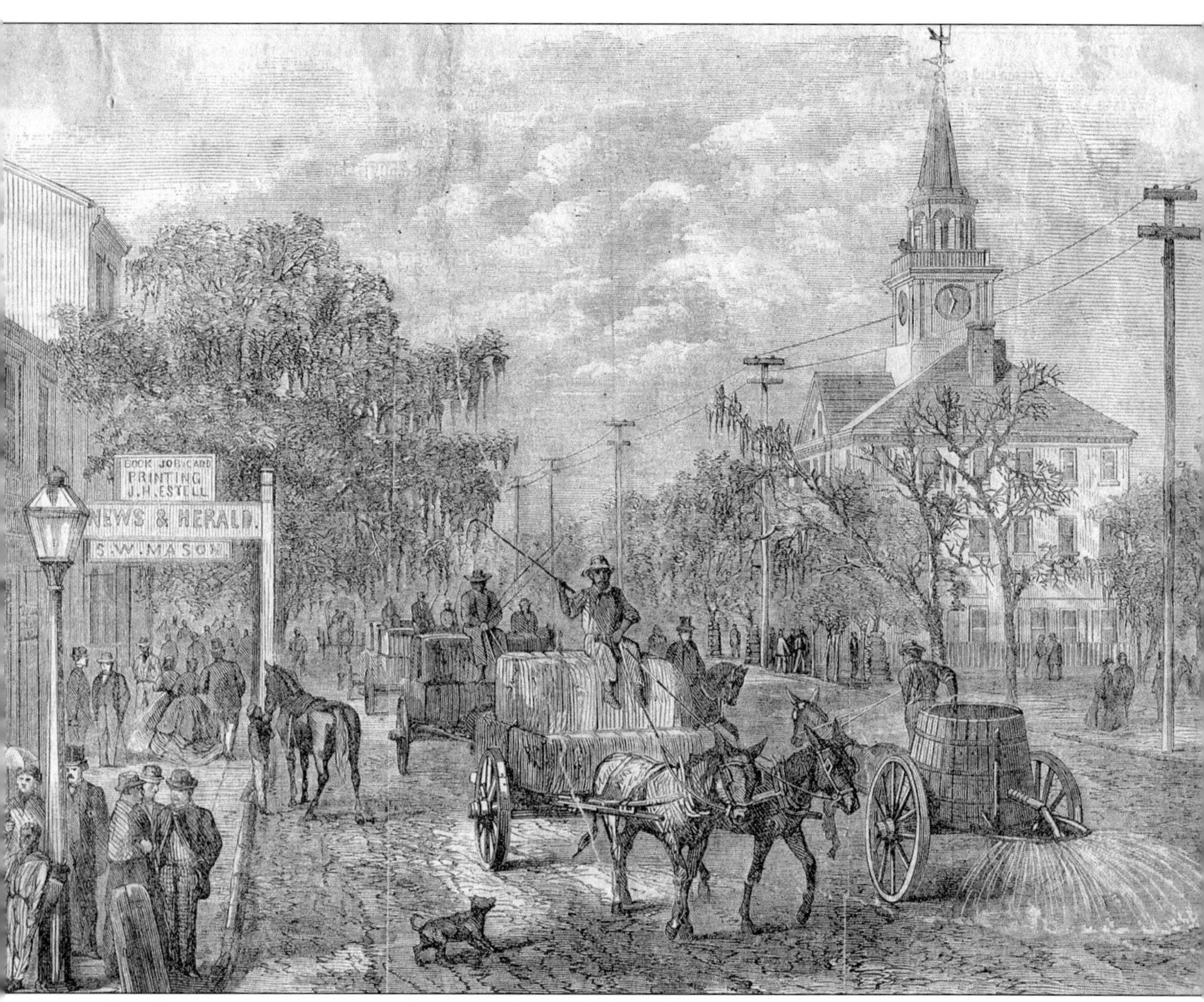

Freight service was permitted in 1869, but it did not begin until 1873. In December, a turntable was built at the corner of Bay and Drayton Streets to accommodate the waterfront freight activity. This print, published on September 21, 1867, in *Frank Leslie's Illustrated Newspaper*, shows Bay Street immediately west of its intersection with Drayton. The print also shows that dust was a problem on roads. The same was true on train tracks. Savannah passed an ordinance in 1883 requiring tracks to be watered to keep the dirt down. In both cases, specially-equipped cars did the job.

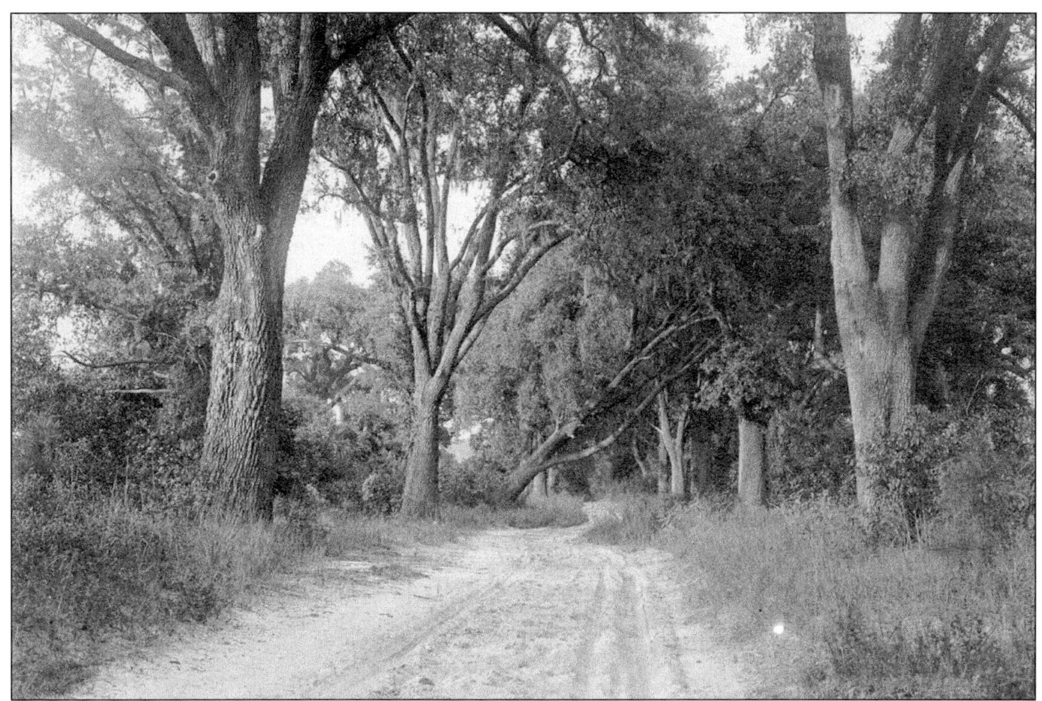

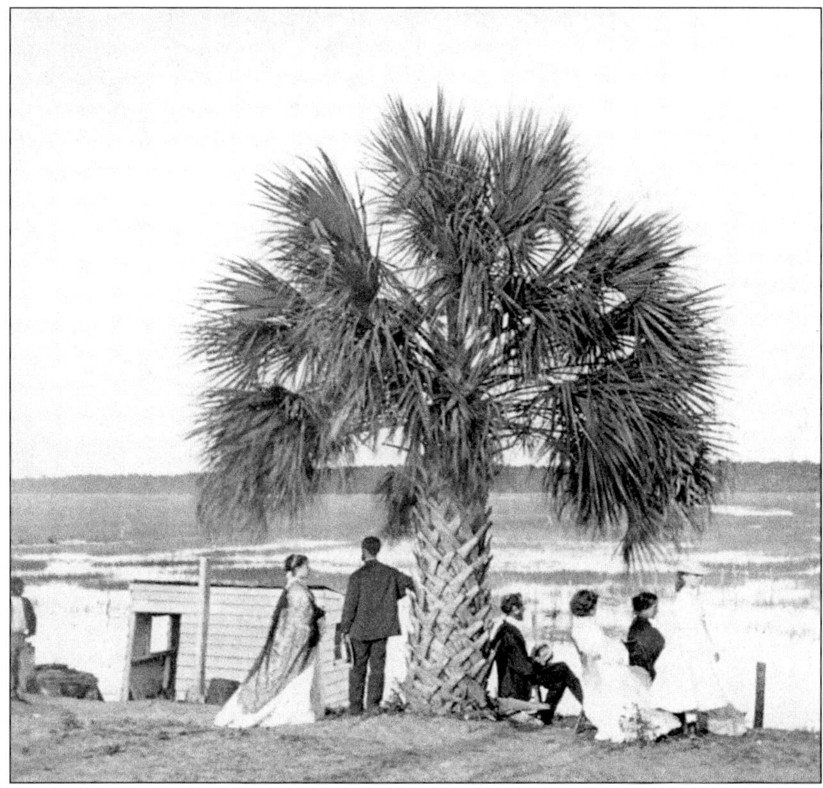

Excursion trains operated to Isle of Hope in March 1870. The top picture illustrates the potential difficulty of travel over sandy, rutted roads for those fortunate enough to have their own transportation. Streetcars eased the difficulty. The bottom picture shows a group relaxing at Isle of Hope.

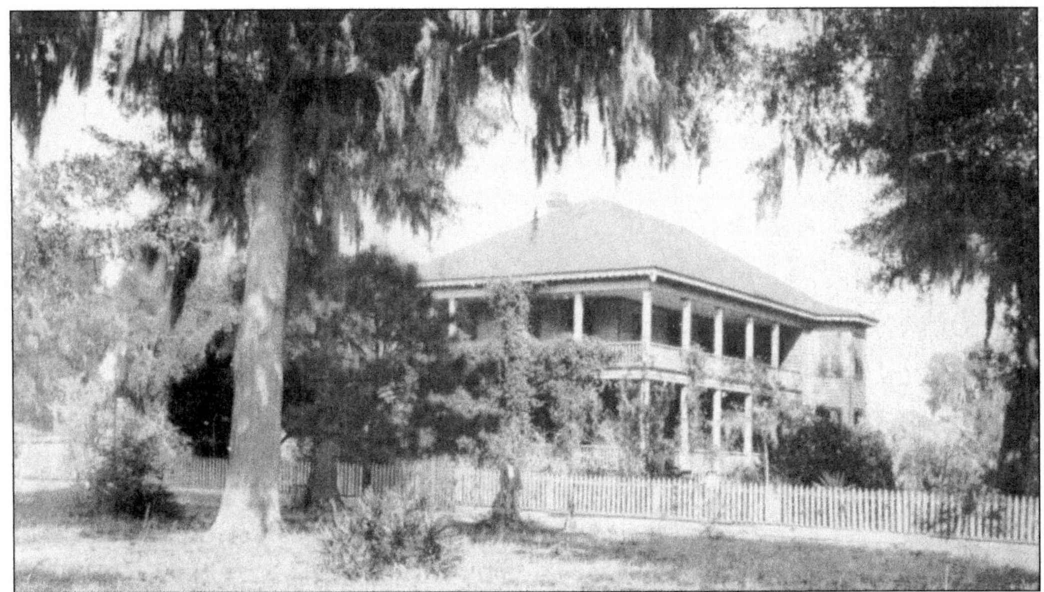

The line to Montgomery was opened in April of 1871. According to an account by Florence Olmstead, daughter of Colonel Charles H. Olmstead, her father bought one of 31 lots on Burnside Island offered for sale by John Schley. He used the streetcar line to Montgomery as an enticement to buyers, building a road across the marsh to connect Burnside Island to the railroad. This photograph shows the Olmstead home.

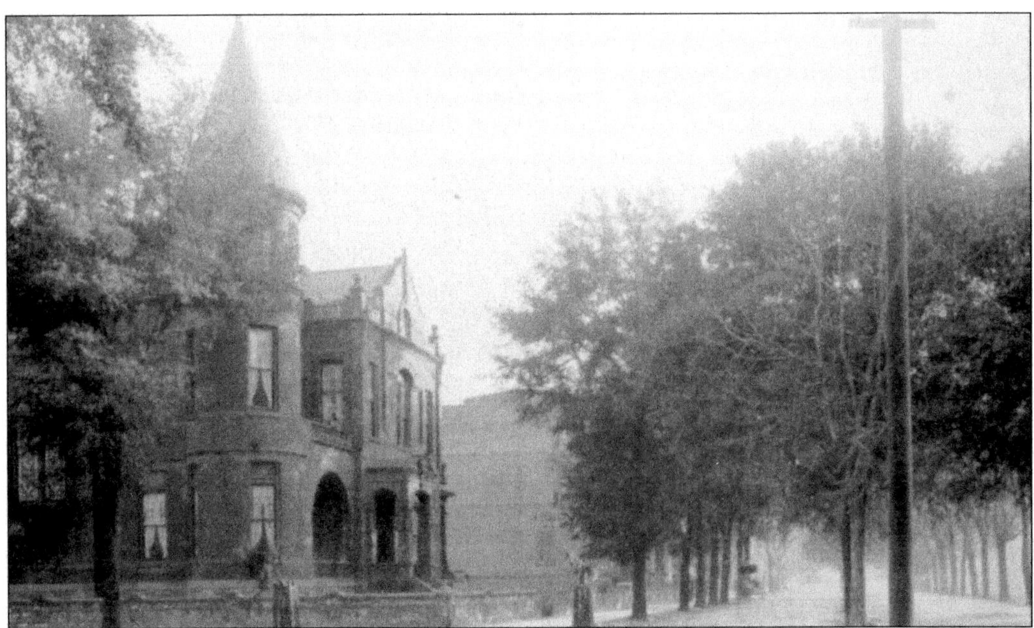

Work was begun on a line through Drayton Street but was halted by an injunction brought against S.S. & S. by the city attorney. An editorial in the *Savannah Morning News* stated that this line would "destroy the only street now available through the center of the city." This is a view down that peaceful road.

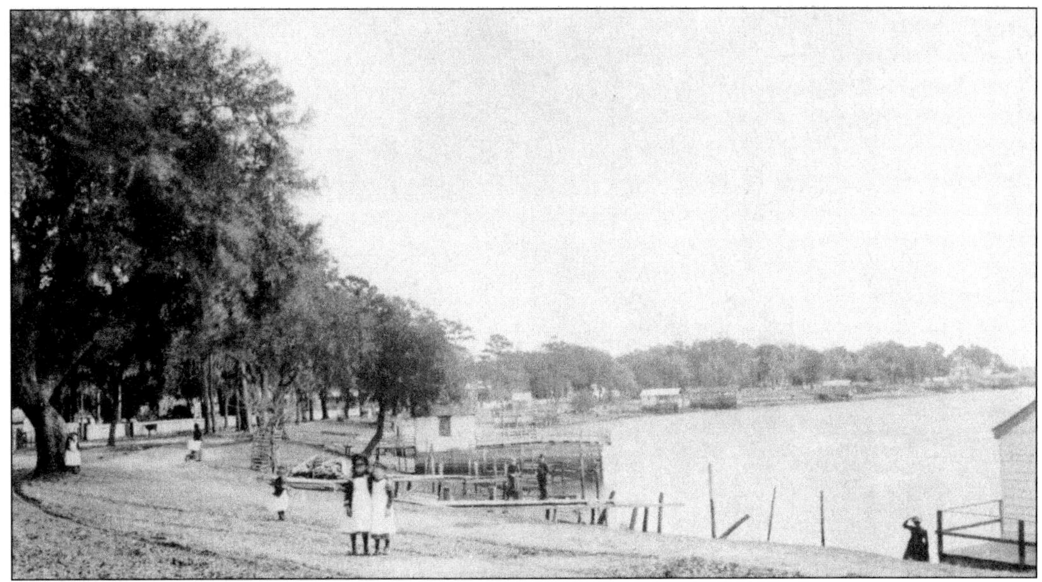

The Savannah and Thunderbolt Railroad Company (S. & T.) was incorporated in December 1871. Its line was to run down Abercorn Street to Anderson Street and then on to Thunderbolt, Beaulieu, and Montgomery. Before construction on the lines was completed, S.S. & S. was making arrangements to purchase the new company. The two merged in February of 1874. This is a scene at Isle of Hope, one of this line's destinations.

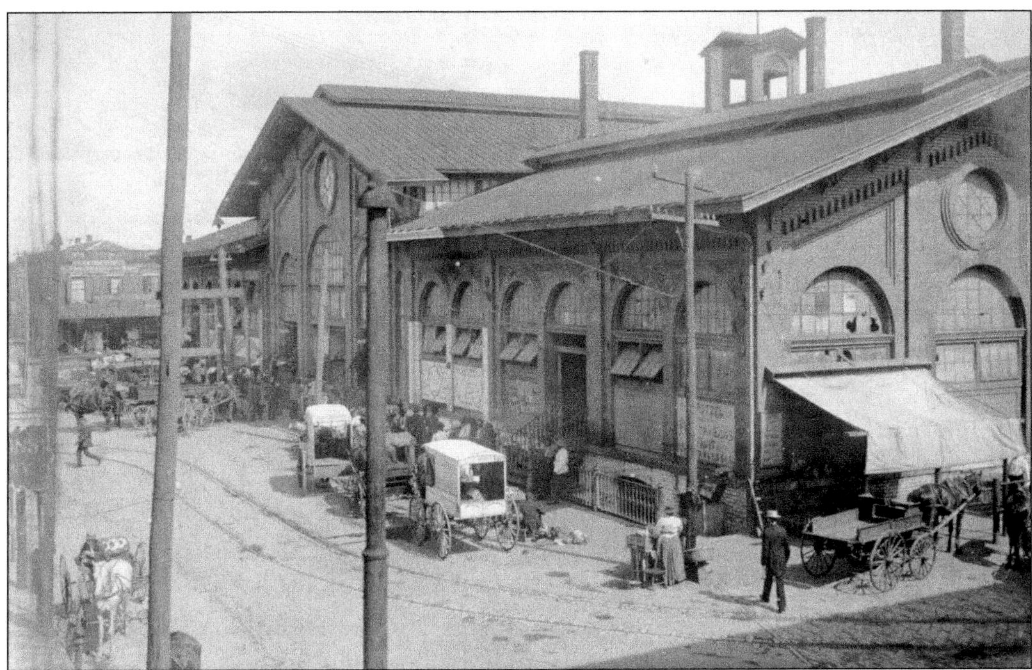

Throughout 1872, plans were made for new lines. They included lines through Montgomery Street to a point south of Anderson Street and another through St. Julian Street. This photograph shows the tracks around the City Market on St. Julian Street.

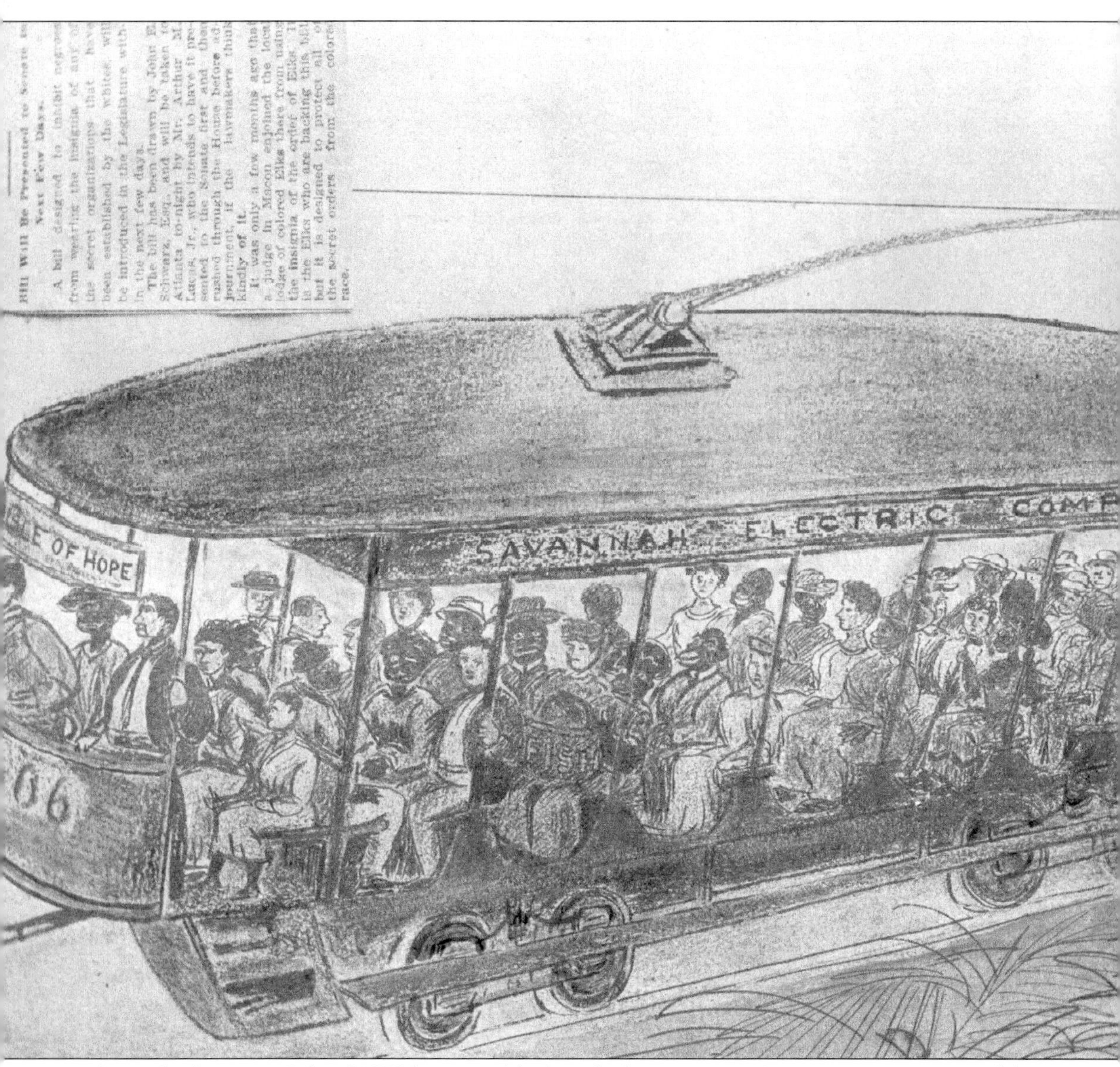

A riot broke out in July of 1872 between black and white patrons. Some cars were reserved for "whites only," while the streetcar company ran the same schedule for black patrons. A charge was brought against the company, stating it did not provide an adequate number of "cars reserved for Negroes." On July 26, blacks who boarded a "whites only" car were forcibly ejected. Conditions deteriorated into a full-blown riot with gunshots fired and the police called. A proclamation was issued by Alfred Haywood, the mayor *pro tem*, demanding that rioters halt their activities and "good citizens" help the authorities. Police officers were placed along the streetcar lines to arrest those who violated the orders. The above image is of a note card sent in 1906 to the Savannah Electric Company, which then operated the streetcars. The note requested that Savannah's segregation laws be enforced.

Another company came into being in 1872. The Wilmington Railroad Company was incorporated on October 10, 1868, to run a line from the intersection of Broughton and West Broad Streets to Wilmington Island, with a branch line to Bonaventure and Thunderbolt. Ferry service was to be operated to Wilmington and Whitmarsh Islands. Little happened until 1872, when the company was revamped and its name was changed to the Coast Line. It was required to begin work by October 1, 1873, and run its first car by January 1, 1874. This scene shows a group on a picnic in the now more accessible Bonaventure Cemetery.

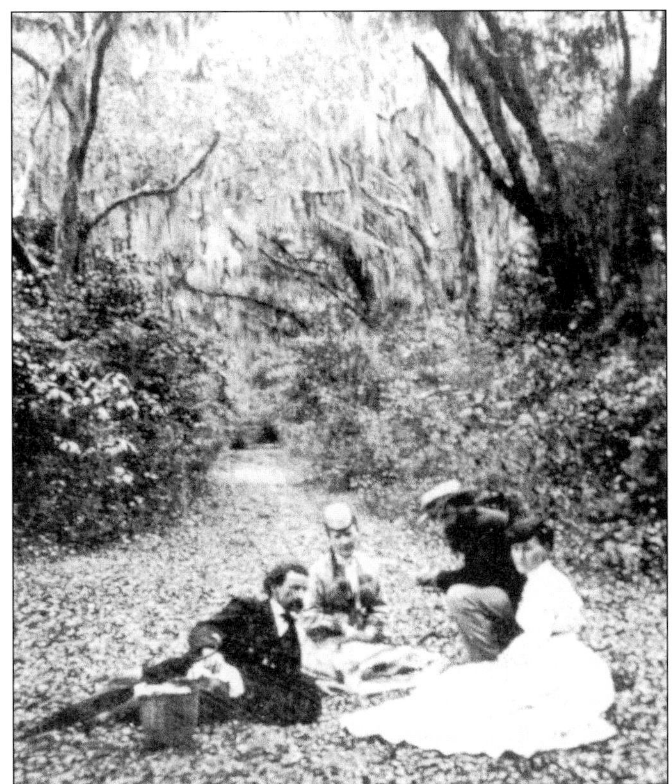

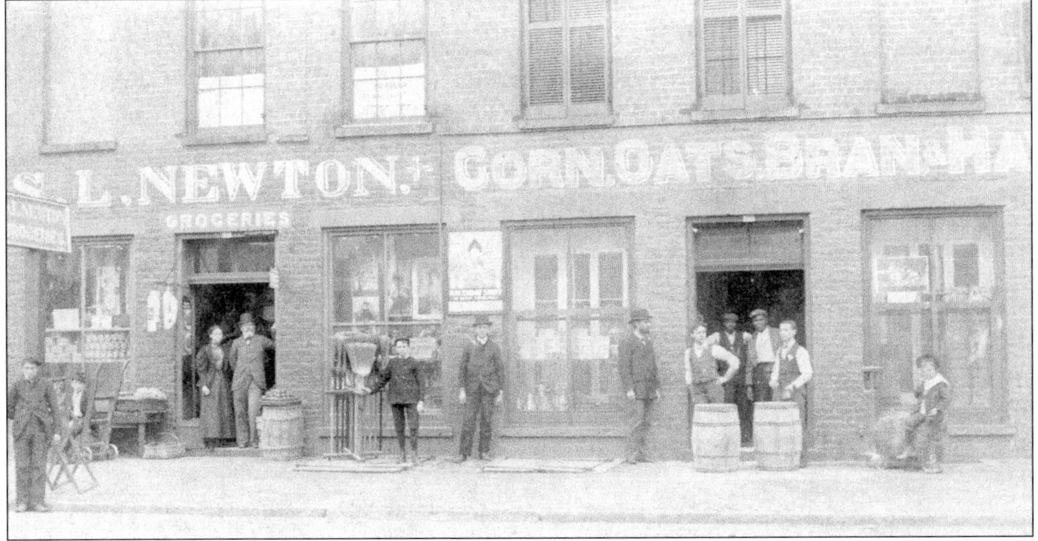

The Coast Line broke ground at West Broad and Broughton Streets on May 12, 1873. The above image shows 201 and 203 West Broughton Street, housing a shop along the new route. The new company survived various court challenges in what the *Savannah Morning News* called "the war between the Coast Line and the S.S. & S," opening to the public on September 15, 1874. In May 1875, the first cars ran to Thunderbolt with stops at Catholic and Bonaventure Cemeteries. A depot was built at Catholic Cemetery and a dancing pavilion and picnic grounds at Thunderbolt.

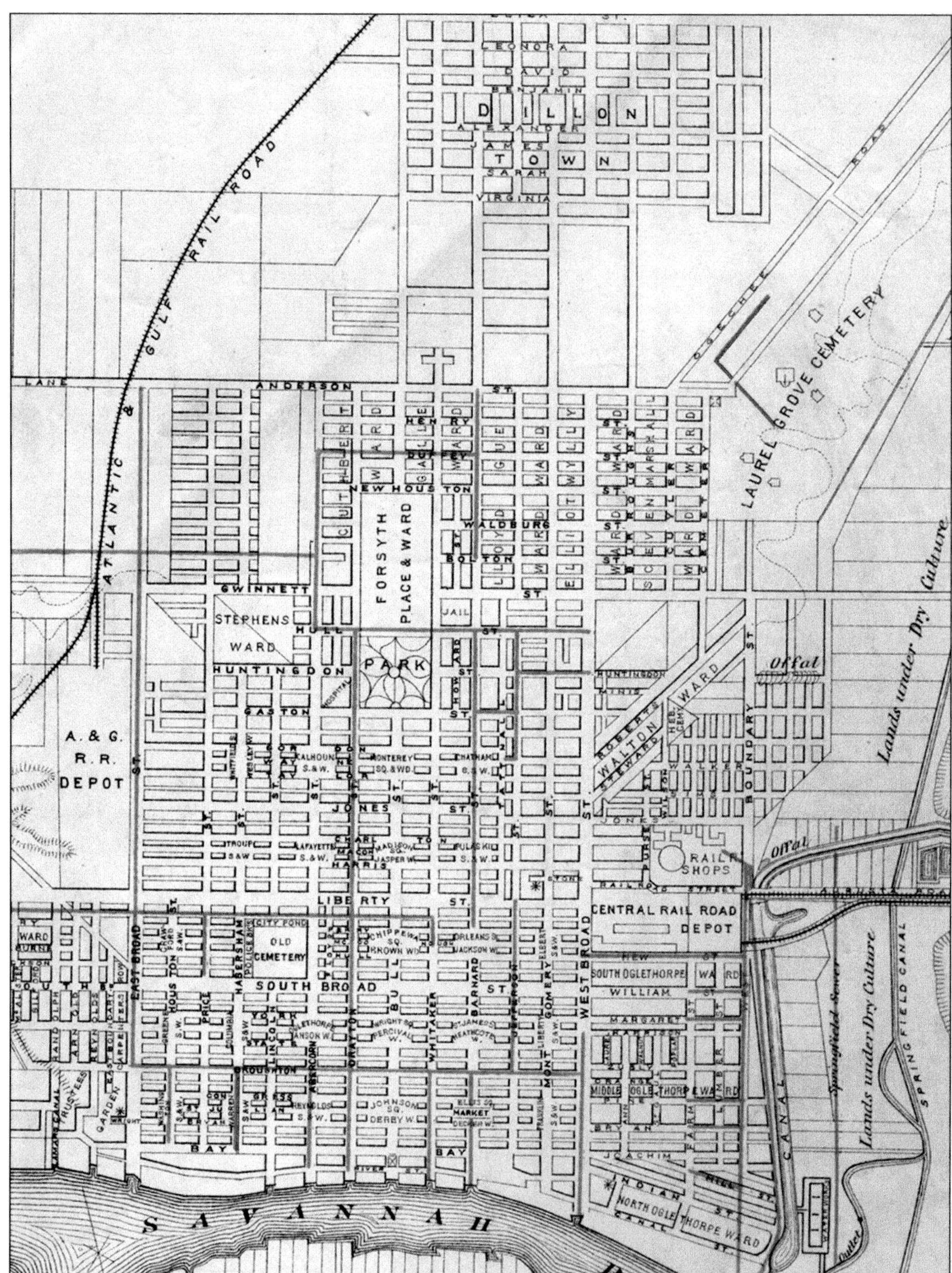

The Superior Court of Chatham County ruled on a debate of right-of-way privileges between S.S. & S. and the Coast Line. The court ruled that although the former had been granted exclusive rights to Savannah's streets, the company lost its claim to those upon which it had not built tracks. The Coast Line received permission to build on any street not used by another company. This 1876 map of Savannah was drawn by the city surveyor, J.B. Hogg.

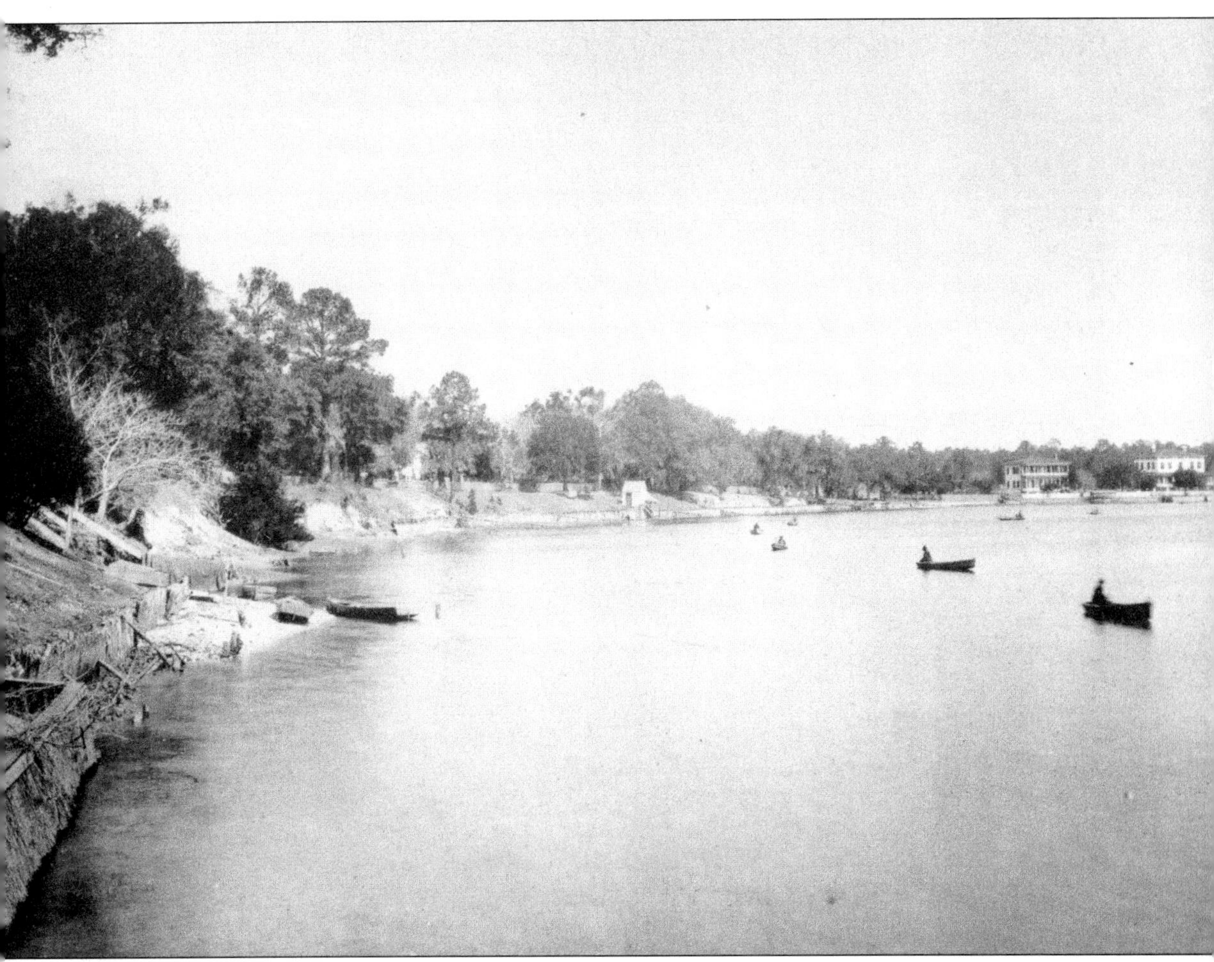

S.S. & S. finished its line to Laurel Grove in the spring of 1875. This line connected the depots of the Atlantic & Gulf and the Central of Georgia Railroads. By July, it had connected its White Bluff branch to its main line. The company went on to focus upon its rural routes, to increase suburban excursions with amenities and entertainment provided. In October of 1875, the board of directors proposed dividing the 60 acres it owned near Montgomery to lease for $1 an acre for a term of 99 years, with the condition that lessees become permanent residents. This is a view at White Bluff in 1893.

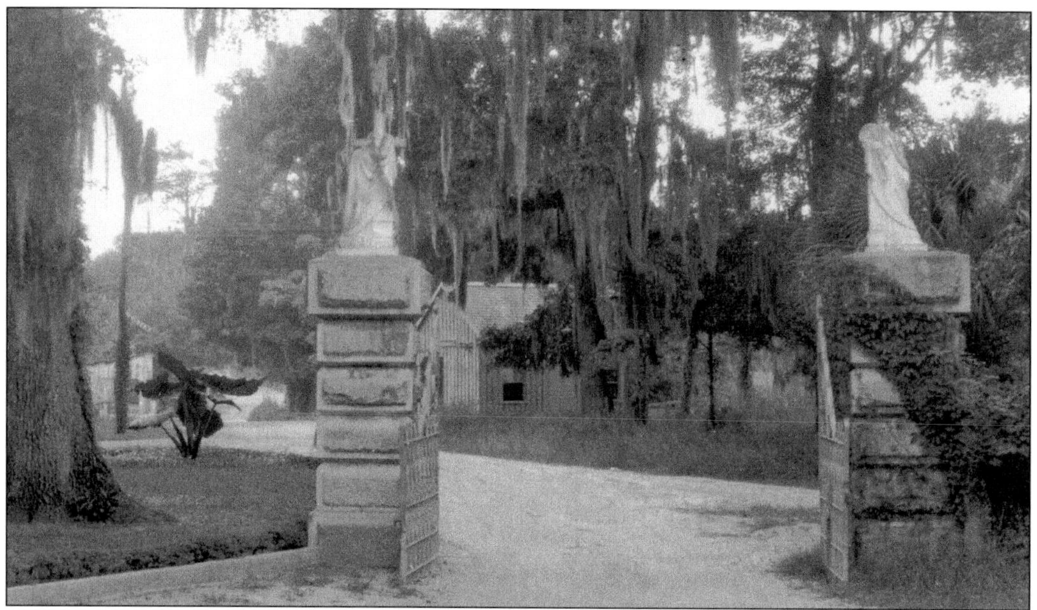

With great fanfare, the Coast Line began operation to Schuetzen Park, located one-half mile north of Bonaventure Cemetery. This spur began at the cemetery's gates and was three quarters of a mile in length. The cost, $2,200, was paid by the directors of the railroad line who were members of the Schuetzen Society, a German club. Profits were to go toward that debt, and when it was paid, ownership of the line reverted to the Coast Line. This is an image through the gates at Bonaventure Cemetery.

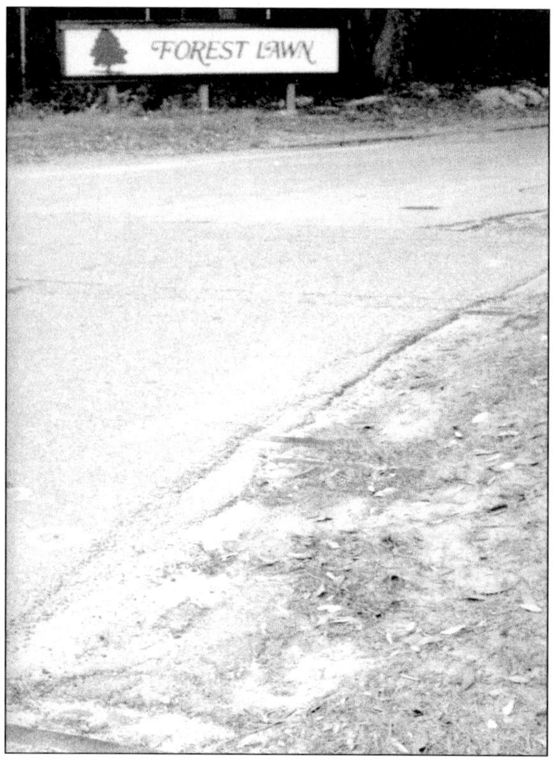

The rails are still visible at Bonaventure. This photograph, taken April 4, 1999, shows the road that leads to the gates pictured above. (Photo courtesy of C. Brauner.)

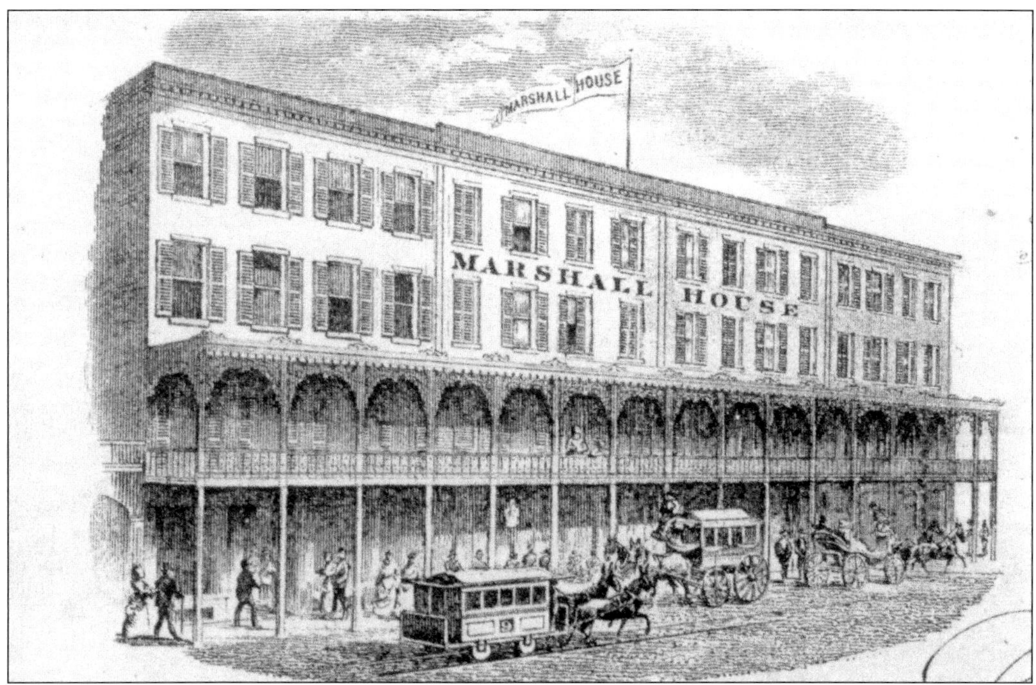

Another company began operation in 1877. The Barnard and Anderson Street Railroad (B & A) was incorporated by Julian Hartridge, George W. Anderson, and Benjamin B. Ferrill on August 23, 1872, to operate horse-drawn cars to Laurel Grove Cemetery. The line formally opened on June 30, 1877, with cars traveling between City Market and Laurel Grove. In the summer of 1878, open cars drawn by double teams were run. The Marshall House, a hotel on Broughton Street, used this image as its letterhead.

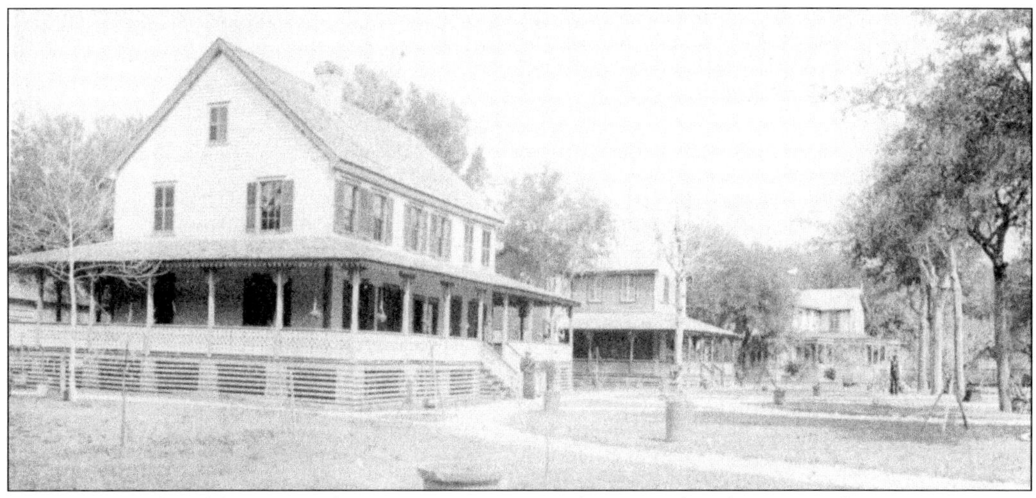

S.S. & S. replaced horses with steam power on its line to Isle of Hope and Montgomery on Saturdays in order to carry freight. The Coast Line's 1877 annual report, given by company president Alfred Haywood, announced a modification on the suburban line. Horses were to replace steam engines for a savings of $2,000. The operating expenses of a horse line were one-fifth that of a steam line. This photograph shows some of the homes on Isle of Hope served by these lines.

Barnard and Anderson Street Railroad Company.

No. CCXXIX.—(O. No. 172.)

An Act to revive, continue in force, and to amend an act entitled an act to incorporate the Barnard and Anderson Street Railroad, and for the purpose of opening a railroad communication from Savannah to Laurel Grove Cemetery, and for other purposes.

Charter revived.

SECTION I. *Be it enacted by the General Assembly of the State of Georgia,* That the above recited act, be, and the same is hereby, revived and continued in force: *Provided,* the said railroad be built, and kept in regular running order, within two years, from the passage of this Act.

Road to be built in two years.

Line of road defined.

SEC. II. *Be it further enacted,* That the road bed shall not extend further north, than the southern line of Congress street, but beginning at a point, at the intersection of Barnard and Congress streets, it may extend southward, along Barnard street, to Liberty street, thence westward, to either Tatnall, or Montgomery streets, thence south, through either Tatnall, or Montgomery street, to Berrien street, thence west, through Berrien street, to West Broad street, thence south, through West Broad street, to Huntington street, with the privilege of extending thence to Laurel Grove Cemetery.

SEC. III. Repeals conflicting laws.

Approved February 22, 1877.

B. & A. applied to the General Assembly to amend its charter in order to extend its tracks to connect the Atlantic & Gulf and Central of Georgia Railroad's depots. This is the passage found in the *Acts and Resolutions of the General Assembly of the State of Georgia, 1877*, granting the request. In addition, B. & A. acquired land on the Ogeechee Road at the battery, part of Savannah's defenses during the Civil War, for the construction of a park and rifle range. A dancing pavilion was built on the top of the earthworks. A condition of sale of the land was that service be extended to what was the "colored portion" of Laurel Grove. On Sundays in the summer, cars left City Market every seven minutes.

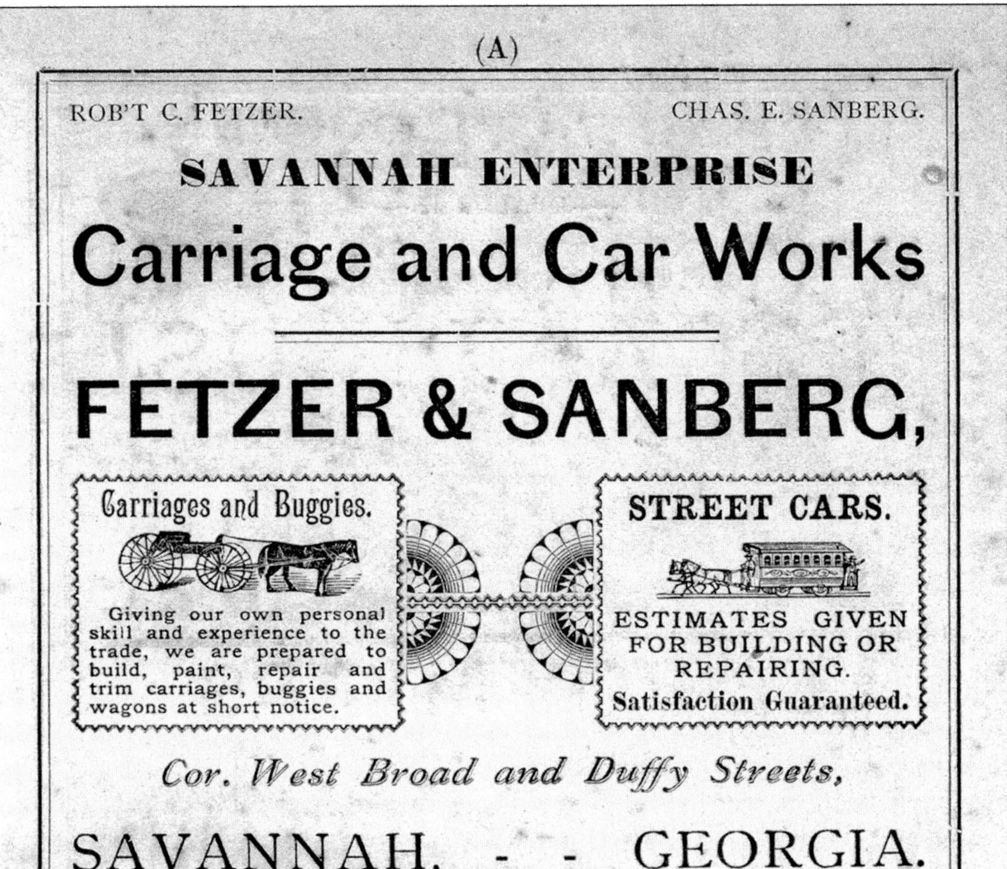

Although cars for the various companies were built primarily in Northern cities, Philadelphia notably, B. & A. often awarded contracts to build their cars locally. Robert C. Fetzer and Charles E. Sanberg of Savannah were contracted to build a number of new cars in 1880. This is the advertisement they ran in the *Savannah City Directory* in 1882.

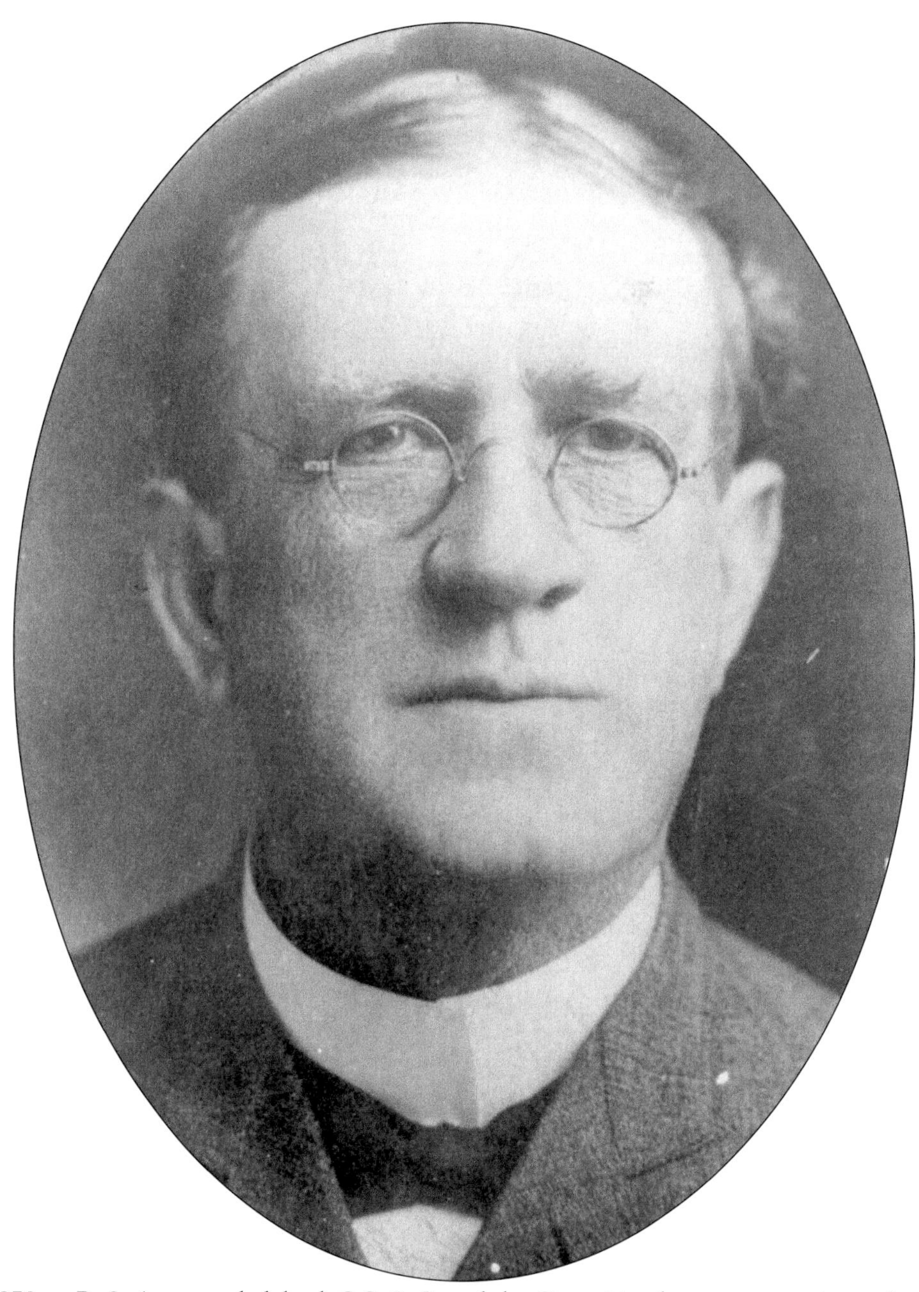

In 1879, as B. & A. expanded, both S.S. & S. and the Coast Line began to experience financial uncertainty. S.S. & S. asked their stockholders to take a smaller percentage of the profits in order to reduce their debts. The Coast Line asked for increased investment. By the end of 1881, Colonel John Holbrook Estill, pictured above, was appointed by the Superior Court to act as receiver for the Coast Line. He gave a bond of $50,000, preventing foreclosure.

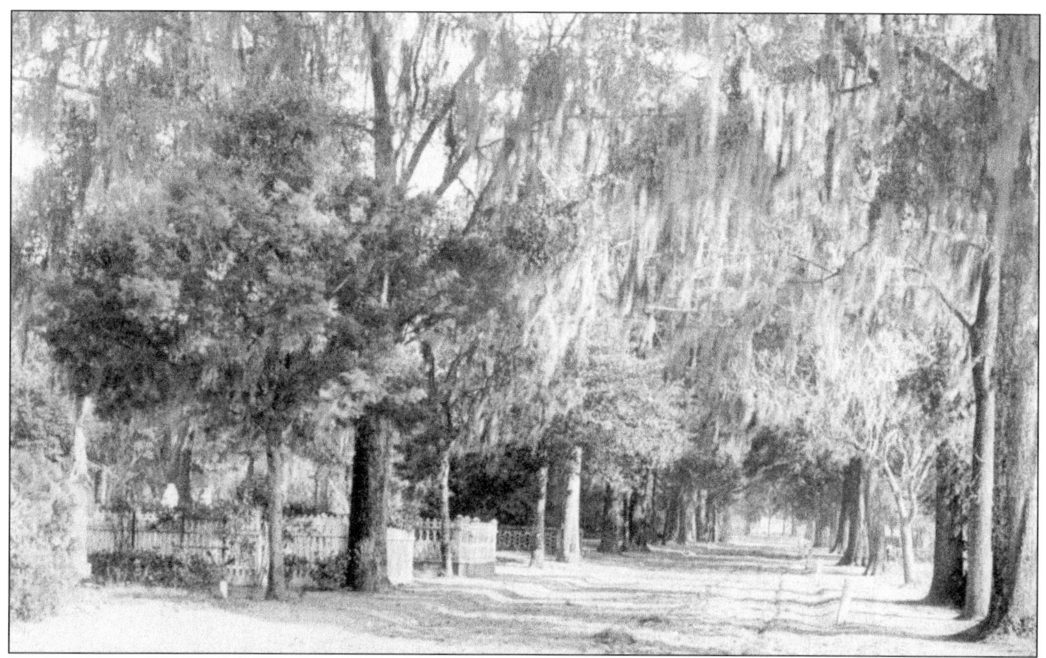

The Liberty Street line opened November 16, 1881, with service from City Market to Liberty Street and onward to the Savannah, Florida, and Western Railroad Company (S. F. & W.) depots on East Broad Street. For passengers going to Laurel Grove Cemetery, a free transfer could be made at the intersection of Liberty and Barnard Streets, with tickets being good on both the B. & A. and the new line. This is a view in Laurel Grove.

In March of 1882, Jacob Rauers purchased the S.S. & S. On April 6, the City and Suburban Railway Company (C. & S.) was incorporated, with the goal of taking control of the assets and franchises of the S.S. & S. Eight days later, this new company also assumed control of the B. & A. Street Railroad. Edward J. Thomas was made the general manager. The board of directors was comprised of Daniel Gugel Purse (pictured at right), Jacob Rauers, A L. Hartridge, and J. H. Estill. The summer months of 1883 saw the C. & S. active in resort promotion. Improvements were made at Montgomery and Isle of Hope. A picnic ground at Cedar Hammock with a dancing pavilion was created for the "exclusive use of the colored people."

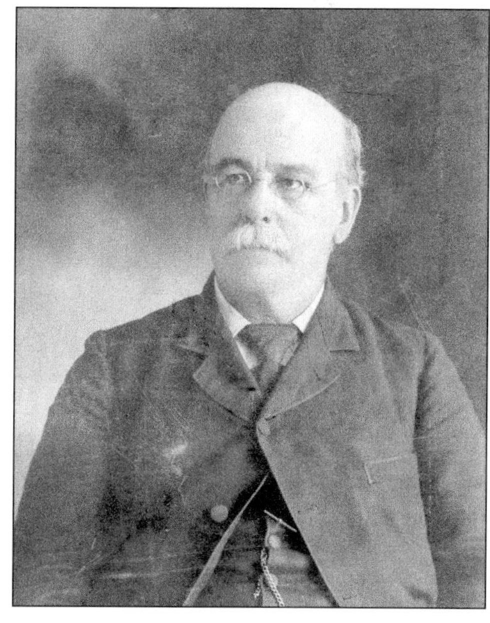

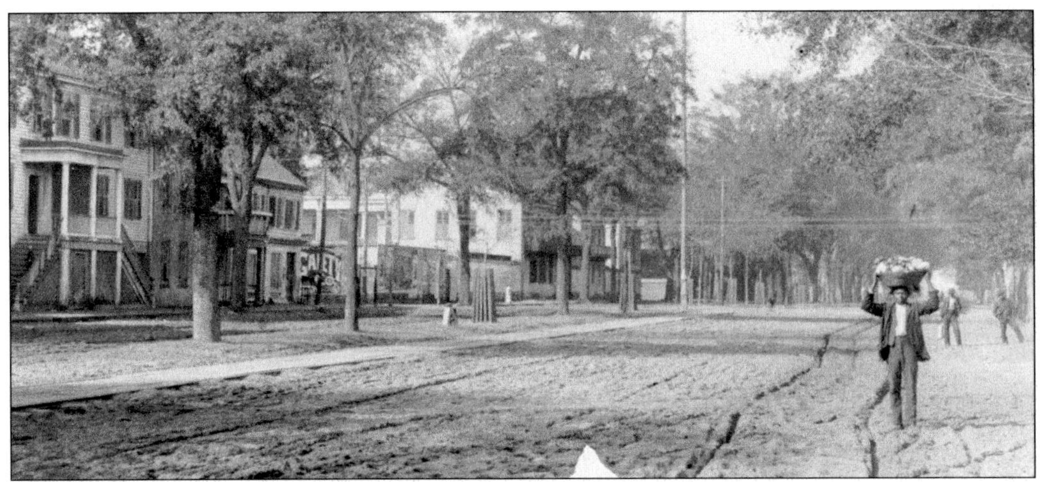

The C. & S. continued with improvements. In 1884, new steel tracks were laid on its suburban lines, existing engines were rebuilt, and new cars were added. A broader change was made in April. Although its basic operations and management remained the same, company ownership shifted. J.W. Fellows & Company of New York bought three-fifths of the company's stock. The goal was to add this line to a system of passenger and freight service between Florida and the North. Over the next four years, the company continued to publish its schedule and experienced no major changes. This image shows East Liberty Street, with tracks running through the center of the deeply rutted road.

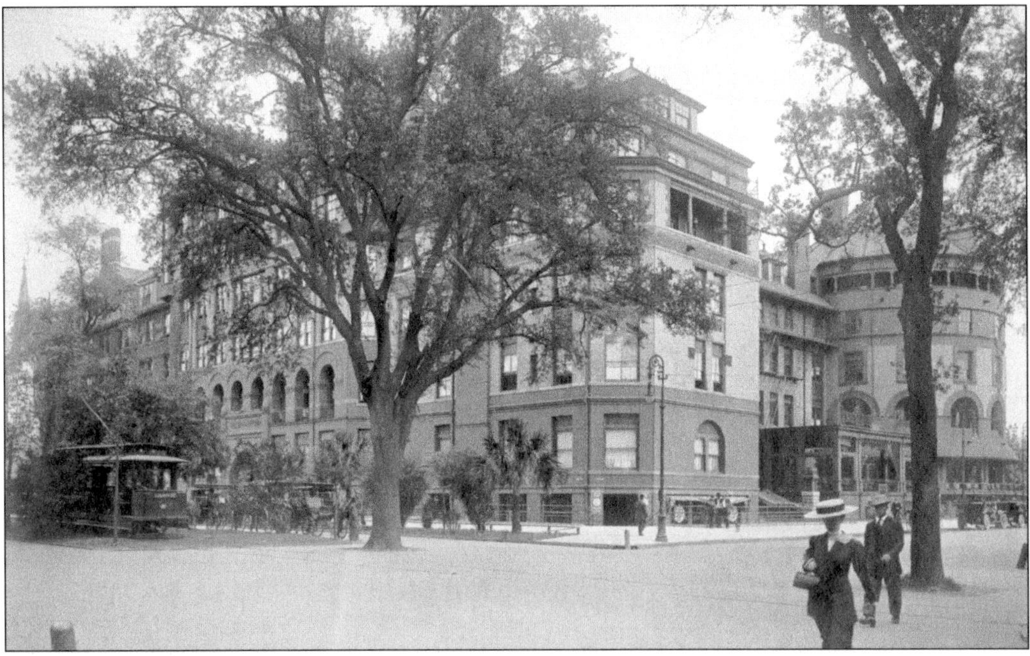

In 1887, the C. & S. offered numerous free excursions to both out-of-town visitors and poor residents of Savannah. Hotel management and local clergy were used to dispense tickets. In 1888, a new locomotive called the *A.L. Hartridge* was built. C. & S. was also authorized to connect its Liberty Street line with the depot for the train to Tybee Island at the foot of President Street. This 1912 photograph of the DeSoto Hotel demonstrates the convenience of streetcars for guests of the hotel.

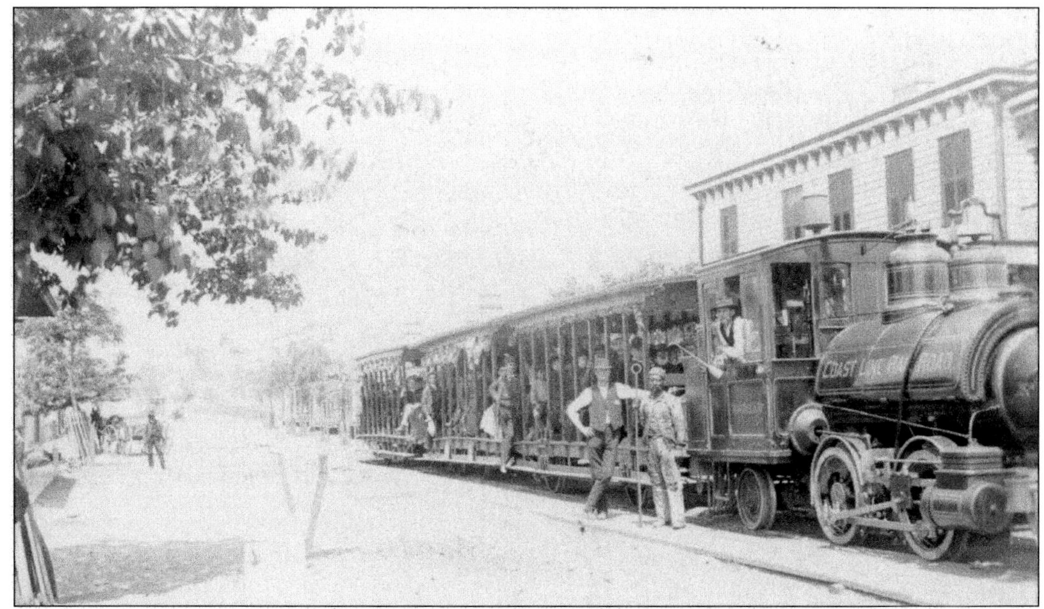

In the meantime, an editorial in the *Savannah Morning News* encouraged the Coast Line to take advantage of the permission it had been granted previously to extend its line through the southern part of Savannah. A preliminary survey was made in February 1887, for a possible extension from Thunderbolt to Warsaw Sound. It changed its out-of-town lines from horse-drawn to steam-powered. The trip from one end of the line to the other now took 20 minutes. Above is a Coast Line train with open cars.

SUBURBAN RAILWAYS.

Coast Line Railroad.

Suburban Sunday Schedule.

Cathedral Cemetery, Bonaventure and Thunderbolt.

SCHEDULE FOR THIS DAY

CITY TIME.

Leave Savannah 8 a. m., 9:35 a. m., 10:35 a. m., 11:45 a. m., 2 p. m., 3 p. m., 4 p. m., 5 p. m., 6 p. m., 6:50 p. m.

Leave Bonaventure 7:20 a. m., 9:05 a. m., 10:05 a. m., 11:05 a. m., 12:40 p. m., 2:40 p. m., 3:30 p. m., 4:30 p. m., 5:30 p. m., 6:30 p. m.

Leave Thunderbolt 7:10 a. m., 9 a. m., 10 a. m., 11 a. m., 12:35 p. m., 2:35 p. m., 3:25 p. m., 4:25 p. m., 5:25 p. m., 6:25 p. m.

Round trip to Bonaventure 20c.; round trip to Thunderbolt 25c.; round trip to Cathedral Cemetery 10c.

Take Broughton street cars 25 minutes before departure of suburban trains.

R. E. COBB, Superintendent.

At the same time that these improvements were being discussed or implemented, the Coast Line was in court, arguing against the city selling its property because it would then enter bankruptcy. A year later, the company was still publishing its schedule in the newspaper.

State of Georgia

County of Chatham

To the Superior Court of said County:

The petition of Albertina Graul shows that the Coast Line Railway Company, a corporation of said County, has damaged your petitioner to the extent of Fifteen Thousand Dollars by reason of the following facts. On the 28th day of May 1887 Lewis Graul was a passenger on the train of defendant running from what was then known as Scheutzen Park, in said County to the City of Savannah, having paid fully the amount due the said defendant for his passage as a passenger as aforesaid; and whilst on said train as a passenger as aforesaid and whilst same was in motion a sudden and severe jerk was given to the car upon which said Lewis Graul was and said Lewis Graul was thereby violently thrown from said car and fell under the wheels thereof. That said wheels passed over the legs of the said Lewis Graul, cutting same off and from the effects of which the said Lewis Graul in a few days died.

Petitioner shows that at the time the said Lewis Graul was entirely free from fault and negligence and the accident resulted from a failure on the part of the said defendant to exercise ordinary and reasonable care to prevent said accident.

Petitioner shows that said defendant was using at the time of said accident, for the accommodation of its passengers, open cars used and intended for Street Railways and to be drawn by horses, but upon this occasion an engine was used in place and instead of said horses. That said defendant failed to furnish sufficient cars to accommodate its passengers; that being unable to obtain a seat in said cars the said Lewis Graul was compelled to ride upon the side platform of one of said cars and while stand-

Accidents and bodily injury were a danger. This document shows the court case brought against the Coast Line by Albertine Graul in 1887. Chatham County Superior Court ruled that a company could be held liable for inadequate equipment and poor decisions made by its employees. This case also documents that, with the proper equipment in place, horse or steam power was used over the same line.

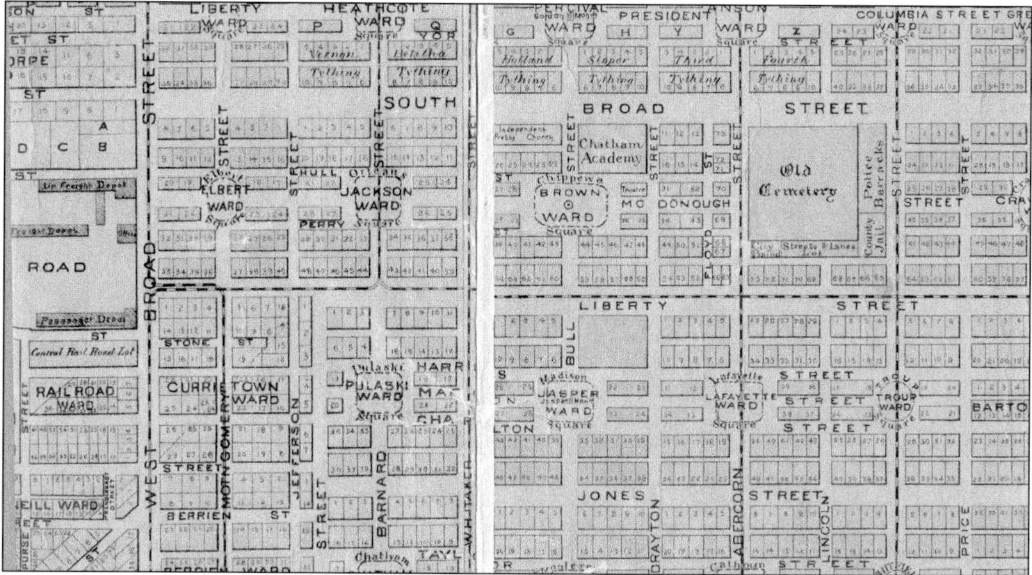

Competition among the companies was enlivened with the emergence of the Savannah Street and Rural Resort Railroad (S.S. & R.R.). This company was referred to as the Belt Line. City Council granted permission on September 21, 1887, for the company to operate horse-pulled streetcars along the following route: from near the Ogeechee Canal up Indian Street to West Broad, along West Broad to Bay Street. Here the line branched with one running through Bay to East Broad. The other ran through West Broad to Liberty, where it turned onto Montgomery running out to Seventh Street (now Thirty-seventh Street). It continued east to Habersham and on to Bolton. The first car ran on January 9, 1888, from the Exchange to the canal. The line from the Ocean Steamship Wharves to S. F. & W. depot opened on February 6, 1888. By March, the Central of Georgia Railroad passenger depot was also connected.

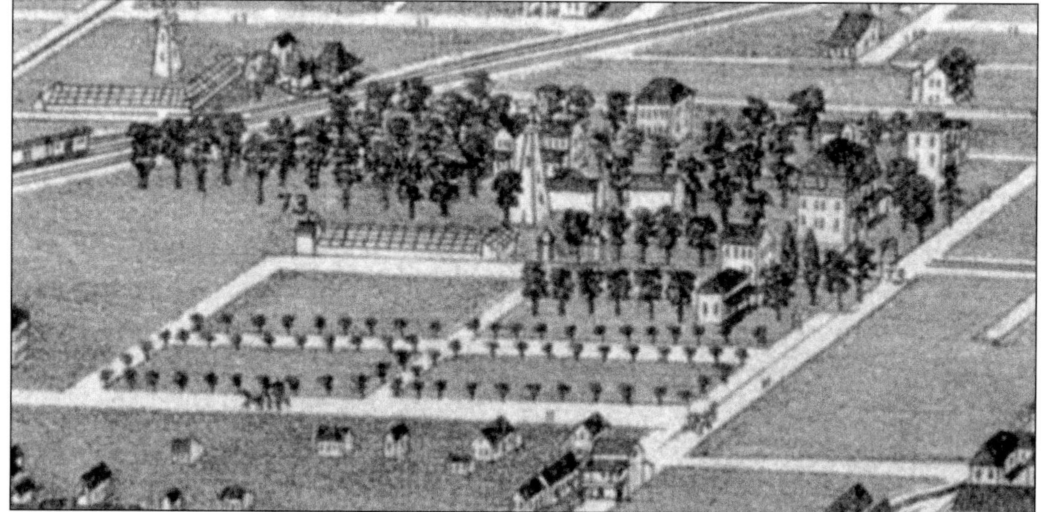

The extension through Southville (north of Seventh Street, at Habersham), Maupas's Dairy, Riesling's Gardens, Schwarz's Place, Seiler's Concordia Park, and to the company's stables was next. The newspaper marveled at the numbers of people traveling on this line "to see the new part of the city, which has been heretofore almost inaccessible except to those who own vehicles."

Except for the C. & S.'s threat of legal action to maintain its exclusive rights to its streets, the new company was well received, according to newspaper accounts of the day. The 6 miles of new track covered new areas, and competition among the lines caused travel time to drop. The five men responsible for this new company were Henry C. Cunningham (pictured at left), Horace P. Smart, Charles H. Dorsett, J.C. Shaw, and, once again, J.H. Estill.

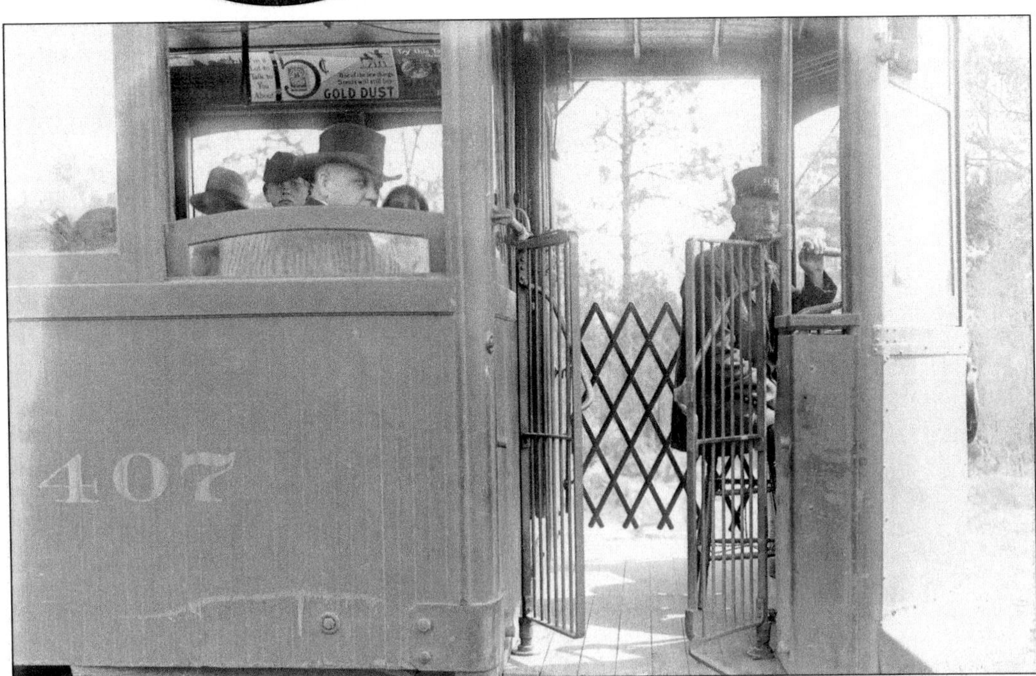

As 1888 came to an end, three main companies were operating streetcar lines in Chatham County. They were all horse-drawn or steam-powered. The first mention of electrification of the lines was made by the S.S. & R.R. in 1887, as it investigated various possibilities. Electricity was not used, however, until 1890.

Two
SUBURBAN DESTINATIONS

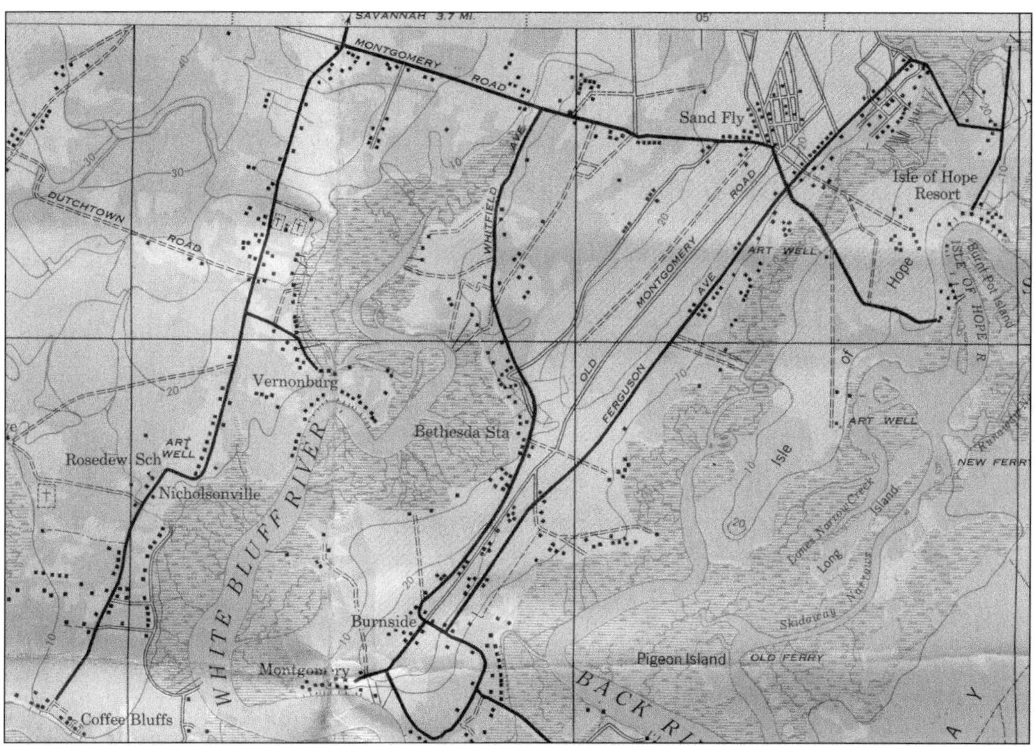

One of the early stated purposes of the streetcar companies was to open suburban areas to individuals who might not otherwise have the means to travel out of town. Areas billed as resorts were popular spots to go when escaping the heat of the city. This is a 1945 map of much of the area discussed in the following pages.

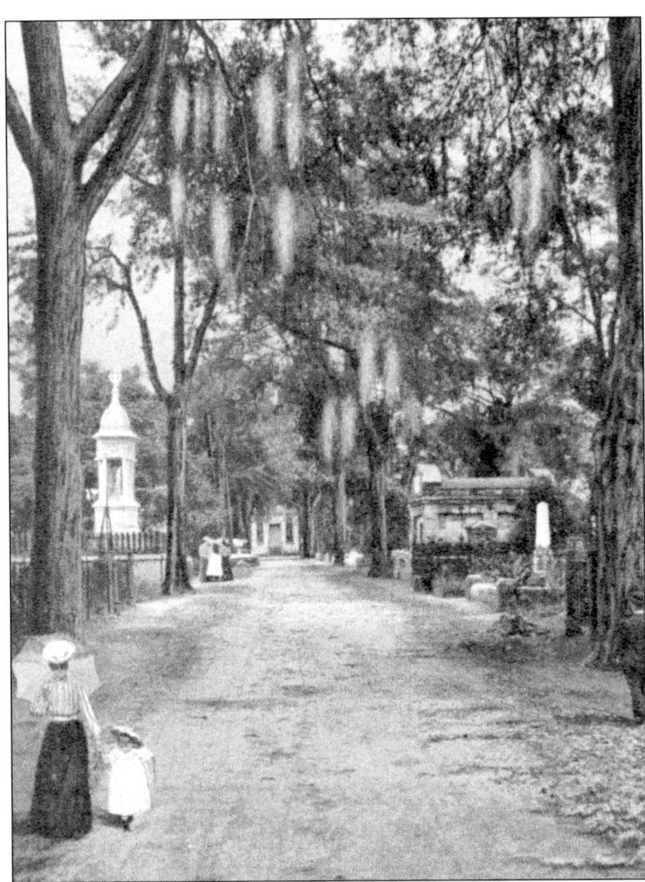

One of the first stops on the way to Thunderbolt was Catholic Cemetery, 2 miles from Savannah and reachable by the Coast Line.

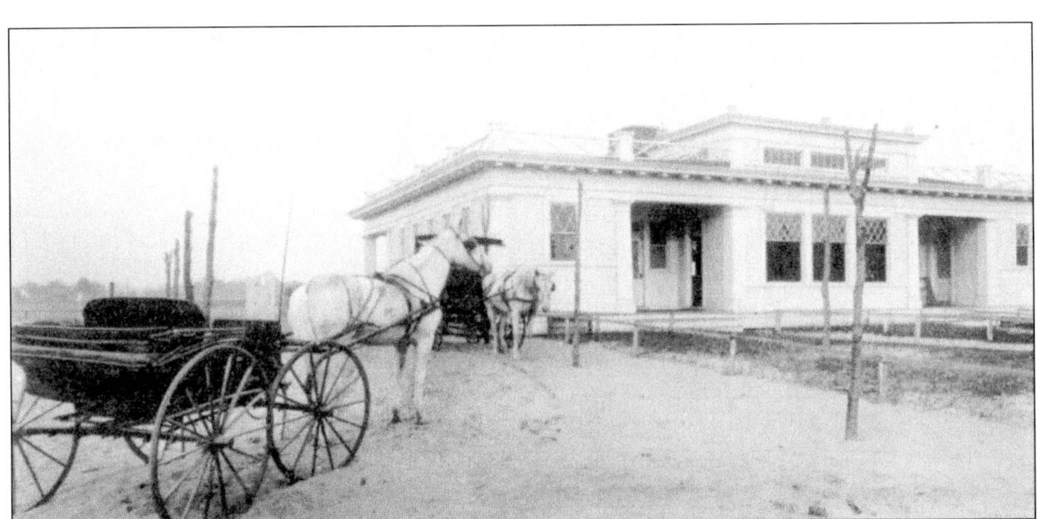

The Savannah Golf Club was the next stop. The club was incorporated in 1899, and in 1900, the club bought and rented land bounded by the Central of Georgia right-of-way, Garrard Avenue (now Goebel), Lawton Avenue, and Catholic Cemetery. Later, the rented land was purchased. The first clubhouse was on Gwinnett Street.

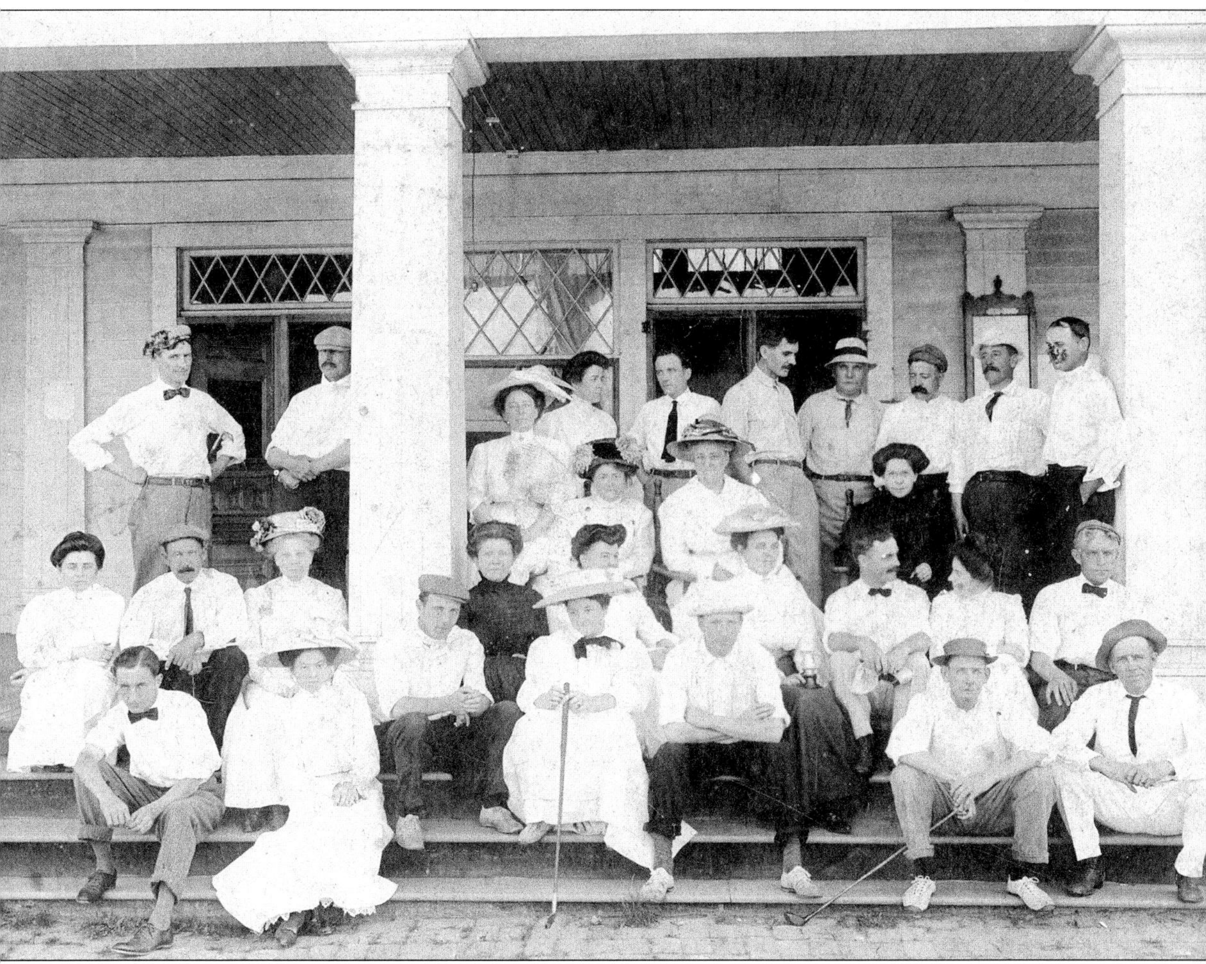

Charter members of the Savannah Golf Club included H.C. Cunningham, John A.G. Carson, Edward Karow, and C.S. Saussy. The photograph, *c.* 1910, shows a group of golfers on the clubhouse steps.

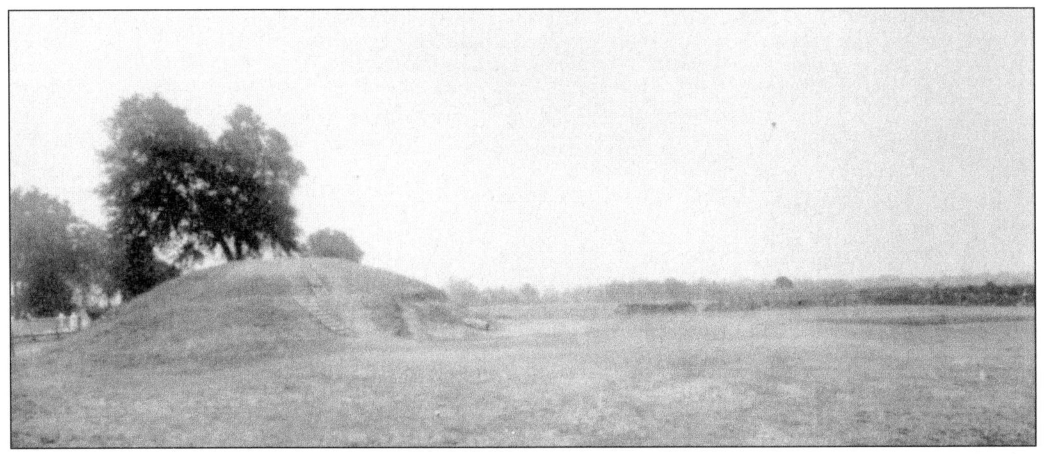

The golf course was built on the site of what had been Confederate fortifications, with the mounds used as hazards.

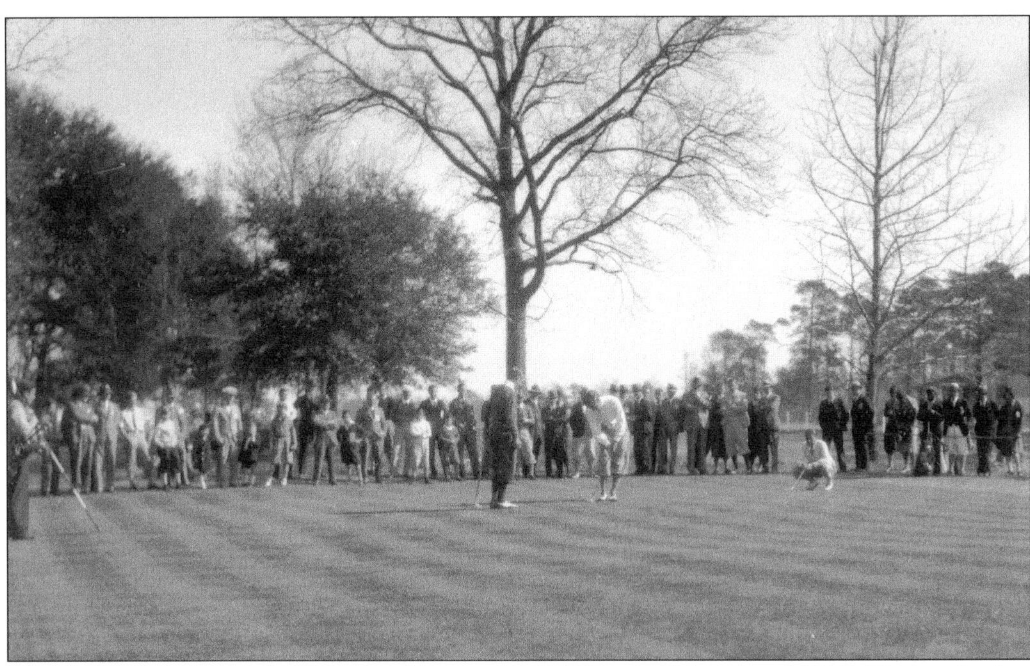

This is the turnout at the links for the Savannah Open in February of 1930. This is the last tournament that Atlanta native Bobby Jones lost before his "Grand Slam" victory, which included winning the Walker Cup, the British Open, the British Amateur, the U. S. Open, and the U. S. Amateur, a feat not since repeated.

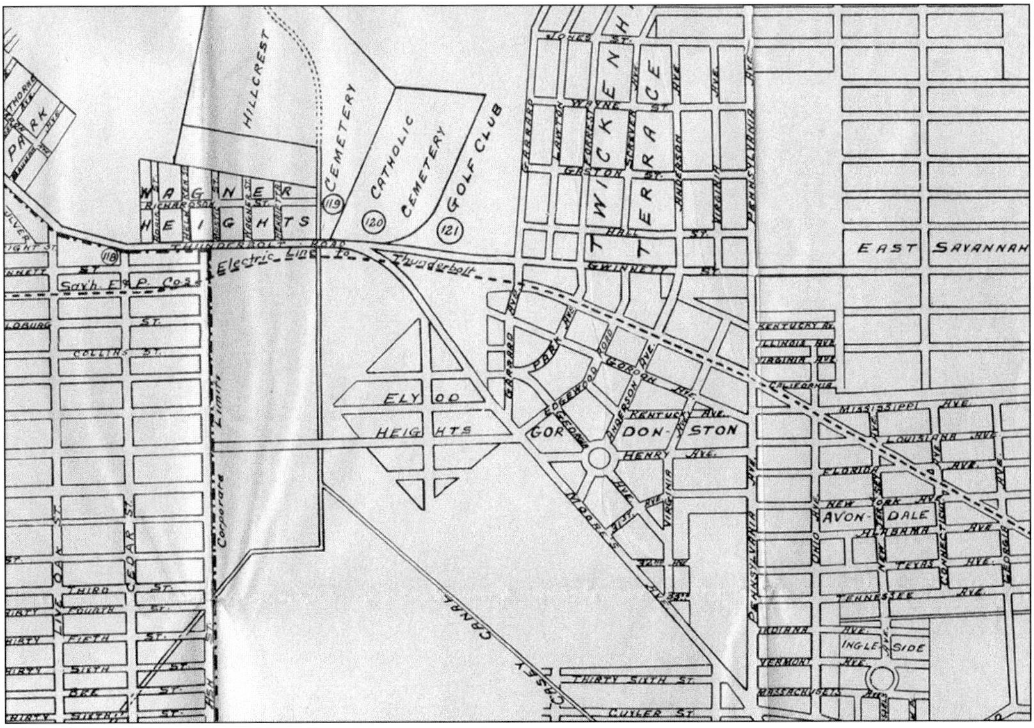

The first residential areas just outside city limits to be reached on the line to Thunderbolt were Gordonston and Twickenham Terrace. This map shows the eastward spread of neighborhoods.

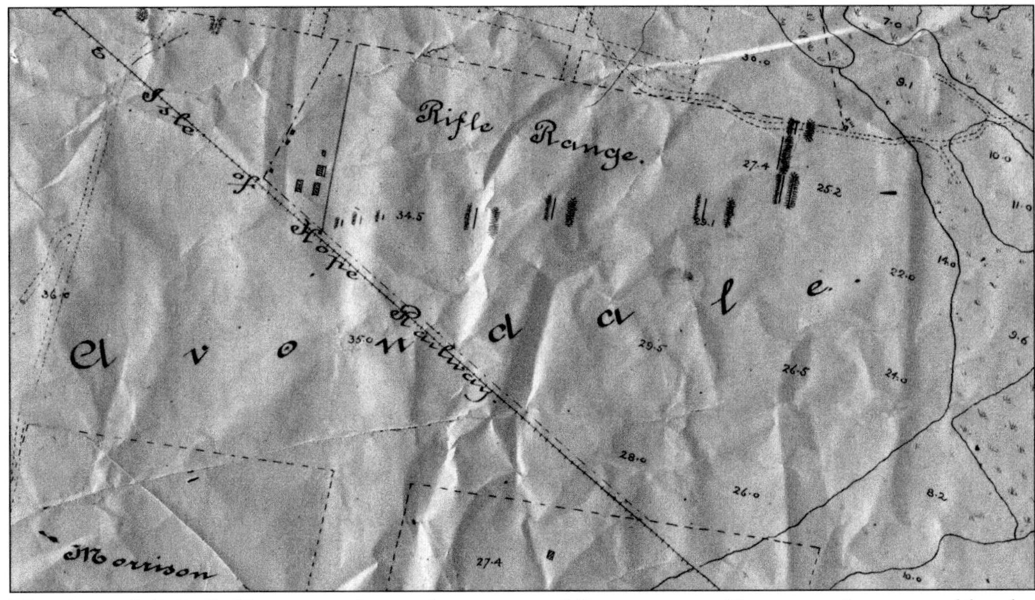

The Avondale Rifle Range was located just west of Bonaventure Cemetery. It was used by the Savannah Volunteer Guards. This plat from 1903 shows land features and backstops for targets.

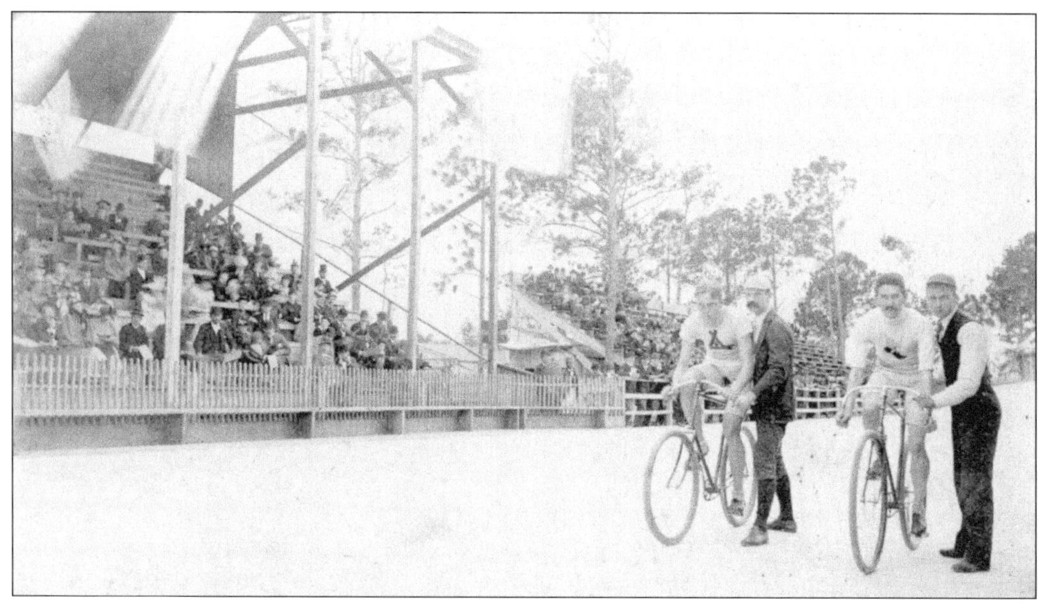

The Savannah Coliseum, a mile outside of Savannah, was the location for bike races.

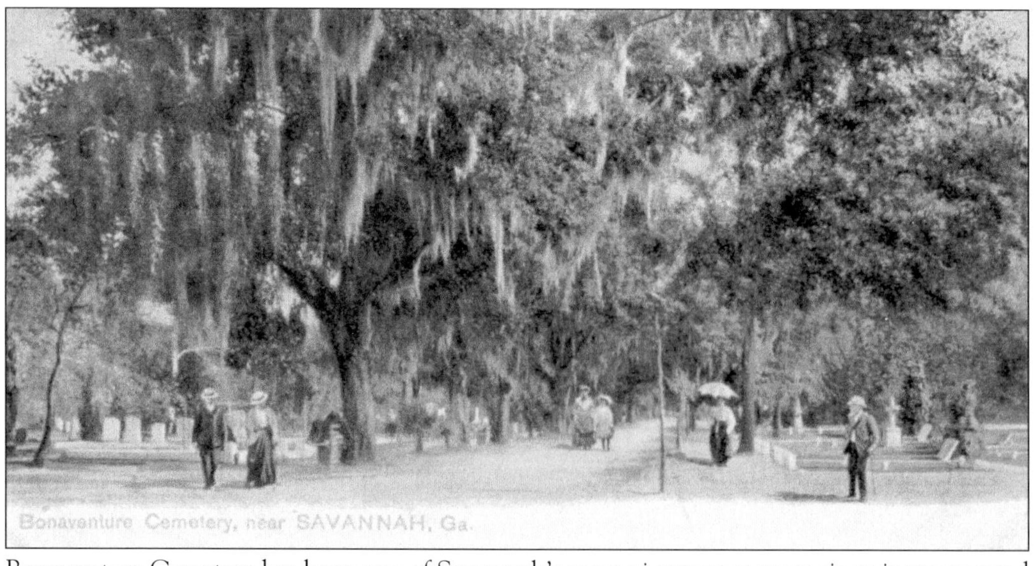

Bonaventure Cemetery has been one of Savannah's most picturesque spots since it was created in 1846. This postcard is postmarked 1906.

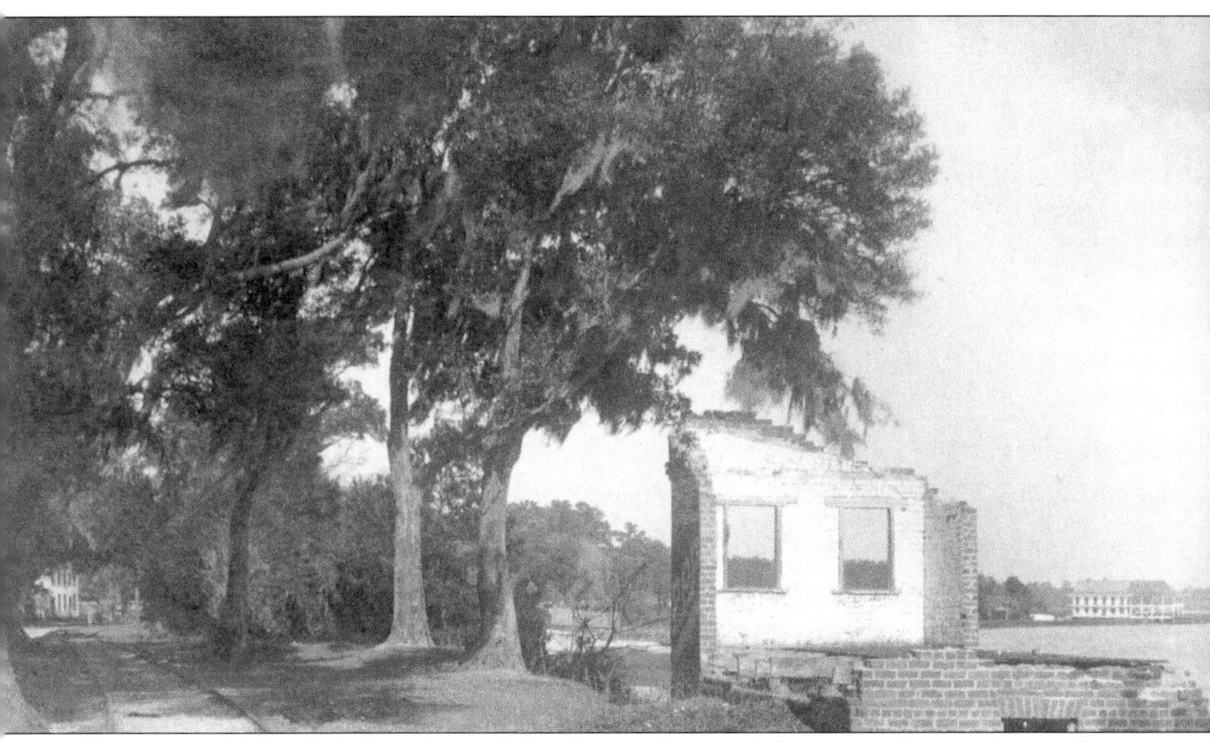

The town of Thunderbolt is located 5 miles southeast of downtown Savannah, on the Wilmington River. This was one of the early resort destinations. The streetcar lines brought people out of Savannah to enjoy the ocean breezes as well as the entertainment that sprang up as patronage of the line increased. This is a view looking north toward Thunderbolt, showing the tracks as they continue on to Isle of Hope. The yacht club is in the distance.

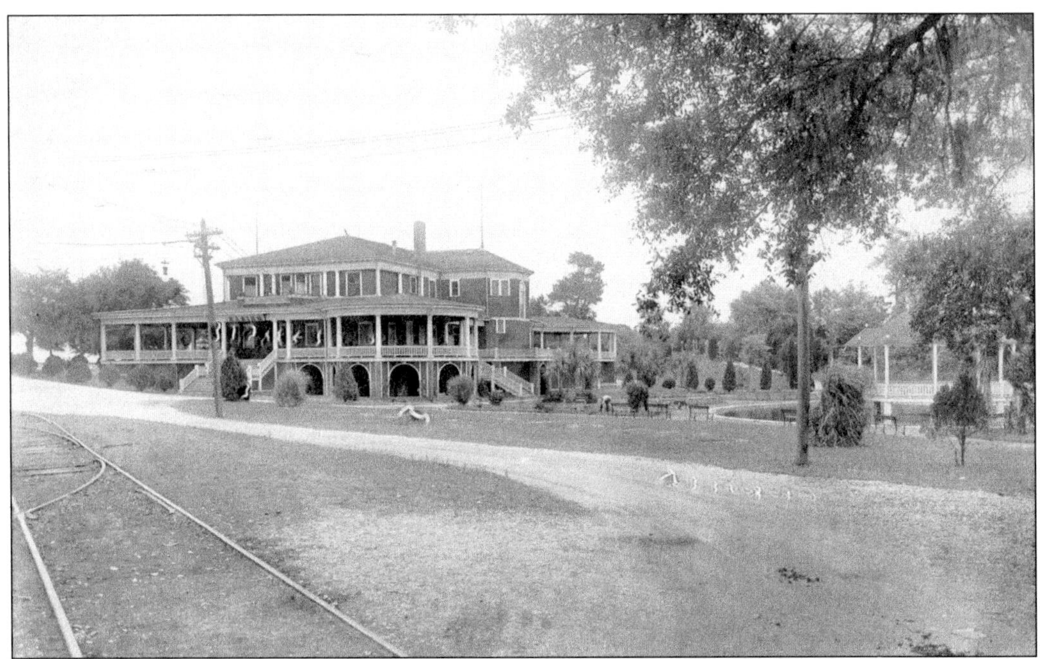

The casino at Thunderbolt, pictured above, was built as an attraction to increase business on the streetcar line. The building and grounds were the site for a number of amusements. Bandstands (one in the center of the pond, shown here, and another on a pier), a miniature railroad, a roller coaster, a merry-go-round, and one of Savannah's first moving picture houses were part of the entertainment to be found at Thunderbolt through the years.

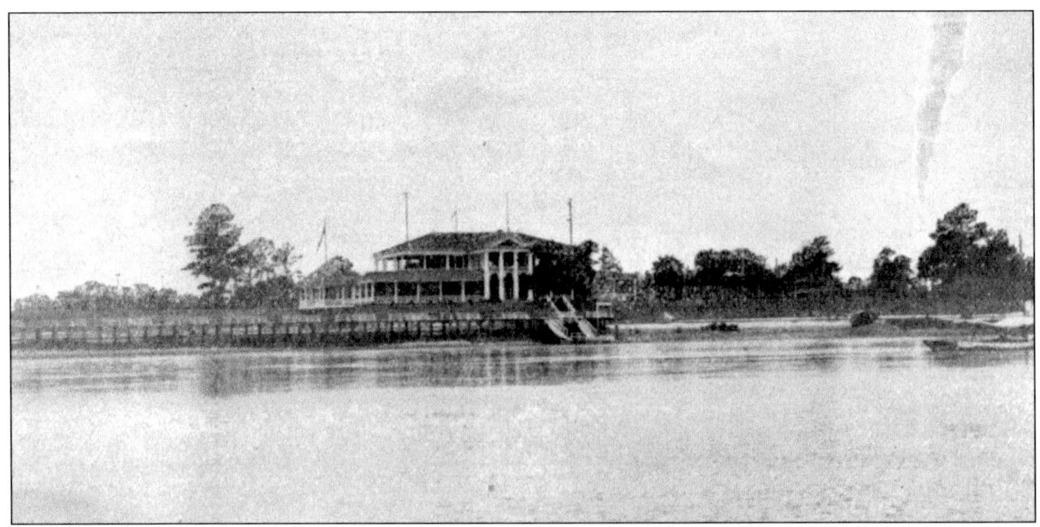

In 1930, Savannah Electric and Power Company sold the casino to Michael M. May. Within the year, it burned to the ground. The fire began in the basement sometime after 2 a.m. on Sunday, November 2, and was out of control by the time firefighters arrived from Savannah.

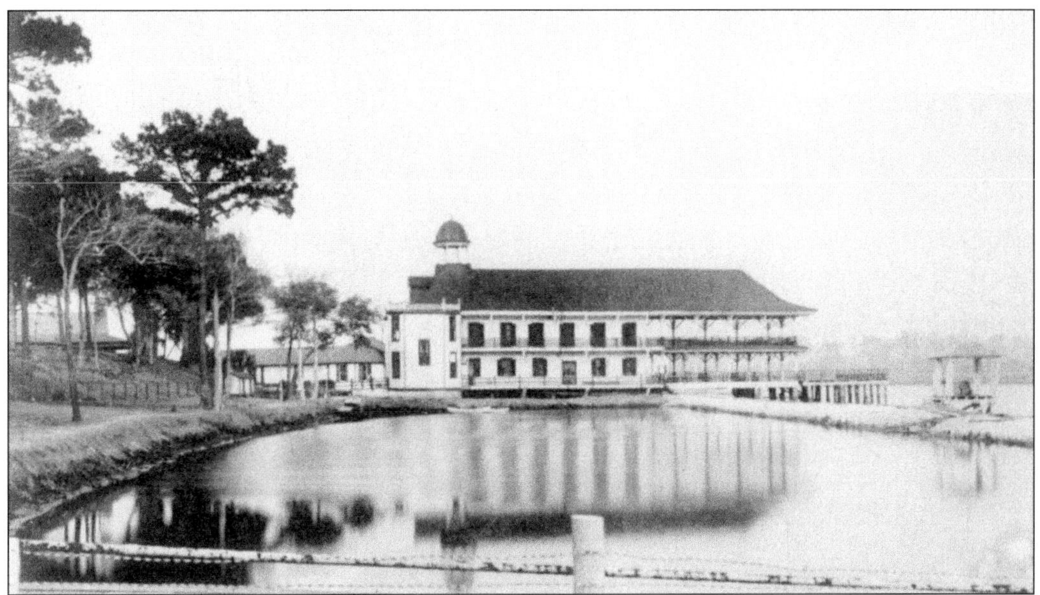

The Regatta Association of the State of Georgia was formed in 1869 and renamed in 1876 as the Savannah Yacht Club. Its early headquarters were in Montgomery and, later, on Wilmington Island. It 1897, it was located in Thunderbolt with facilities including billiards, shuffleboard, a bowling alley, and a swimming pool. A platform over the marsh connected the boathouse and bowling alley to the pavilion. The club was inactive from 1915 until 1936, when it purchased land on Wilmington Island. The photograph above shows the club around 1893, while the postcard below is a view across the Wilmington River.

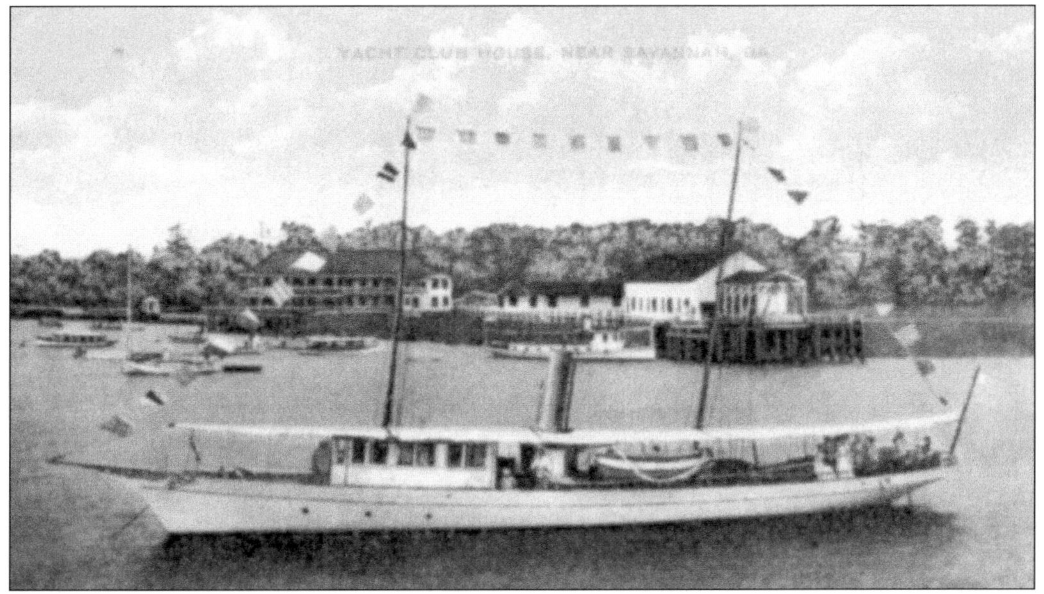

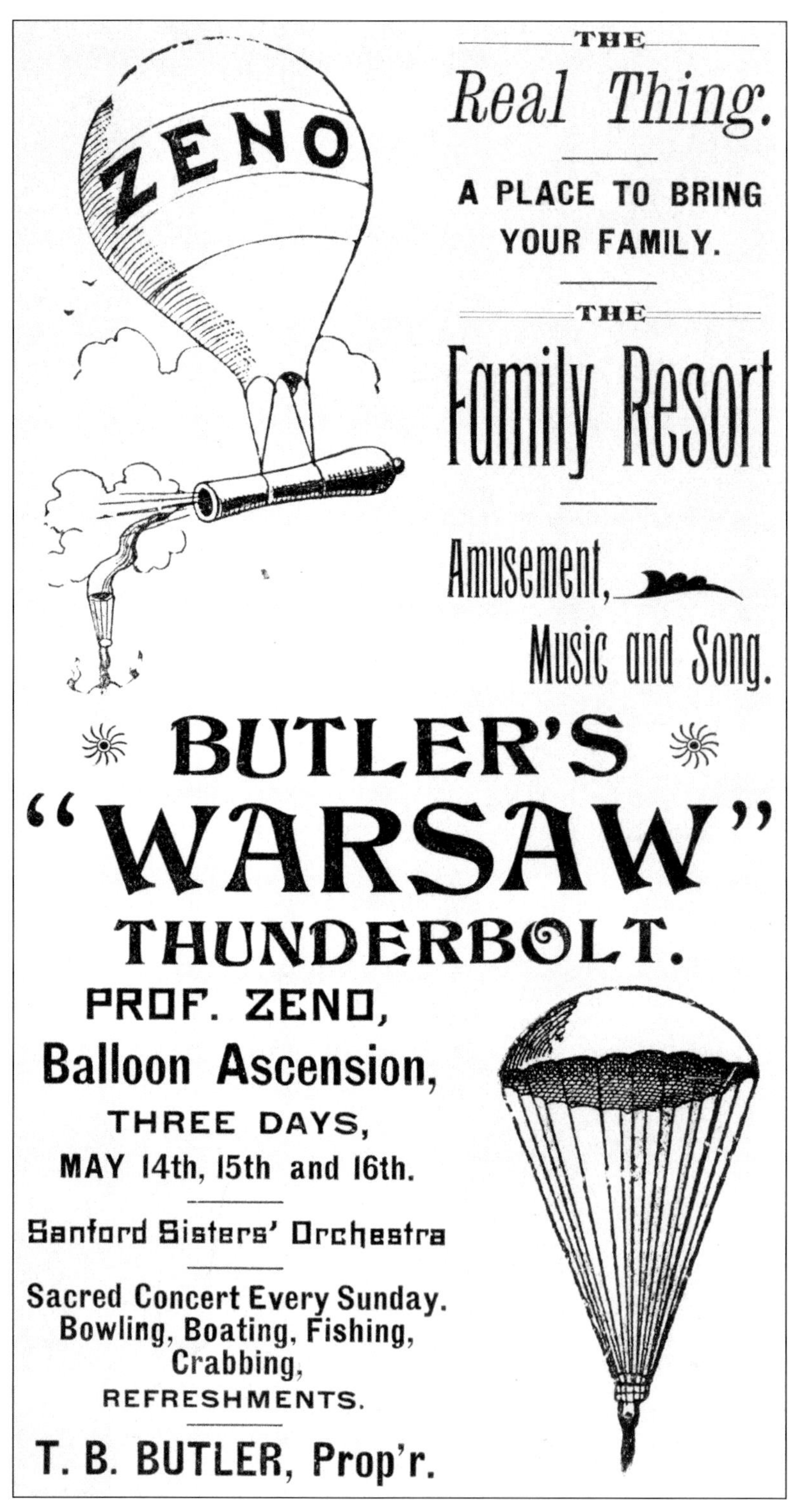

This is an advertisement for the festivities held for May Week in 1895.

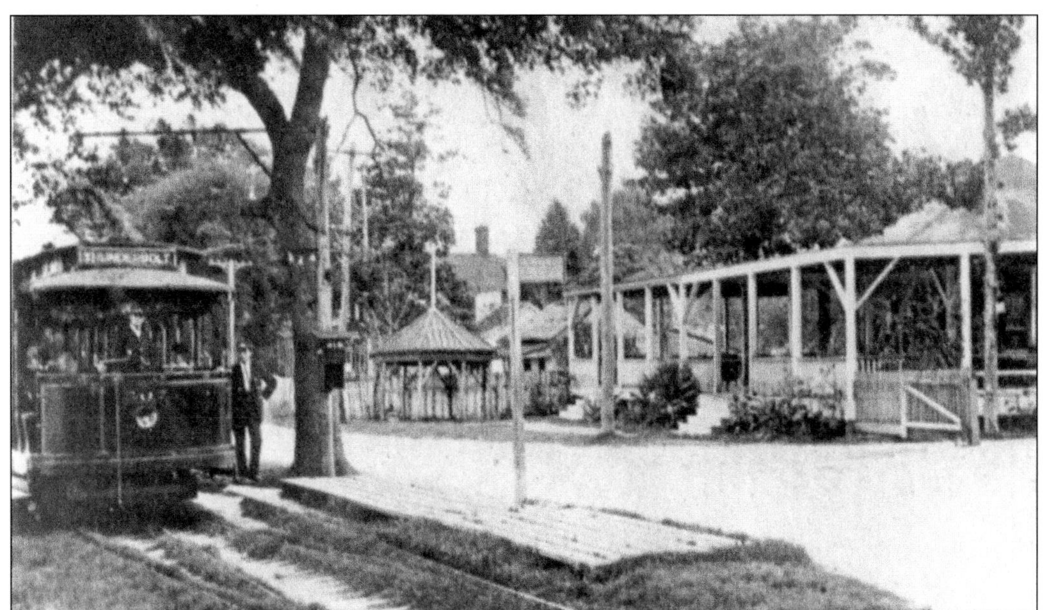

Bannon Lodge, a popular lodge and restaurant, was built around a large oak tree. In 1939, the building was razed by the estate of Mrs. Anna M. Bannon. This photograph shows the porch and outside seating that was available to diners.

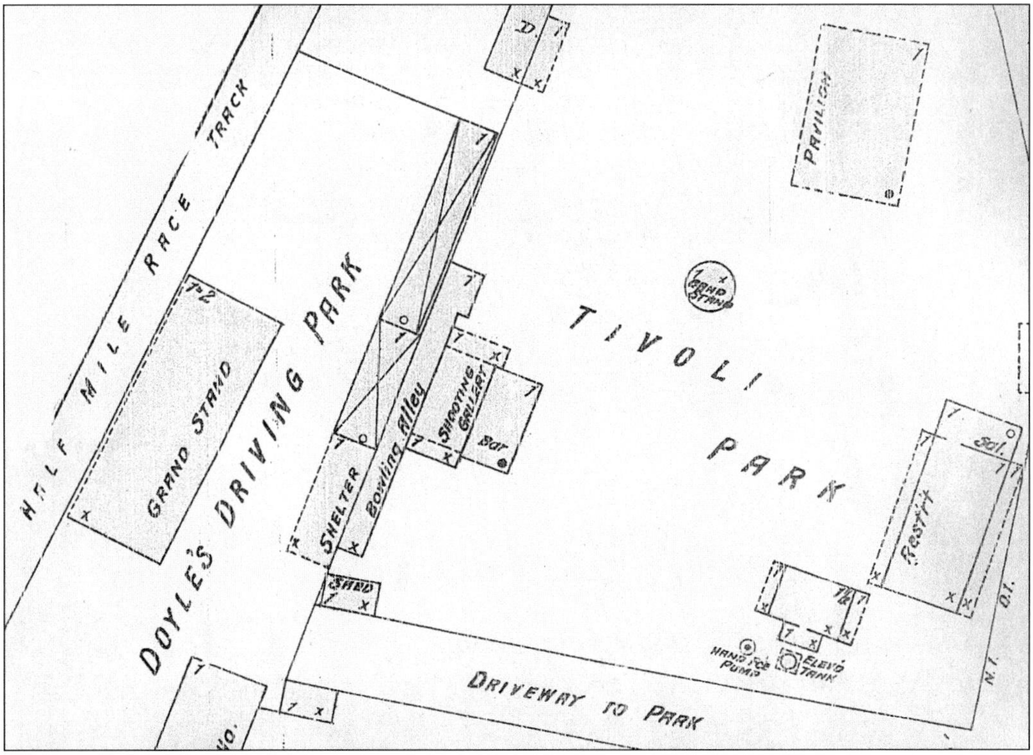

One of the area's fastest half-mile horse tracks was to be found at Thunderbolt. Capt. Michael J. Doyle was the proprietor of the track. The 1916 Sanborn Fire Insurance map shows a section of the track and the grandstand, along with other amusements.

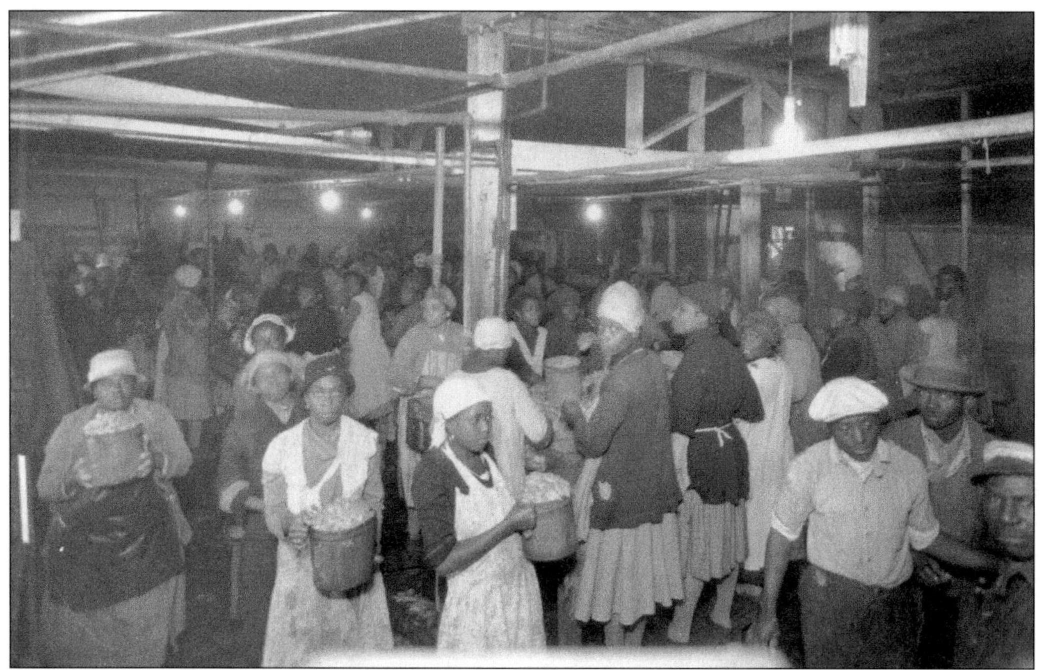

Streetcars enabled workers to go to where the jobs were located. These photographs, taken in the early 1930s, show workers at the Maggioni Shrimp Factory in Thunderbolt. The facility was a multi-building operation that extended over the bluff and included separate peeling and packing structures. A number of other buildings along the river were dedicated to similar purposes.

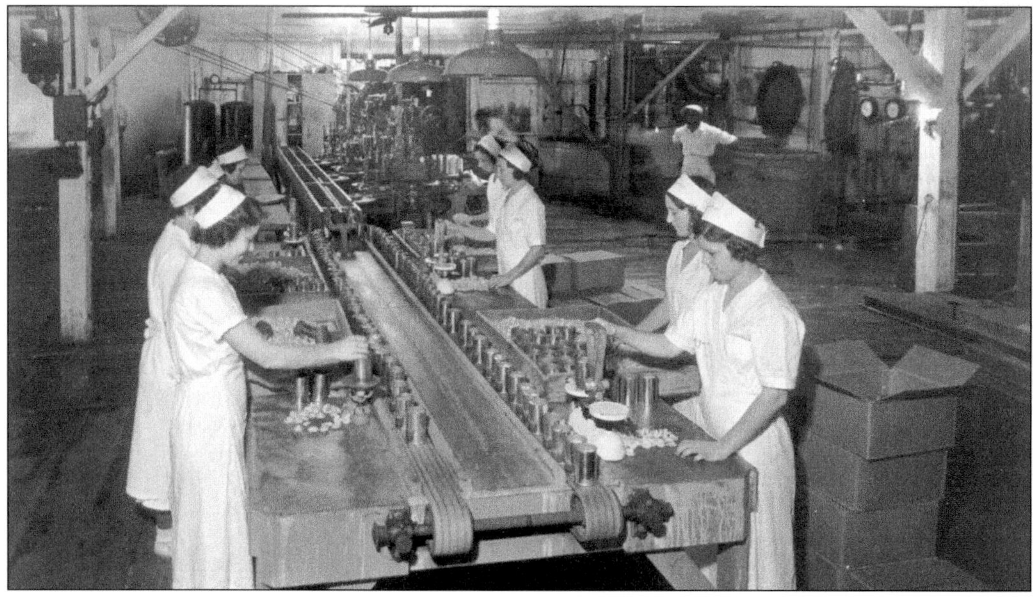

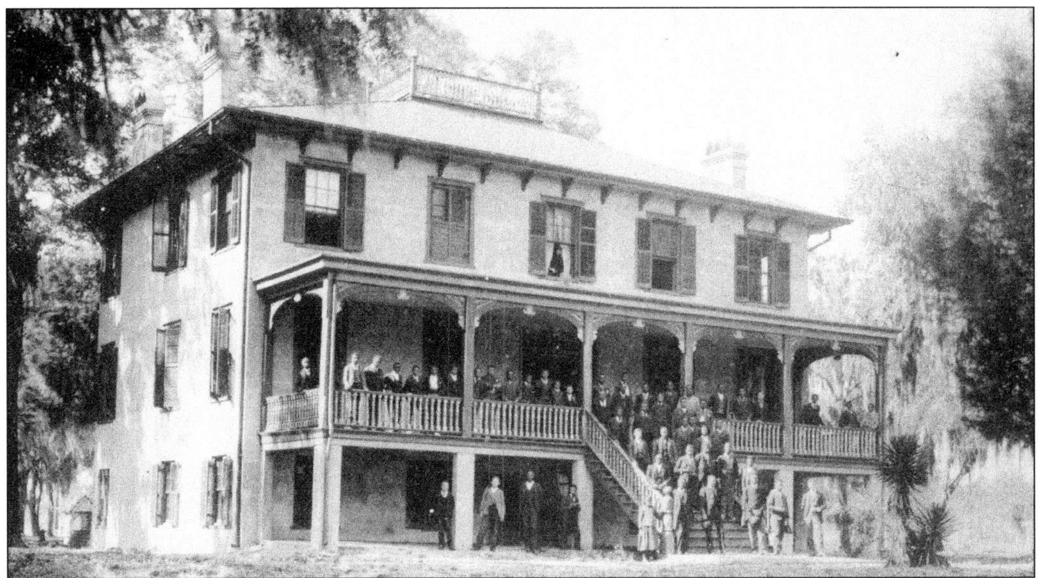

In 1890, the General Assembly "established in connection with the state university, and forming one department thereof, a school for the education and training of colored students." This school was named the Georgia State Industrial College and situated in Chatham County, a half mile southwest of Thunderbolt. As of 1933, the campus was composed of 20 buildings on 120 acres of land, including 50 used for agricultural purposes. The school is now Savannah State University. The campus could be reached by the streetcar line running between Thunderbolt and Isle of Hope. These two images show students and buildings around 1893.

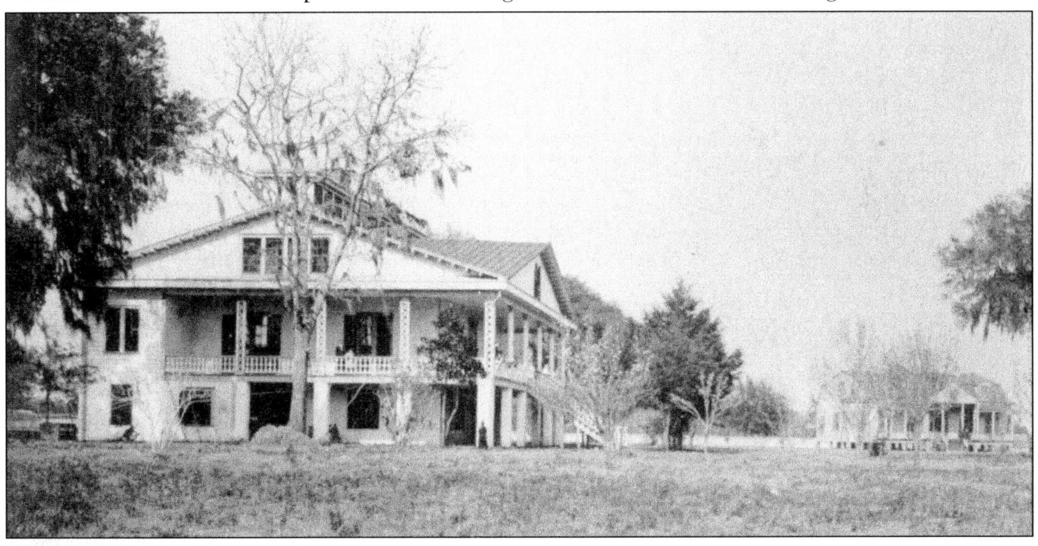

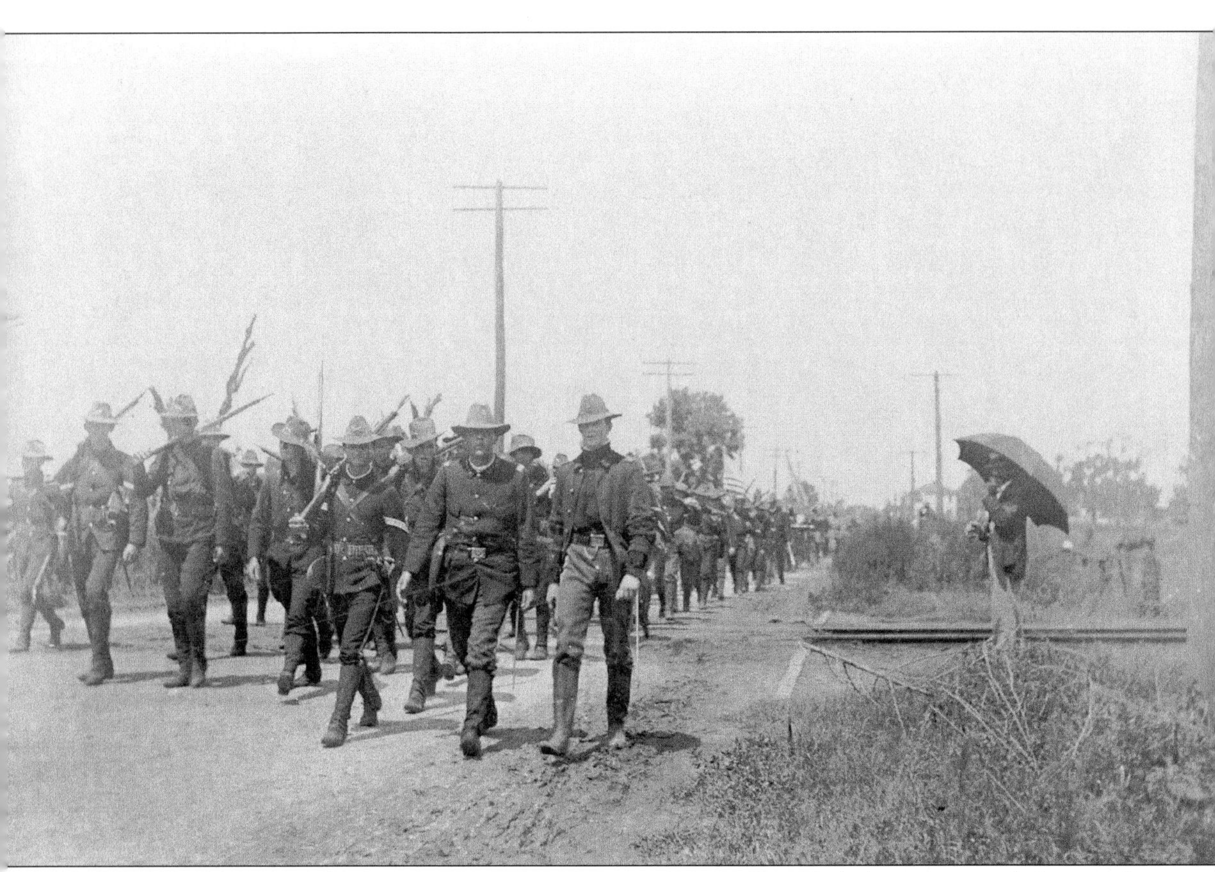

Prior to the Spanish American War, troops camped in Thunderbolt and around Savannah waiting to be sent to Cuba. Toward the end of 1898, approximately 13,000 troops were in the area. Many of them viewed Savannah through the windows of the electric streetcars. This group of soldiers, possibly from the 3rd Nebraska, was on its way to the transport, the *Minnesota*, taking them to Santiago.

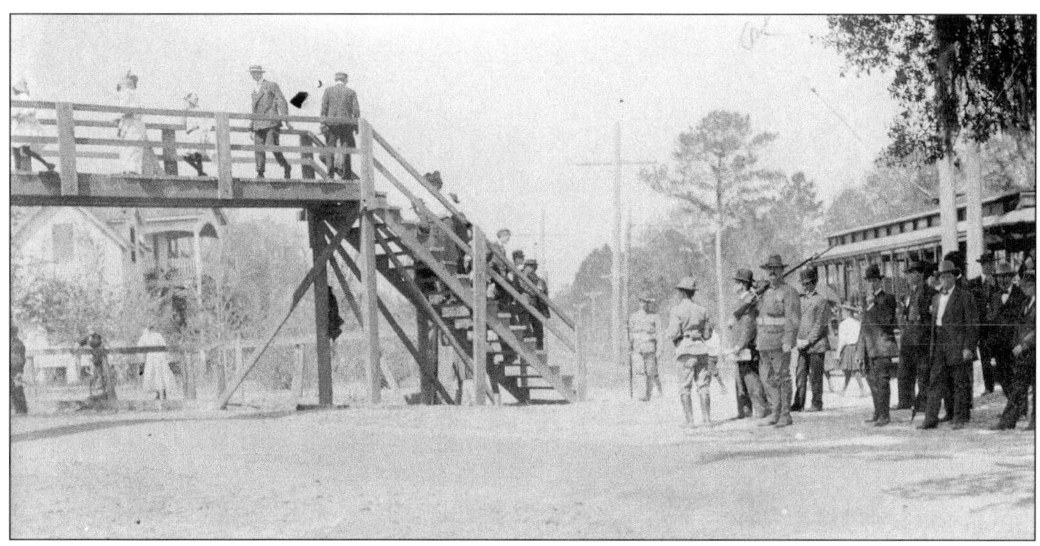

In 1908, 1910, and 1911, automobile road races were held, attracting international competitors and large crowds of spectators. These two photographs show streetcars at a pedestrian bridge over the race course. The 1910 racetrack crossed the streetcar line in two places, so bridges were built at both crossings, and a train ran between them. An estimated 60,000 spectators turned out for the race. Since people traveled from Savannah throughout the day, the outbound trip did not present the logistical challenge the return trip did. All rolling stock was put into service. In all, approximately 8,000 people rode the streetcars every hour.

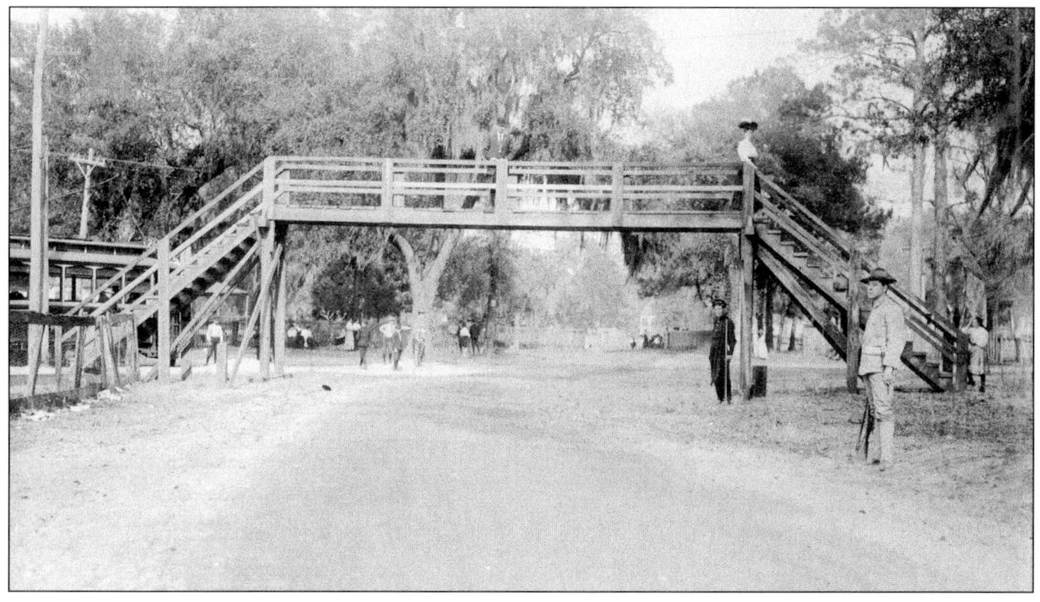

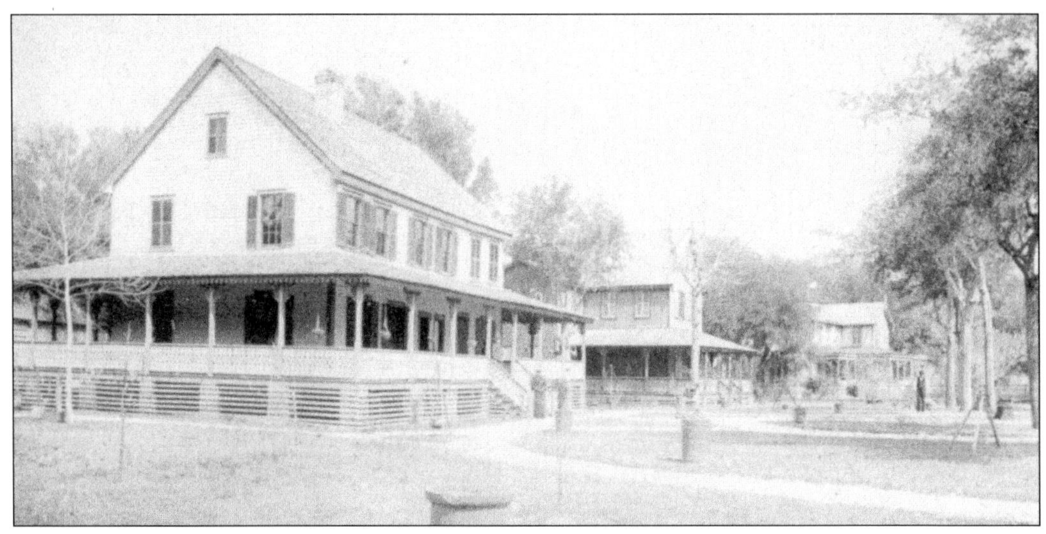

Isle of Hope, located about 9 miles south of Savannah's downtown, was the terminus for the S.S. & S. To the east is Skidaway River, where the Savannah Yacht Club held some of its annual regattas. While the island was home to year-round residents, it was promoted as a resort by the streetcar companies that ran there. Above is a view of some of the homes as they were around 1893.

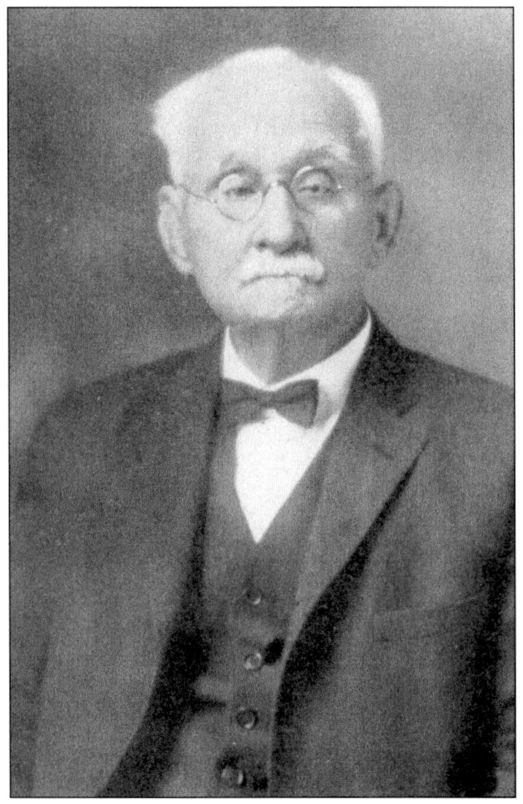

Savannah experienced a number of yellow fever epidemics, and suburban areas were seen as the healthy places to stay. People believed that yellow fever struck urban areas at night, so many left Savannah but remained within commuting distance, taking the train to town for their daily activities. Major Charles S.H. Hardee moved from Savannah, not because of yellow fever, but for general health reasons. He wrote about this in his book, *Reminiscences and Recollections of Old Savannah*. "My health was so impaired that my family physician, Dr. J.M. Schley, advised me to go out and live 'on the salts' for a year." His family moved to Isle of Hope in 1874 and remained there for 46 years.

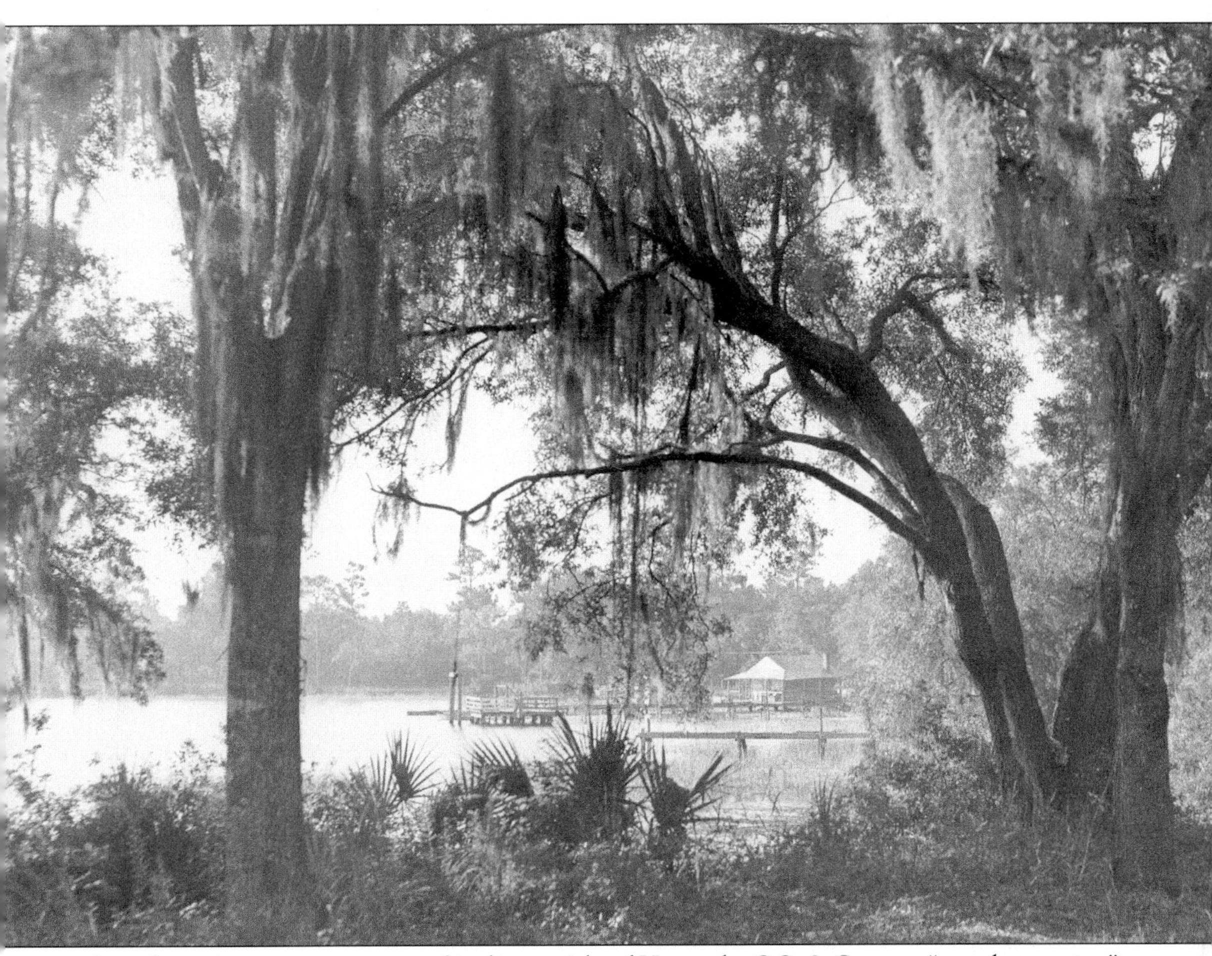

In order to increase patronage of its line to Isle of Hope, the S.S. & S. ran a "grand excursion" each Wednesday. A string band played for dancers on the platform over the water. Rowboats and sailboats were available for rent, and the Wheaton House offered meals. In 1882, C. & S. built a dancing pavilion and, for the swimmers, a large bathing house overlooking the river.

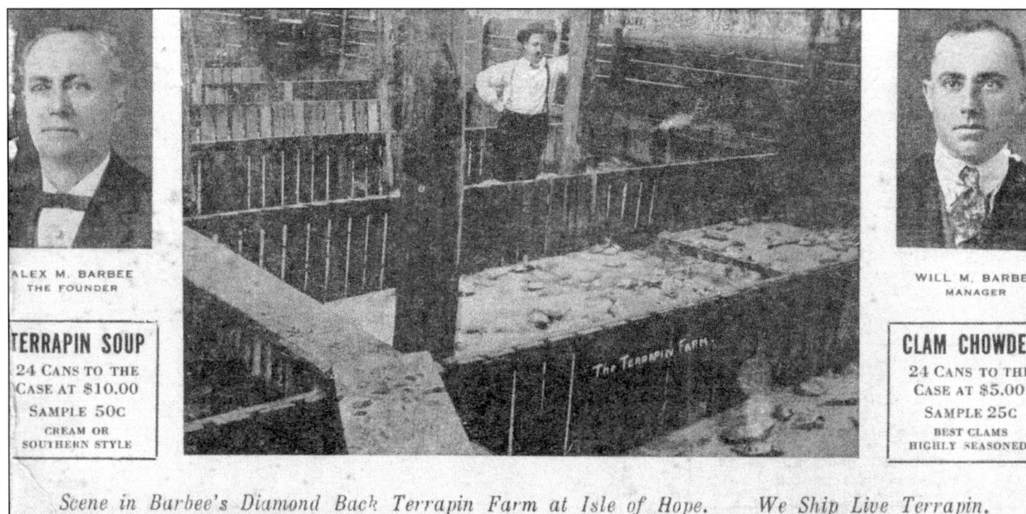

Alexander M. Barbee began his career with the Coast Line Railway around 1878. He was a conductor on the line to Isle of Hope when it was horse and mule drawn and later, when electricity was used. He moved to Isle of Hope in 1888, opening a small store two years later on land belonging to the railway. He made his son, William, a partner upon his 21st birthday. William managed the family business, bringing in prizefighters to perform at the pavilion and holding marathon dances during the Depression. This advertisement shows father and son and the business they ran.

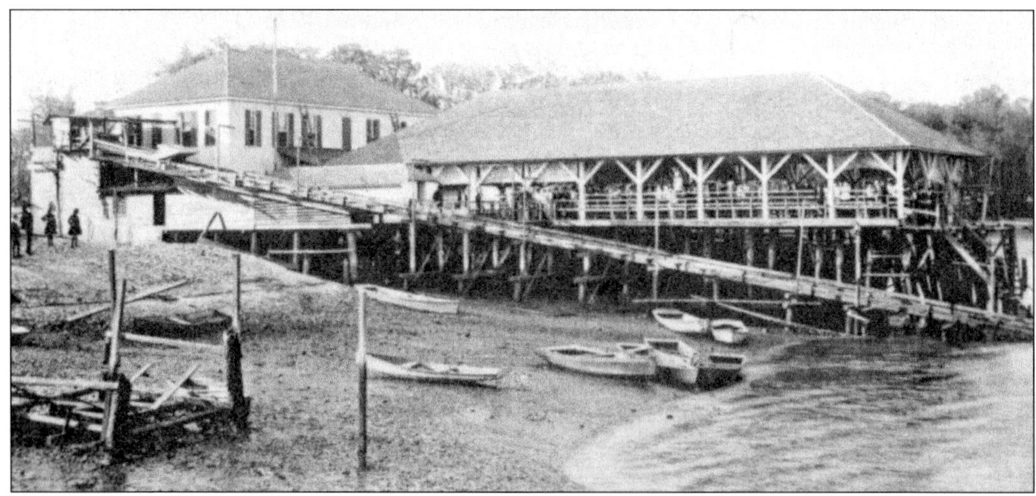

Barbee's Pavilion and Diamond Back Terrapin Farm was founded by Alexander Barbee as an experiment in 1893. The farm was a covered building, 150 feet by 60 feet, divided into 18 pens. The turtles were separated by age and size. An advertisement for the business claims Barbee was the first person to successfully hatch a terrapin. He converted a suitcase into a portable incubator with which he traveled in order to demonstrate his discoveries and promote his business. A trained terrapin, Toby, often traveled with him. Barbee died in 1929.

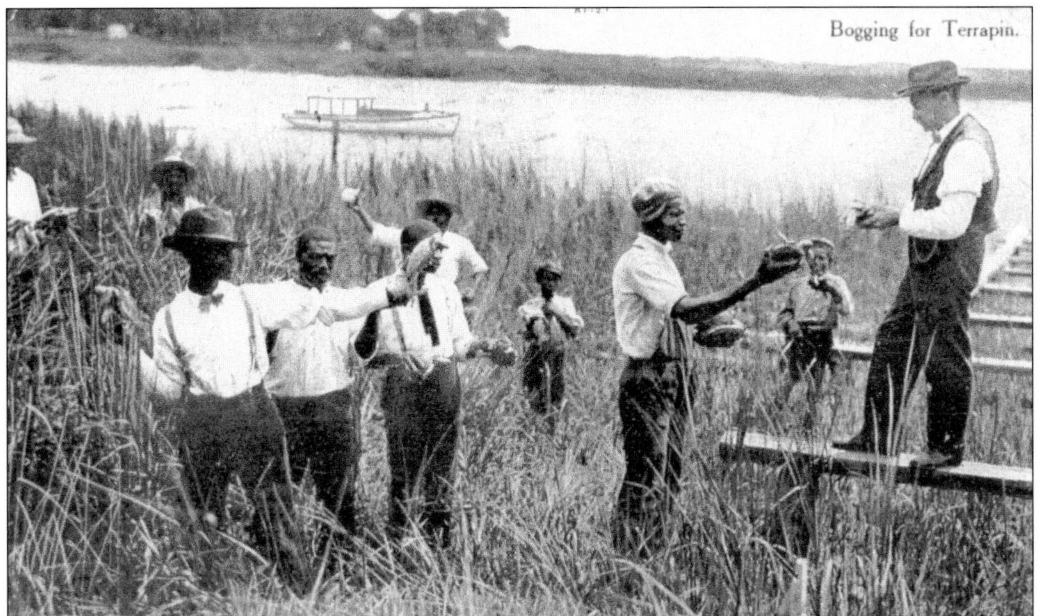

These two postcards illustrate the Barbee family's influence upon the economic and entertainment activities on Isle of Hope. The top postcard was mailed in 1910, and the bottom is undated.

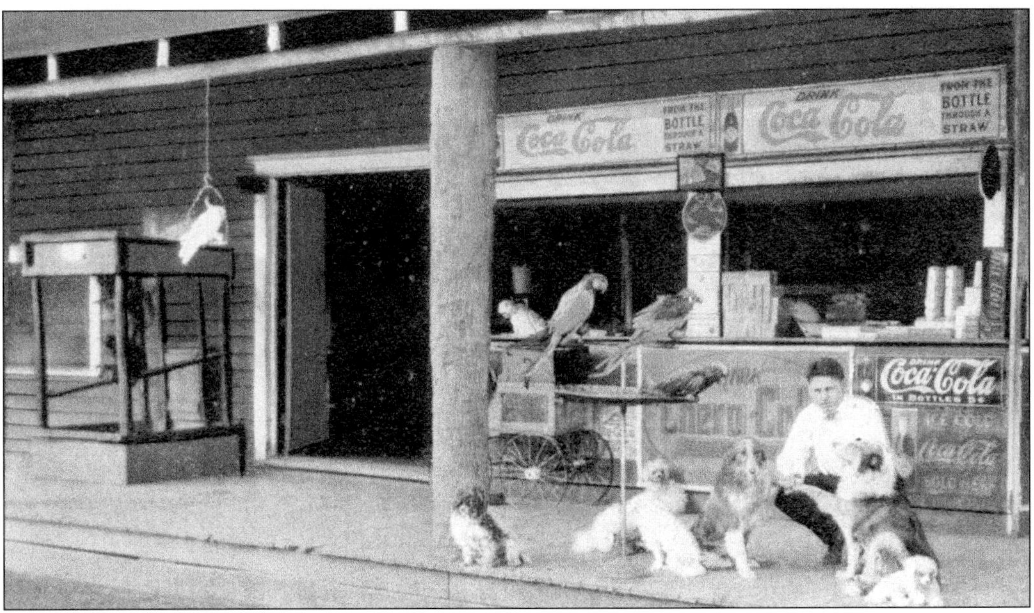

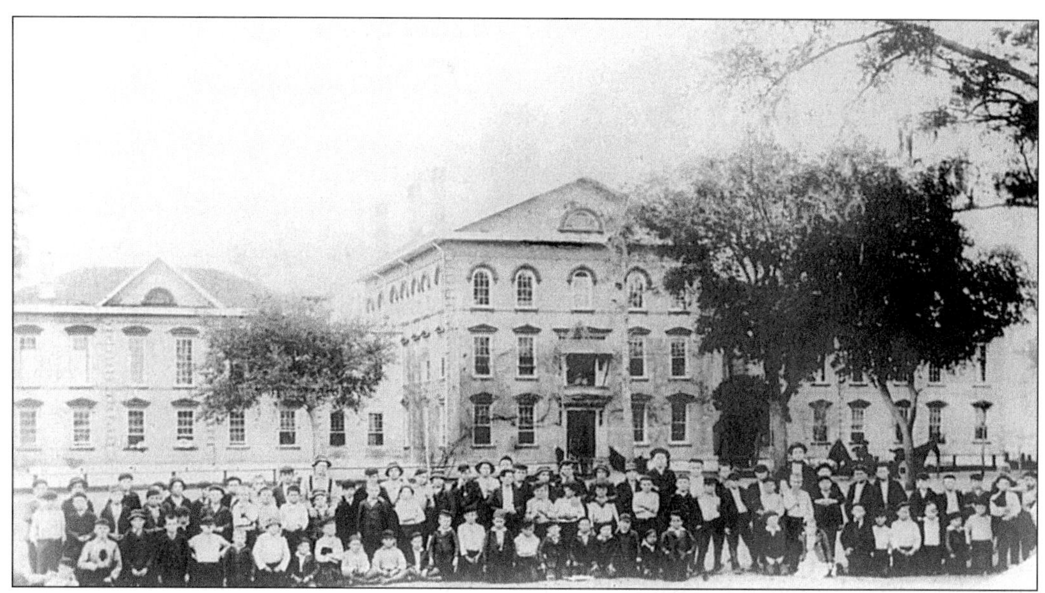

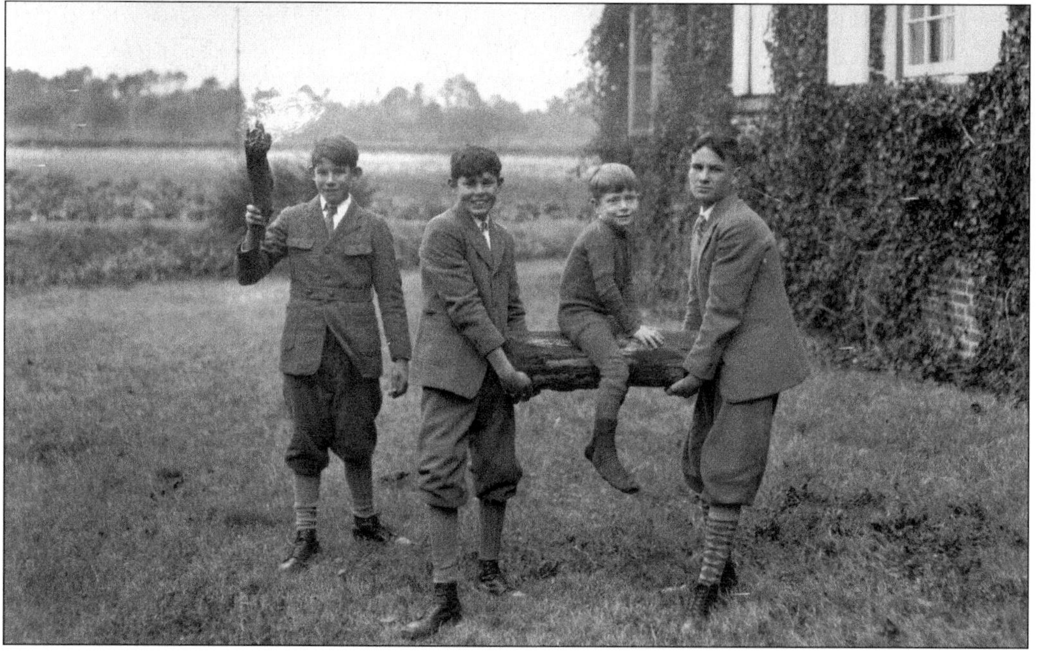

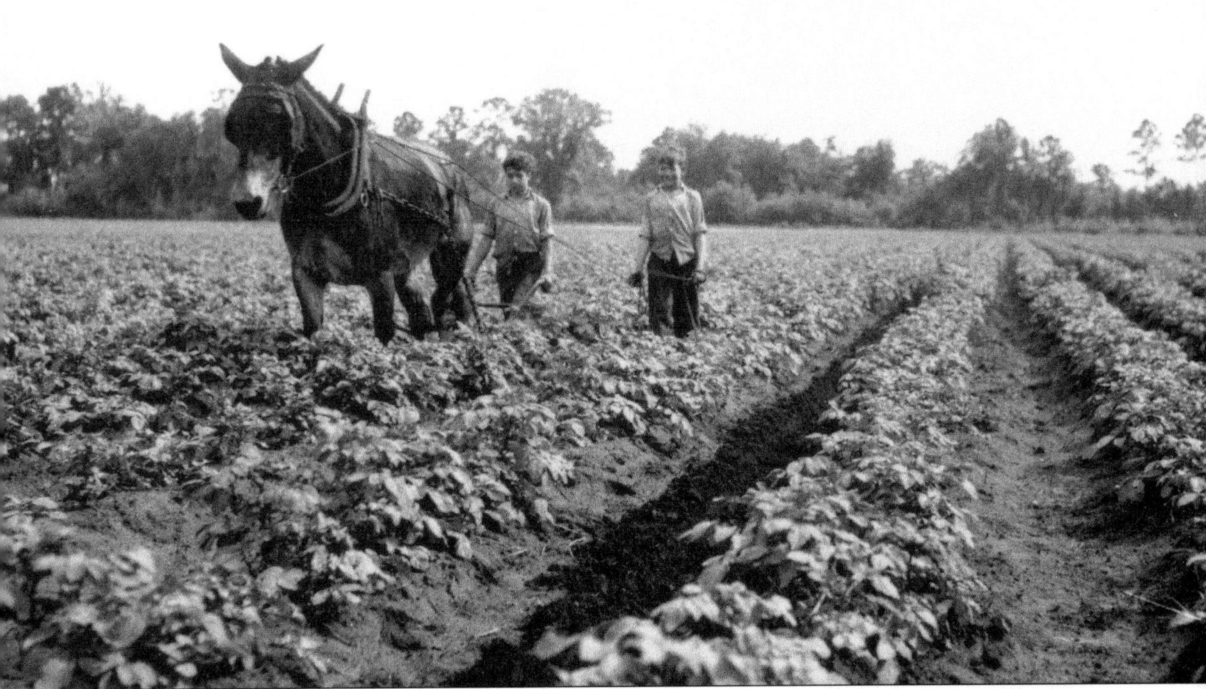

The Bethesda Home For Boys was situated 10 miles from Savannah, on a branch of the west fork of the Burnside River. Founded by the Rev. George Whitefield, Bethesda has operated as a home and school for boys since 1740. These three images (two on the previous page) are from 1915, 1930, and 1940 respectively. Agricultural education played a large role in the curriculum.

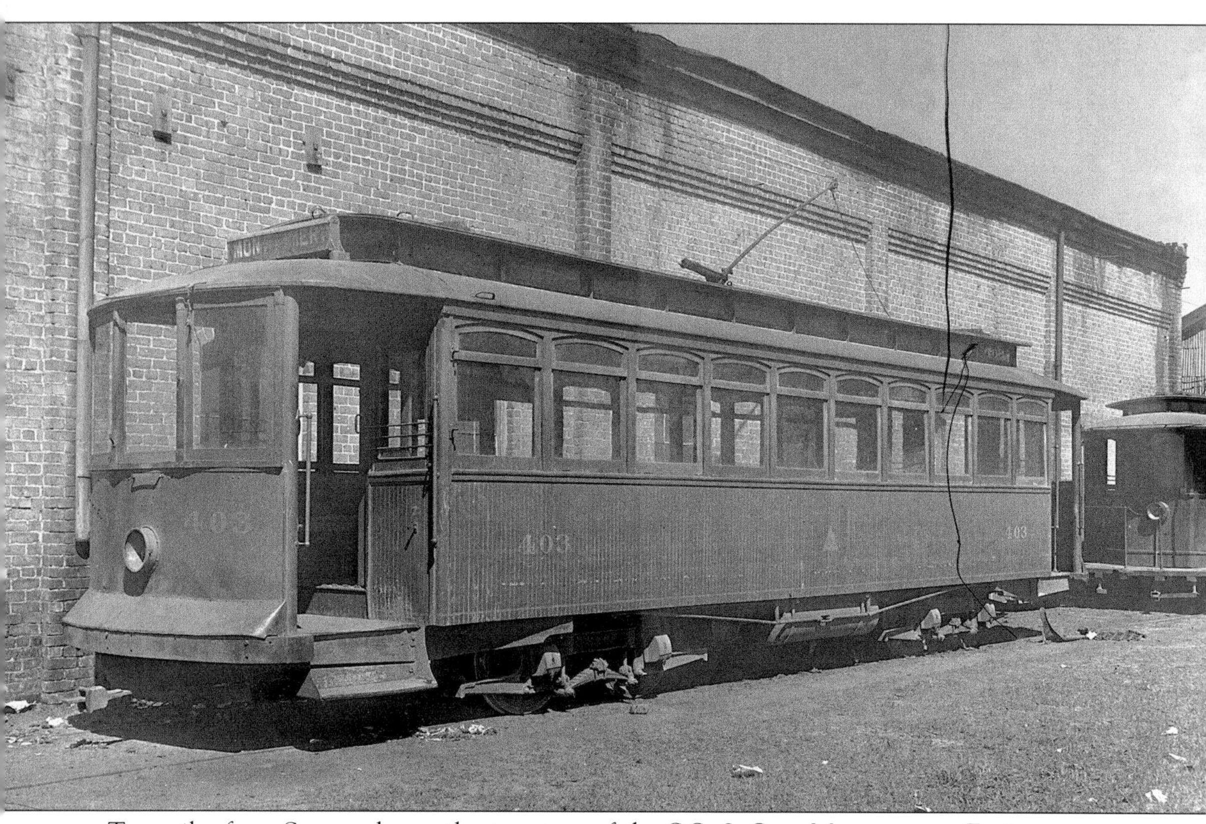

Ten miles from Savannah was the terminus of the S.S. & S. at Montgomery. Enticements to visit Montgomery were provided by the streetcar companies and by private business owners. The C. & S. ran special schedules to accommodate holiday travel to the "salts" and often provided live music. The C. & S. held music programs in the morning and afternoon. Car #403, pictured above, was to make the run to Montgomery.

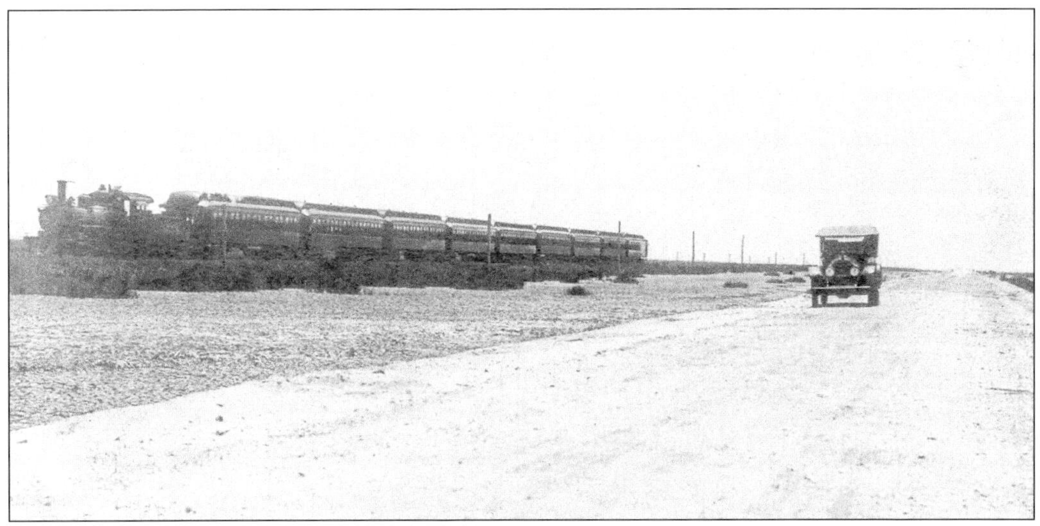

Tybee Island was developed as another resort destination. The train to the island was never pulled by mules or powered by electricity, but it was created and used for reasons similar to those of Chatham County's in-town and suburban streetcar lines. The Savannah and Tybee Railway was incorporated by November of 1885. Construction began in August 1886. The line later became part of the Central of Georgia Railway.

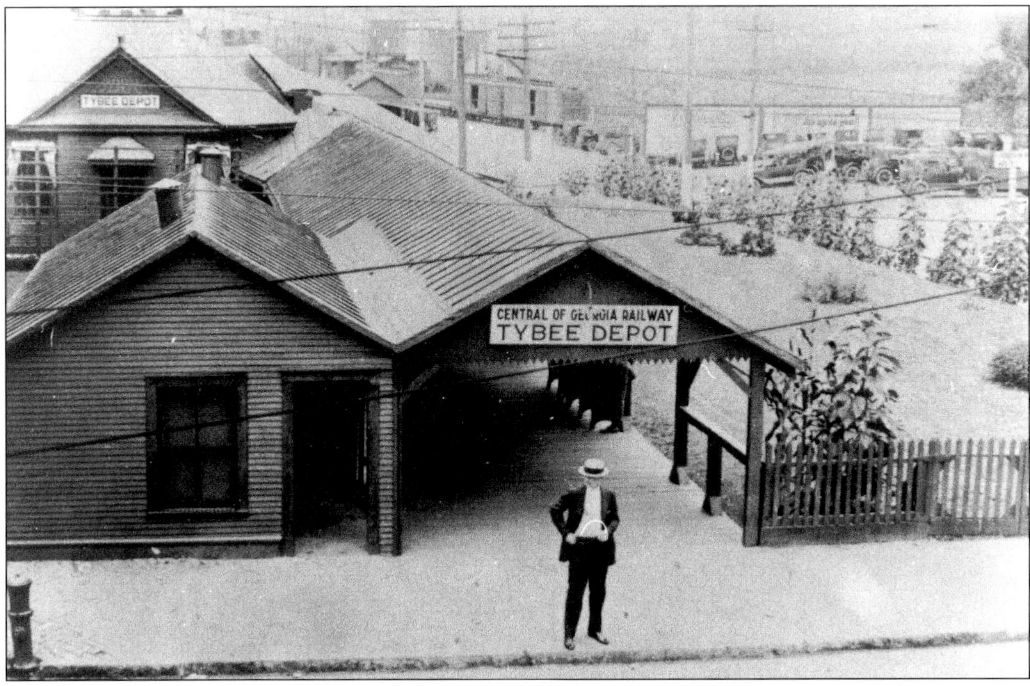

The Tybee Depot stood at 136 Randolph Street, on the eastern edge of Savannah. Streetcars connected the passenger stations on West Broad Street so that out-of-town visitors could easily transfer directly to the train to Tybee. The C. & S. employed an agent to facilitate travel to and from Tybee.

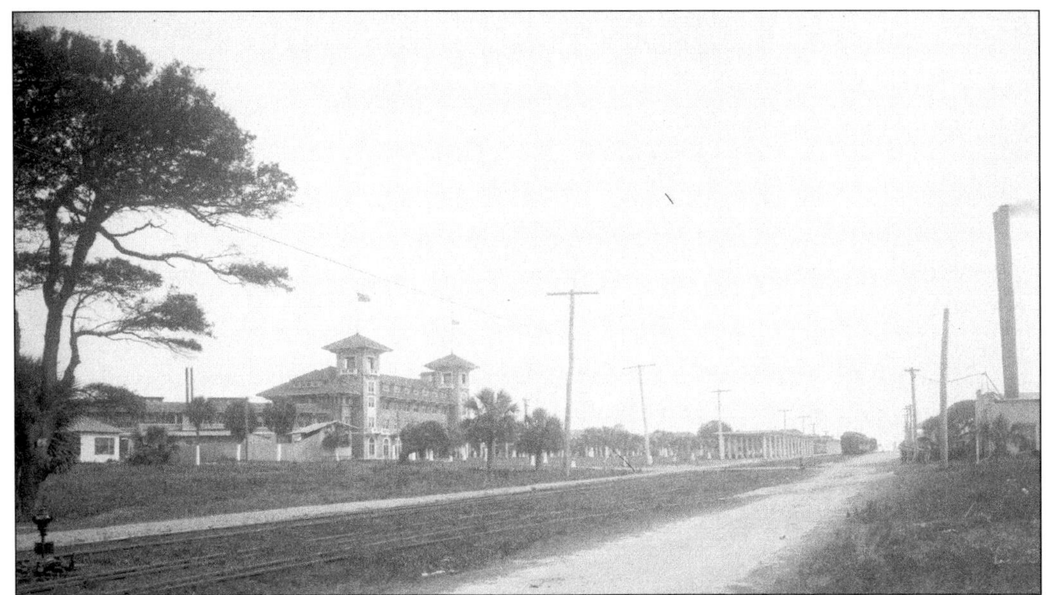

The Tybee Improvement Company was formed to increase the market value of property on the island. Investors included Thomas F. Screven, N.O. Tilton, and J.H. Estill. In 1888, it was decided to divide the Screven land into lots for sale.

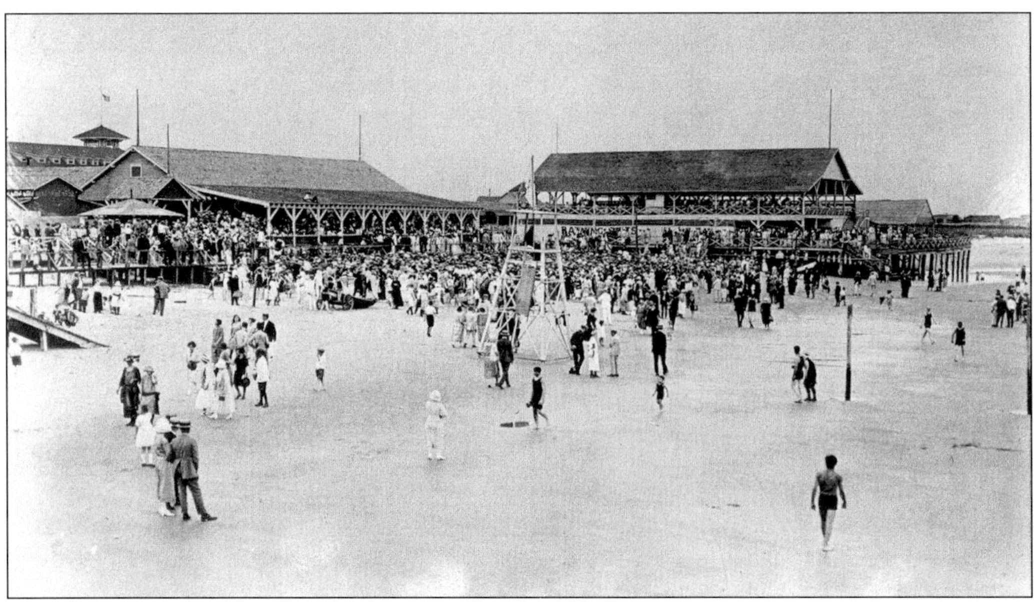

This view of the beach shows the pavilion that stood in 1925.

Three

ELECTRIFICATION: 1889–1902

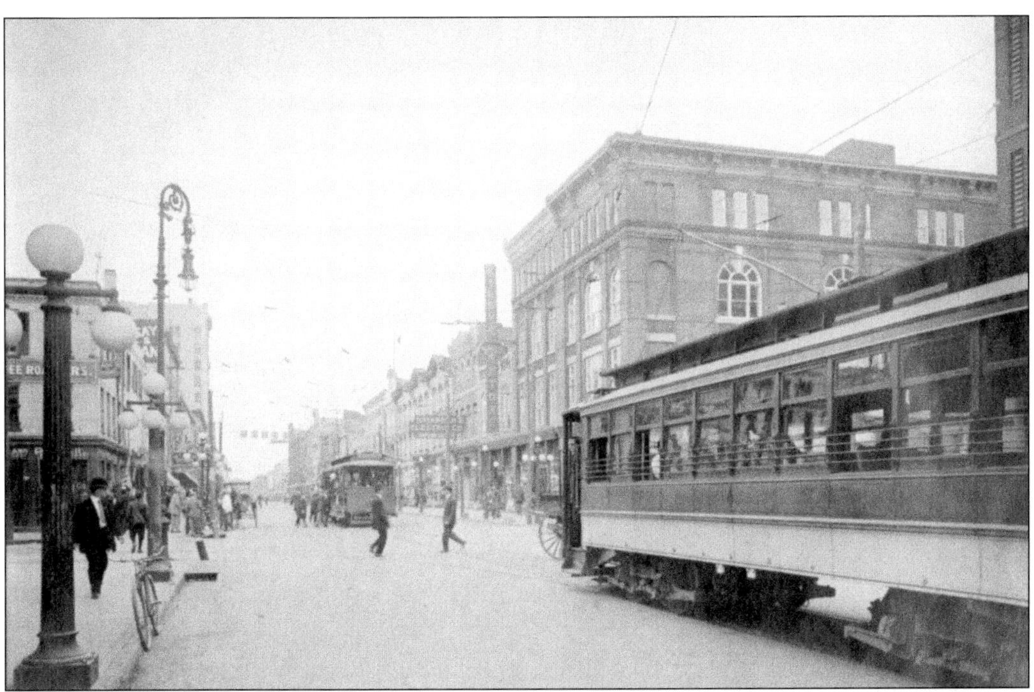

Electrification of the streetcars offered a number of improvements over horse-drawn cars. Electric cars were less expensive, faster, safer (safer for both horse and passenger), and more efficient. The *Morning News* noted the cost as being 50% less per passenger. Speed could vary between 4 and 15 miles per hour, and a larger number of passengers could be carried by adding extra cars, called trailers. This is a view looking east on Broughton Street.

Memorandum of Insurances

Amount		Property		Construction
$2000	on	Office 2nd Avenue		frame
$1,000	"	Machine shop "Repair"		frame
$4,000	"	fixed & movable Machinery		frame
$ 700	"	Sheds outside cars		do
$1.200	"	Stable Whitaker St		do
$ 600	"	Carshed street cars		do
$ 200	"	feed house		do
$ 500	"	Dance Pavillion Battery Park		do
$ 500	"	Stable Battery Park		do
$ 200	"	Car Shed do do		do
$ 500	"	Dwelling at Montgomery	10 miles from Savh	do
$ 250	"	Bar & Billiard room do		do
$ 350	"	Bowling alley do		do
$ 100	"	Kitchen do		do
$ 200	"	Station House do		do
$ 1,000	"	Building Depot Horse Isle of Hope	7 miles from Savannah	do
$ 500	"	Dance Shed do		do
$ 200	"	Small dwelling Anderson & Cemetery St		do

Insurances on Animals

$2000 On animals in the Whitaker St Stables - but loss confined to not over $30 on each animal -

2400 " animals in the Battery Park St Stables loss confined to $60 on each animal

$600 " animals in the Liberty St Stables, loss confined to $2 on each animal

$5000 @ 2½ $125. Prem

Business expenses varied. In addition to construction and maintenance, there were costs such as insurance, new equipment, and care for the horses and mules. Among documents in the C. & S. collection is an itemized memorandum of insurance. Listed were amenities at Montgomery, including a dwelling, a bar, a billiard room, a bowling alley, a kitchen, and the station house. Rolling stock included three locomotives, the *Claghorn*, *Rauers*, and *Hartridge*; 13 passenger coaches; a baggage car; a flat freight car; and 40 streetcars.

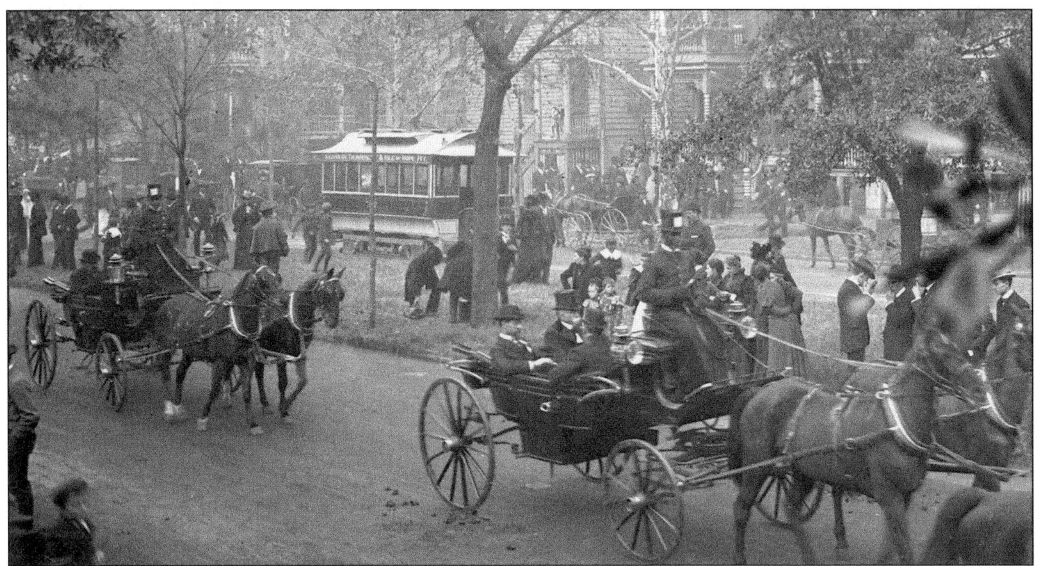

In 1889, the Merchants and Mechanics Land Company received their charter to build and operate a street railroad, the Savannah and Isle of Hope Railway (S. & I.), from Savannah to Isle of Hope with branches to Thunderbolt, White Bluff, and Rose Dhu. The company was formed by Estill and Dorsett, who built the line but then leased it to the Electric Railway Company (ERC), which was formed in September of 1890. The line built was urban, but combined with leased lines, it was a suburban system.

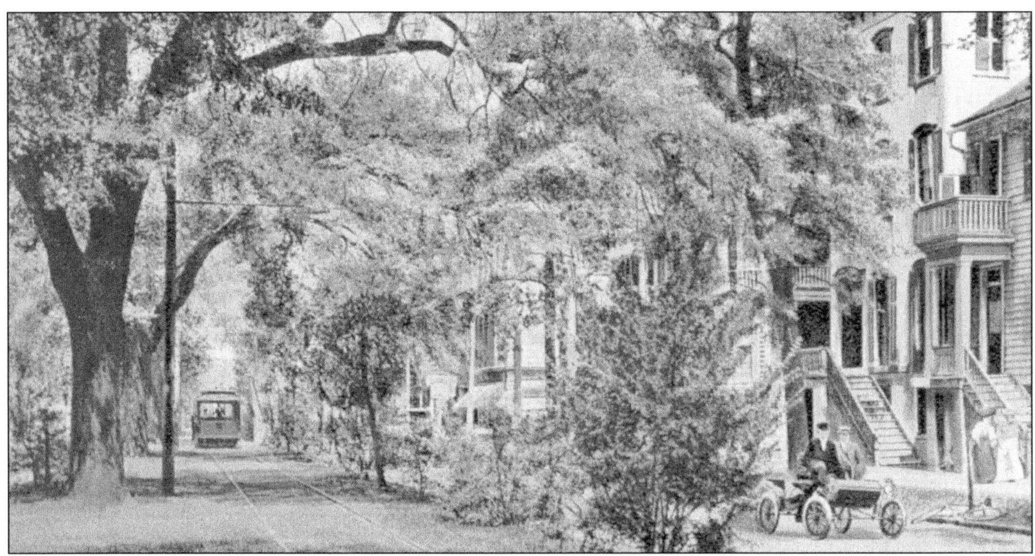

The Belt Line was bought by a group of investors from Nashville, Tennessee, who came to be referred to as the Nashville Syndicate. Isaac C. Rhea was their local representative. Later, the previous local owners would buy an option to repurchase their stock after the benefit of electrification showed a promise of financial gain. This is a view of Liberty Street.

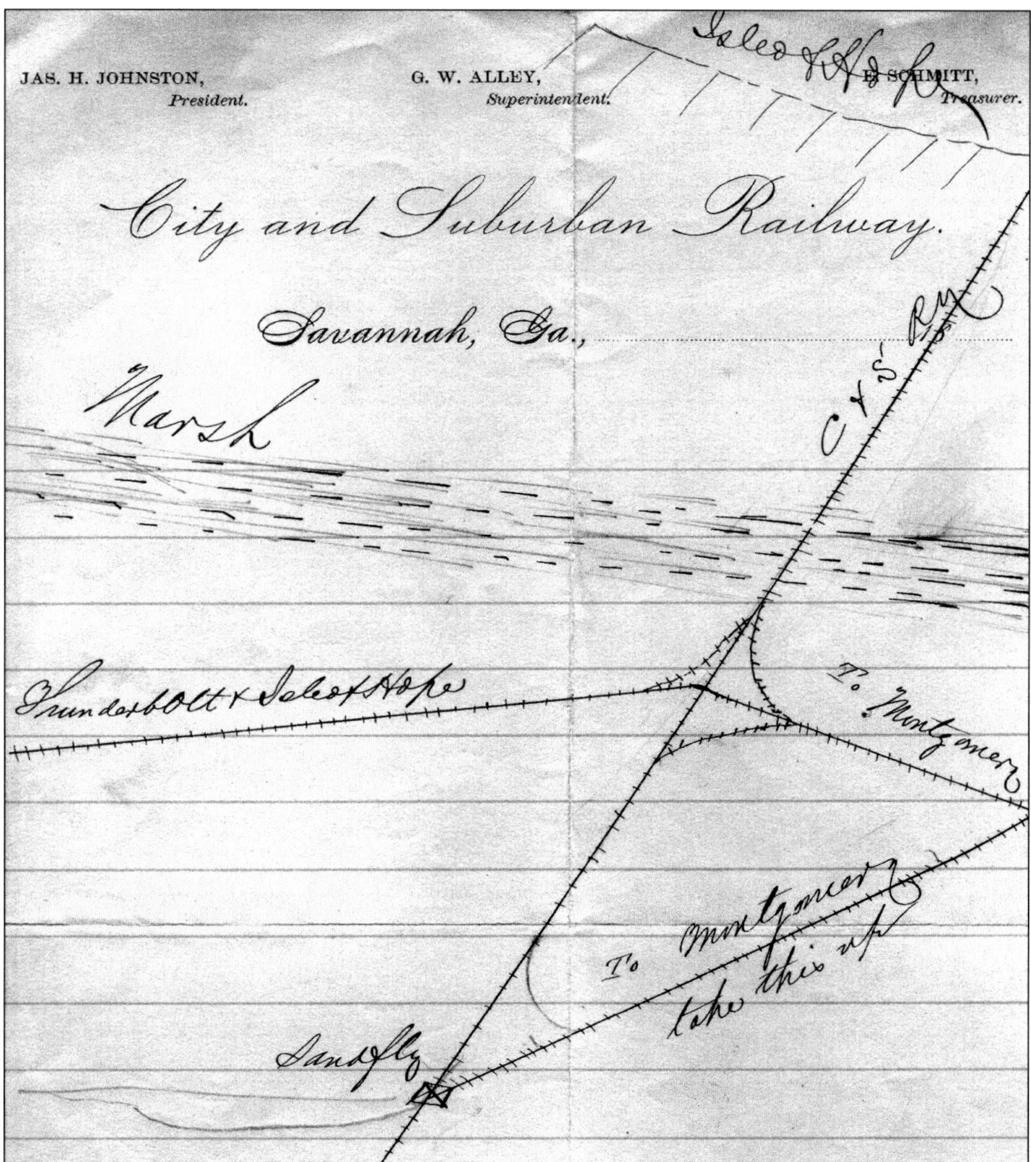

The Coast Line was extended from Thunderbolt to Isle of Hope. The 5-foot gauge rails covered a distance of 2.75 miles between Thunderbolt and Sand Fly in order to connect with the C. & S. Work began on each end to meet in the middle. The C. & S. line from Savannah to Sand Fly would be left in operation, and upon completion of the Coast Line, two railways would provide the service.

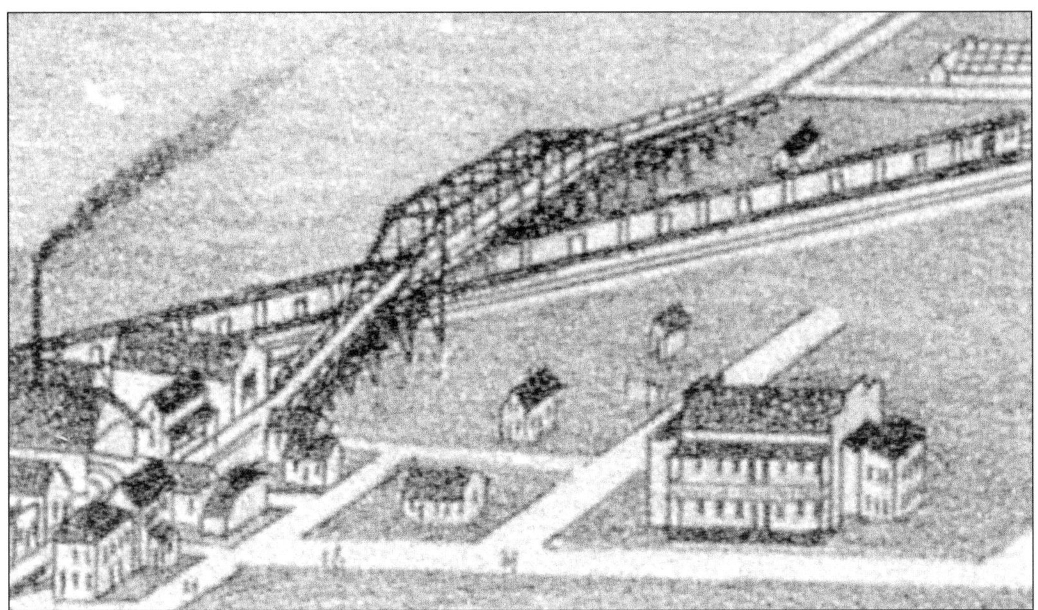

The right to operate by electric motor power through overhead wires was granted to the Belt Line, C. & S., and the Coast Line by City Council. Rhea said work to electrify the Belt Line would begin immediately. The power plant was to be located on the site of the current stables, at Habersham and St. Thomas streets, near the S.F. & W. tracks. Work on the conversion was progressing in October, with plans for completion by Christmas. George Parsons, owner of a controlling interest in C. & S. and the Coast Line, had not declared his intention to electrify these lines to the suburbs. *The Morning News* described him as slow at decision making but quick in action once a decision was made.

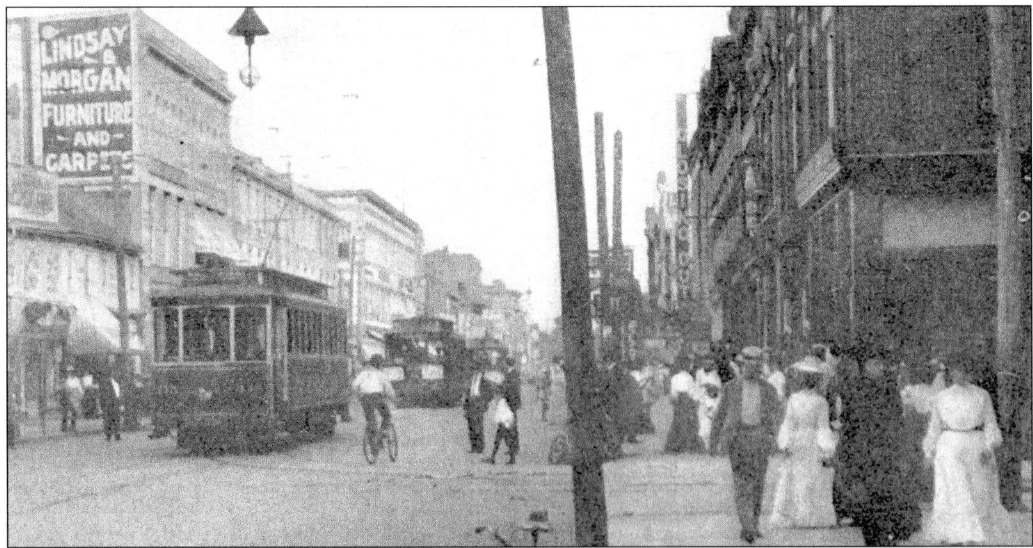

In 1888, the Belt Line had an iron bridge over the right-of-way of the S. F. & W. tracks near Thirty-seventh Street. The first car that traversed this bridge elicited a great deal of public interest. The newspapers called it "quite a curiosity" and commented on the number of people who rode the Belt Line to get a look at it. By February, the new line on East Broad Street was opened to the public.

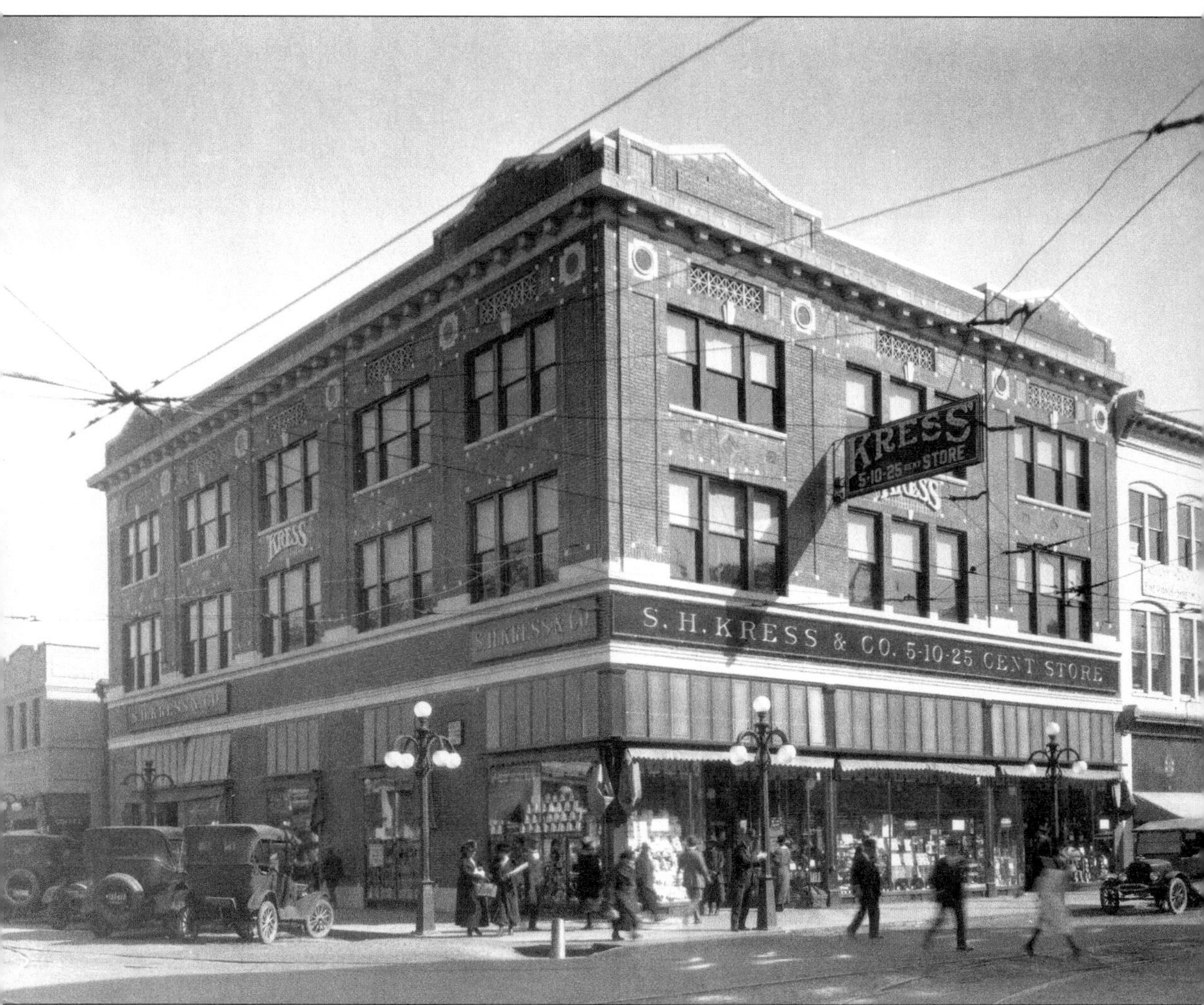

Officials of the various companies involved described how the new electrified system would work. Poles would be erected on both sides of the street to support a network of cables. The electrified cable would run parallel to the track, 19 feet above the ground and would be supported by the cables stretched across the street between the poles. Horse-drawn cars would remain in use to prevent interruption of service. Existing cars could be modified by the attachment of a motor, pole, and trolley (the grooved wheel at the end of the pole in contact with the overhead cable). Smaller cars could be used as trailers, pulled behind the powered car. In November of 1890, eight motorized cars arrived. Four more were expected. This photograph shows the overhead wires on Broughton Street.

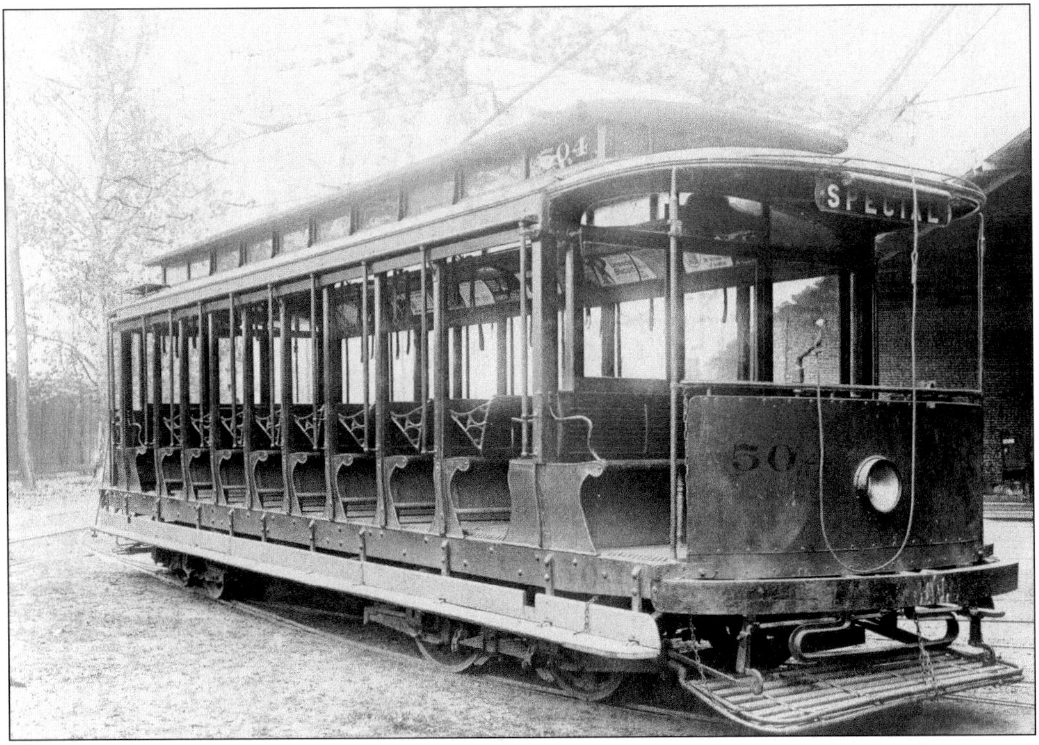

The first electric-powered streetcar in Savannah ran along the tracks of the Belt Line on November 24, 1890. The streets were lined with people, anxious to witness this modern marvel. A motorman controlled the speed that reached 12 miles an hour, allowing the circuit to be made in 42 minutes. The *Morning News* considered the conversion to electric power on the Belt Line a "wonderful stride in its advancement."

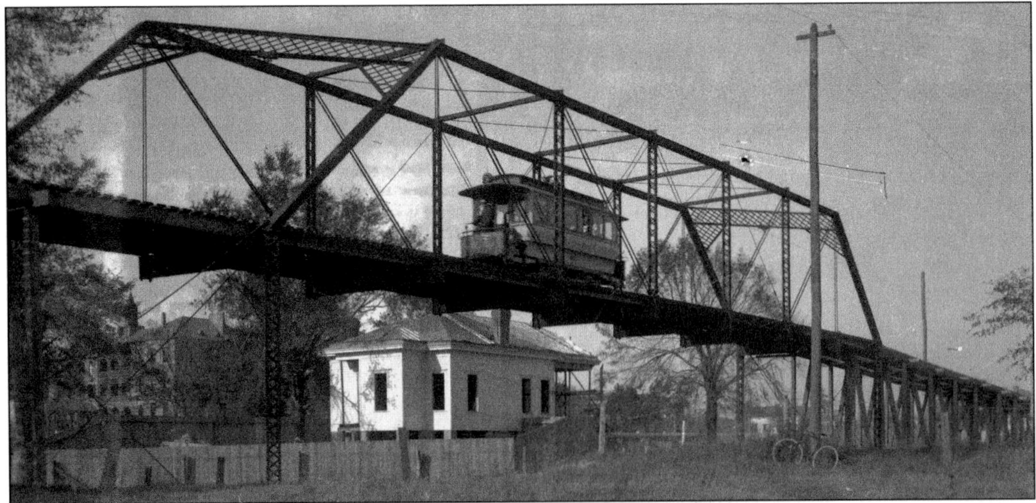

According to an account in *The Morning News*, "When the bridge near the company's headquarters was reached a test of the power of the current and the facility of controlling the car was made. The grade of the bridge is very steep. When midway in its ascent, the car was brought to a standstill and remained as if fixed to the track. A turn of the controller was made and the car went on up the grade in its steepest part as easily as on ground level."

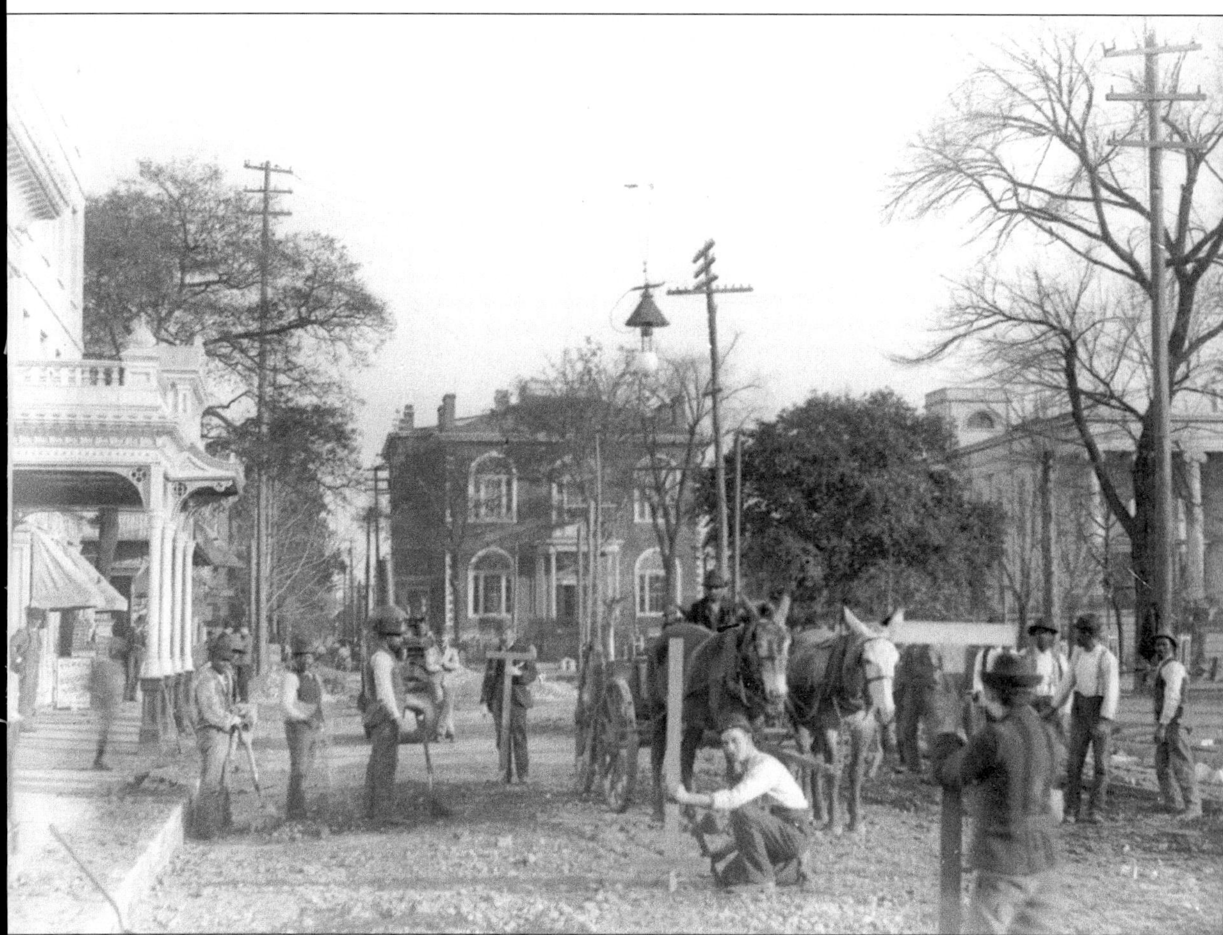

Possibly as a result of advantages due to electrification of lines, the General Assembly saw a flurry of activity having to do with street railroads during the last few months of 1890. Some of the resulting charters or amendments came to fruition in their original plan, while others were modified or abandoned. The General Assembly, on December 9, 1890, approved a 50-year charter for the ERC of Savannah. Jacob S. Collins, W.K. Wilkinson, Robert M. Hicks, W.F. McCauley, Thomas Nugent, Jefferson Randolph Anderson, Walter G. Charlton, William M. Mackall Jr., and Hugh Logan were named as incorporators. The route was to begin just east of the market, on St. Julian Street, and wind through town to the corporate limits out Ott Street. Permission was granted to extend the line to the wharves of the S.F. & W.

City of Savannah
Office City Engineer

W. J. Winn,
City Engineer.

Nov 29th 1892

Statement of the cost of Paving Grading and otherwise improving that portion of Balto. St lying between East Broad & West Broad &

Paid for	90684 Bus Oyster shells @ 4	3627
" "	6205 7/10 Lin Feet Streight Curb @ 31/4¢	1939
" "	81 6/10 " " Circular " @ 60/4¢	49
" "	Time of hands setting Curb	407
" "	" " " Grading Setting Curb & Paving Intersection	151
" "	" " W. H. Cosgrove Plumber lowering Water Pipe	17
" "	" " hands Grading & Shelling	781
" "	" " Teamsters " & Hauling Shells	1378
" "	Cost of Material & Labor building 10 Catch Basins	737
" "	" " 9000 Brick for paving Intersections	108
" "		$9191

As more companies formed and competed for the rights to certain streets, city council became less willing to grant any request made. The council members were divided into two camps. Some wanted a consideration to be paid by the railways, while others were willing to grant free rights-of-way with some restrictions and conditions imposed. In some cases, the railroad companies seemed to be pitted against one another in their offers to improve their chance of being granted the street for which they applied. Competition between the Belt Line and Enterprise Railroad arose over their mutual desire to run tracks through Drayton Street. Enterprise offered to assume the job of paving the road with asphalt if allowed to run a double track through the street.

Cost of Shelling & Grading Bolton St
from Abercorn to East Broad St
42966 Bus Shell @ 4 1718.64
Time of Hands Grading & Shelling 331.06
" " Teamsters Hauling 693.00
Total $2742.70

Total Area 49878.0 Sqr feet
Area of Plank 2029.9 "
Bal Area of Shells 47848.1 " = 5316.4 Sq Yds

Cost of Shelling from Abercorn to
East Broad St Per Sqr Yd $0.51.5

Belt Line Ry Co
Montgomery St 60x2 = 120
Barnard St 60x1⅞ = 112
Habersham St 55x2 = 110 342 ft = 38 Yds $19.57

Electric Ry Co
Price St 55x2²⁄₁₀ = 121 ft 13⁴⁄₁₀ Yds $6.90

Coast Line Ry Co
Habersham St xing 41⁷⁄₁₀ x 2²⁄₁₀ = 91³⁄₁₀ 10.1
Price St xing 43³⁄₁₀ x 2²⁄₁₀ = 95 10.6
Part Not Planked 798.0 = 818⁷⁄₁₀ Yds $421.6

City & Suburban Ry Co.
Habersham St 48⁶⁄₁₀ x 2²⁄₁₀ = 106.9 ft = 11.9
Part not Planked 663.8 675.7 Yds $347.98

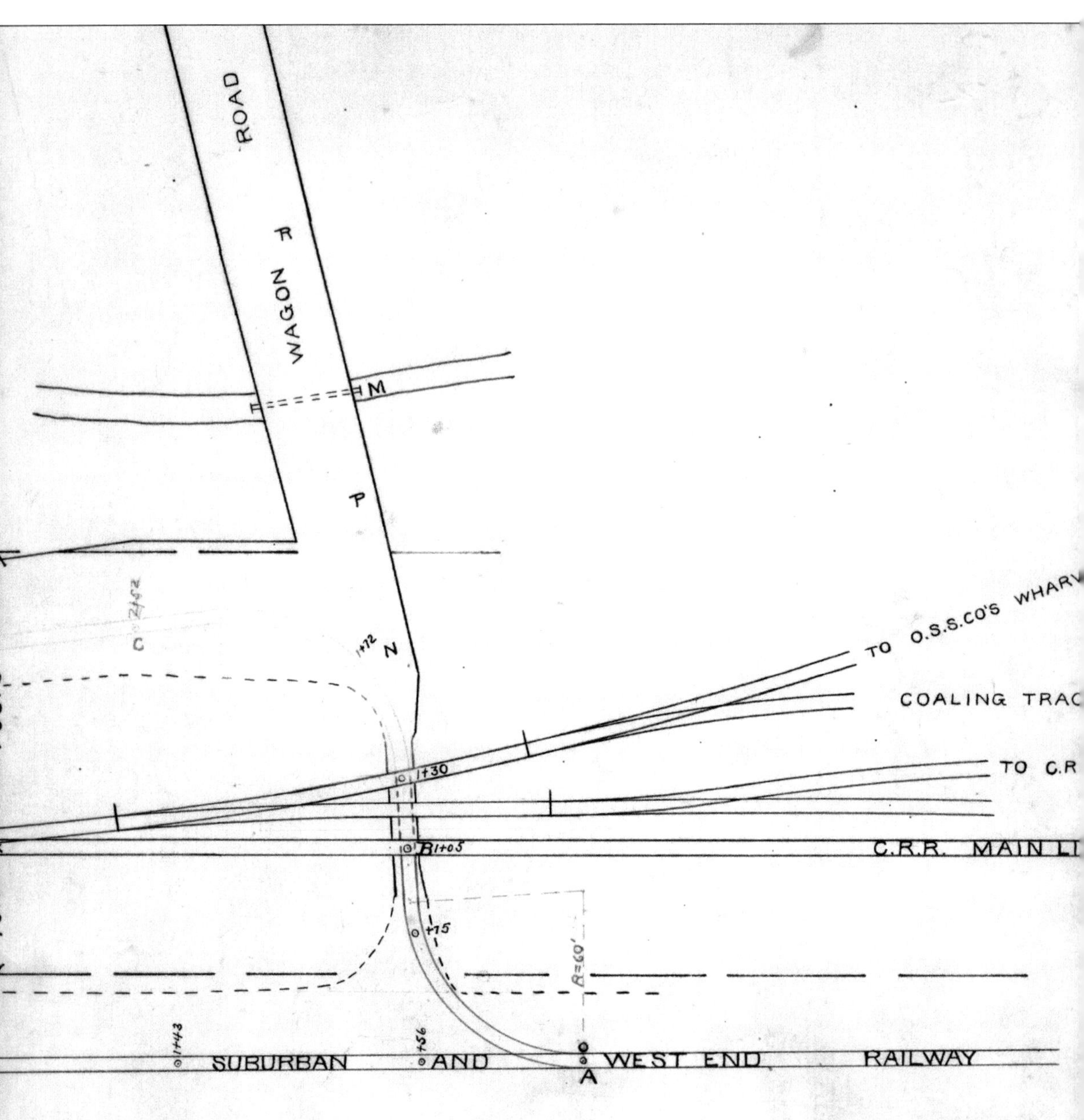

The Suburban and West End Railway was incorporated on December 27, 1890. It would operate lines from western Savannah out the Louisville and Augusta Roads to Jasper Spring, the Ten Broeck Race Course, and Lincoln Park, a "place for colored people." The line also had the authority to run to Wilmington Island and Thunderbolt.

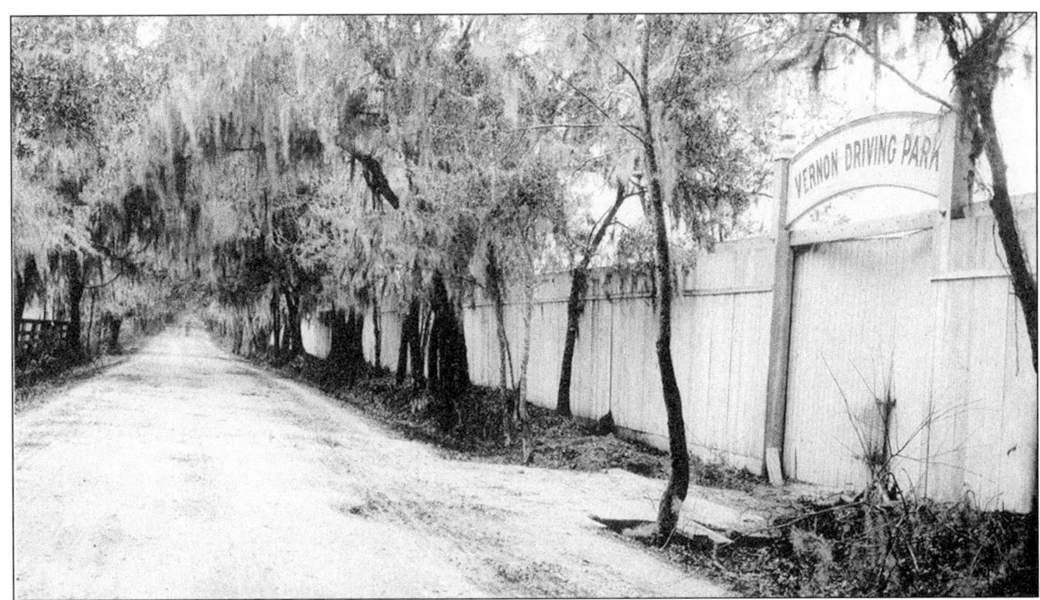

The Vernon Park Railway was incorporated by O.T. Rogers, F.D. Bloodworth, P.D. Daffin, Edward Karow, D.B. Lester, M.W. Dixon, and C.A. Reitze. The line was to go from southern Savannah to Vernon Park, a horse racing track located along the Vernonburg Shell Road, and on to White Bluff, Montgomery, and Rose Dhu. This company was incorporated on December 29, 1890.

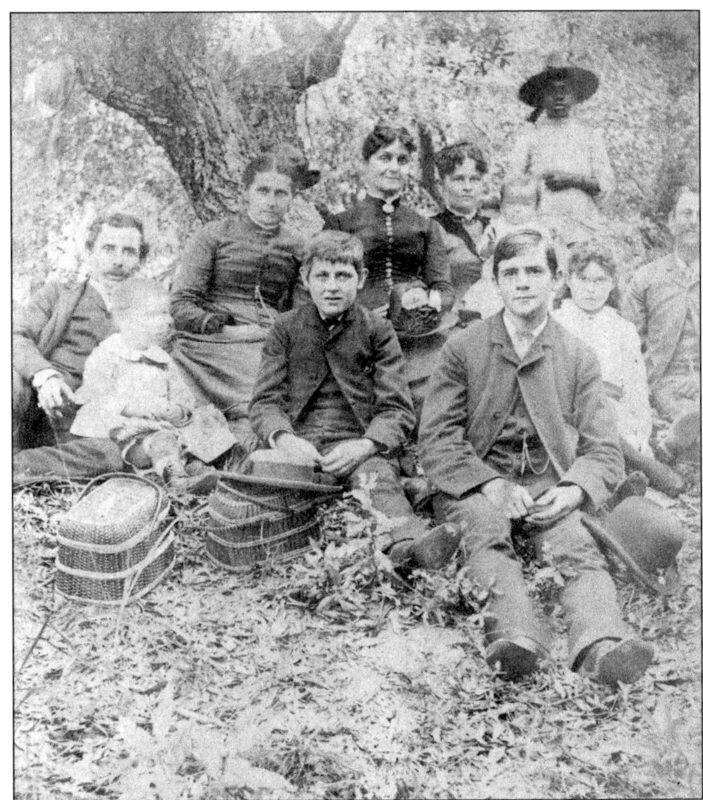

The charter of the S. & I. was amended in 1890 by the General Assembly to permit the line to extend roads, including Wheaton and Waters. By late August 1891, a regular schedule was run from Savannah to Thunderbolt. The line ran 3.25 miles, beginning at Habersham and Estill (now Victory) at a junction with The Belt Line. Groups, like the one pictured here, could travel outside Savannah to enjoy a picnic along the river.

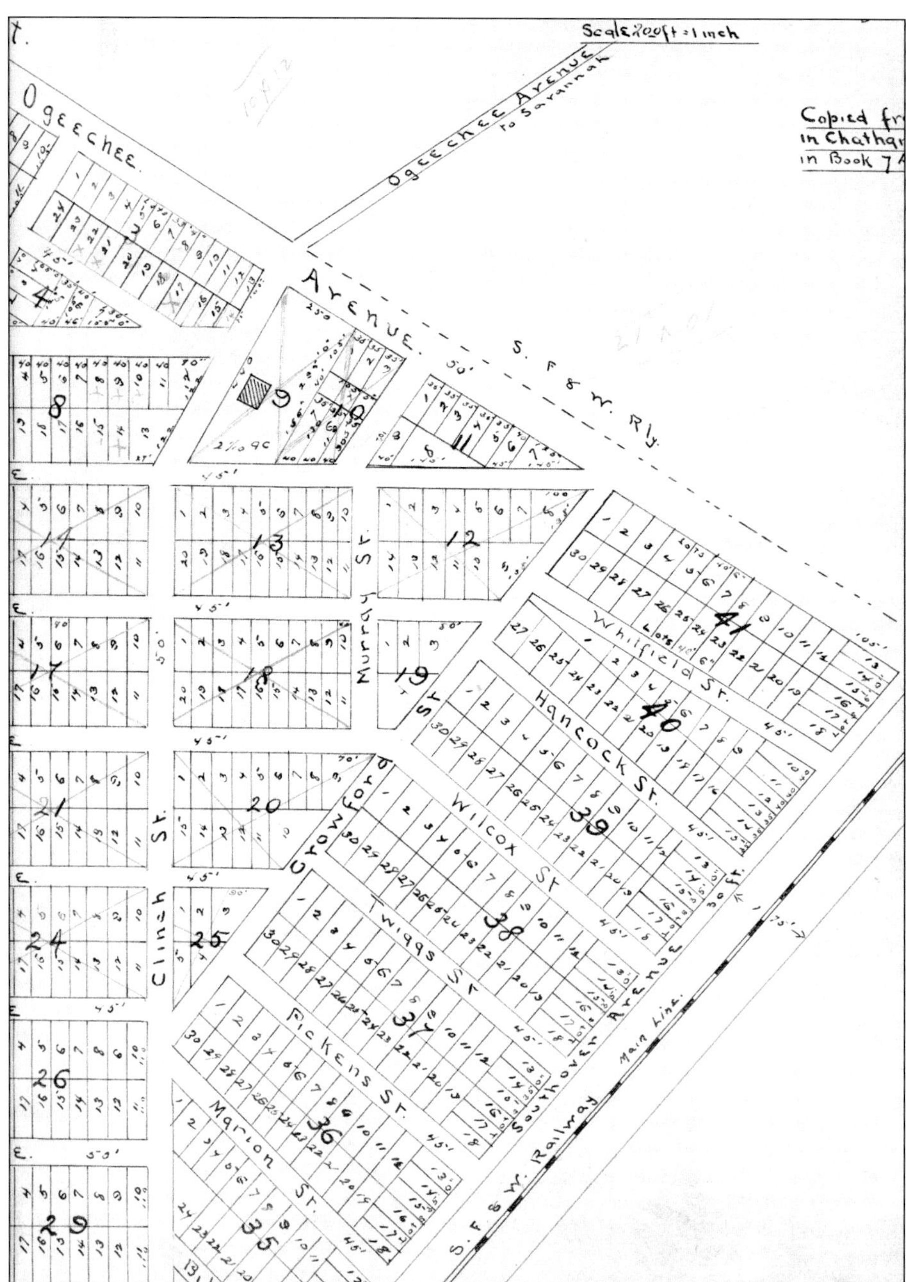

Joseph L. Whatley, Charles H. Olmstead, and Charles H. Dorsett incorporated the Southover Street Railroad on October 9, 1891. This charter specifically granted the right to transport produce and merchandise in addition to passengers. This was to be a city line with branches to the suburbs. Their tracks connected the Belt Line at Montgomery Street with Southover, a development held by the Southover Land and Improvement Company. Work was to begin within a year, with cars running within two years. If this did not happen, the company would lose its charter.

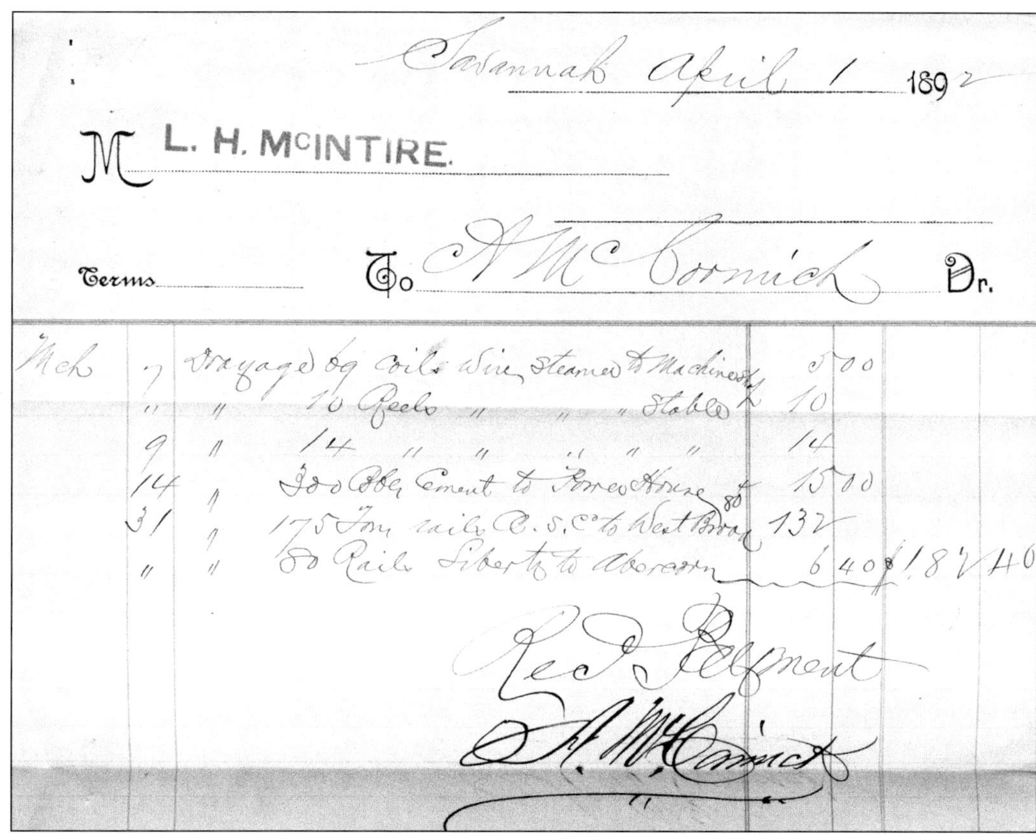

Savannah April 1 1892

M L. H. McINTIRE.

Terms To A. McCormick Dr.

Mch 7	Drayage 69 coils Wire, Steamer to Machinery	5 00	
" "	10 Reels " " " Stable	10	
9 "	14 " " " "	14	
14 "	300 Bbl Cement to Power House	15 00	
31 "	175 Ton rails C.S. Co to West Broad	132 80	
" "	80 Rails Liberty to Abercorn	6 40	182 40

Rec'd Payment
A. McCormick

Work on the Belt Line continued into February 1891. The first car placed on its electric line ran on February 2. The line extended from the office at Habersham and Thirty-seventh Streets to Liberty Street. Six motor cars and four trailers were ordered. The top image is a bill that includes the cost of rails laid along Liberty Street.

The new Electric Railway Company broke ground on Price Street. Fifty workers were engaged in excavating the road from south of Broughton Street to south of Hull Street.

ERC applied for the use of the following streets: Ott Street to Wheaton to South Broad to Montgomery to St. Julian and the south side of the City Market. Six electric cars arrived for the company in July, and a car barn was built between Price and S.F. & W. tracks at St. Thomas Street. The image at right is of a payroll record.

TIME, week ending Saturday, July 30 1892

NAMES.	S M T W T F S	Total Time	Rate per day	AMOUNT $ Cts.
Engineers				
W. D. McIntyre	10 11 10 11 10 10		2.50	15 50
W. L. Williams	10 10 10 10 10 10		2.25	13 50
Carpenters				
J. J. Johnson	10 10 10 10 10		3.50	17 50
W. J. Floyd	10 10 10 10		2.00	8 00
Bricklayer				
John Wilds	11		2.50	2 75
Fireman				
Thomas Maguire	10 10 12 12 12		1.50	6 50
Laborers				
Wm Price	10 5 10 10 10 10			5 50
Frank Campbell	10 11 10 11 10 11			6 35
Wm Thomas	10 11 10 10 10 10			6 10
J. Mungen	10 10 10 10 10 10			6 00
Jack Harris	10 11 10 10 10 10			6 10
H. Grayson	10 10 10 10 10 10			6 00
E. D. Green	5 10 10			2 50
Wm O'Connor	5 10 10			2 50

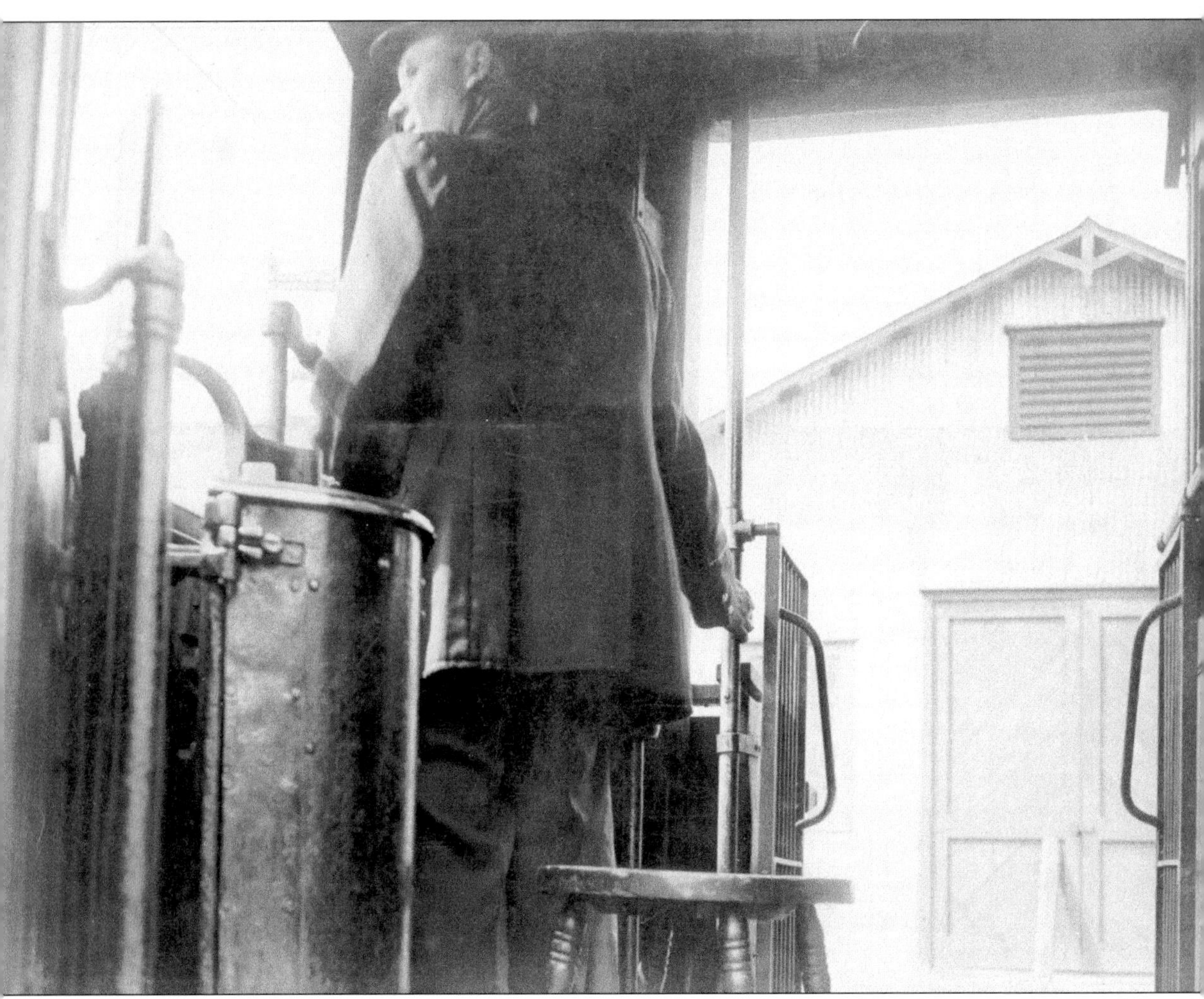

Complaints against C. & S. resulted in a protest signed by some of those "compelled to use the road," including Charles H. Olmstead, A.L. Hartridge, R.S. Claghorn, Julian Schley, and William G. Cooper, among others. These men were all board members and officers of the various lines at one time or another. Suburban residents were dissatisfied by the general comfort, age, and safety of the cars. Poor brakes and dirtiness of the cars were the primary reasons for complaint. In addition, the wood-burning engines spewed dust and ashes over the passengers. The patrons called this the "worst run and poorest managed railroad in the state.

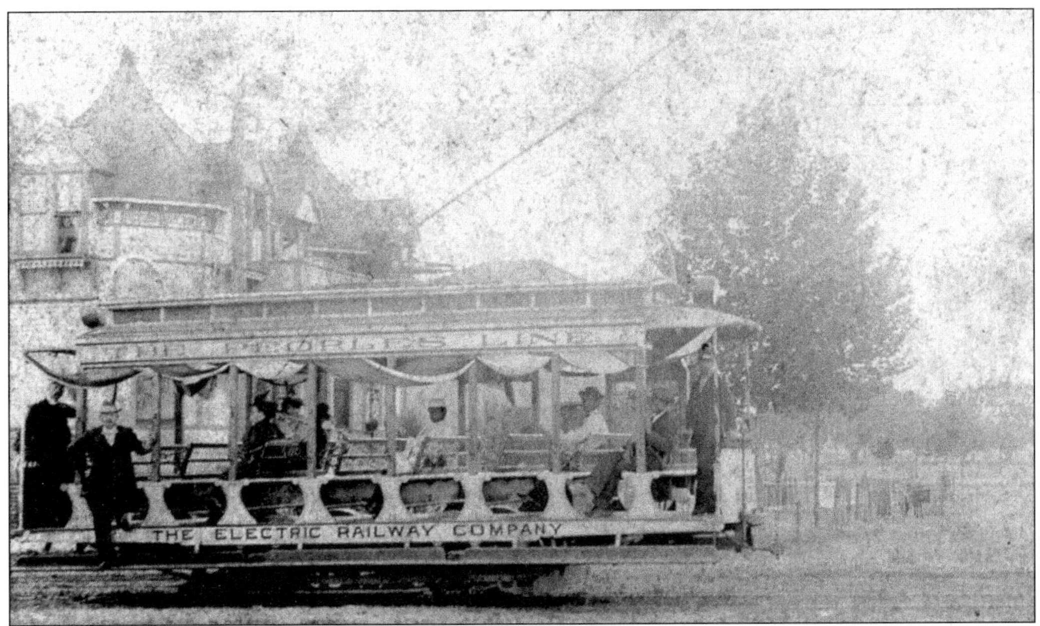

The People's Line was built by the owners of Collinsville. This line began in the neighborhood named for Jacob Collins. The line connected residents with the City Market and western parts of town.

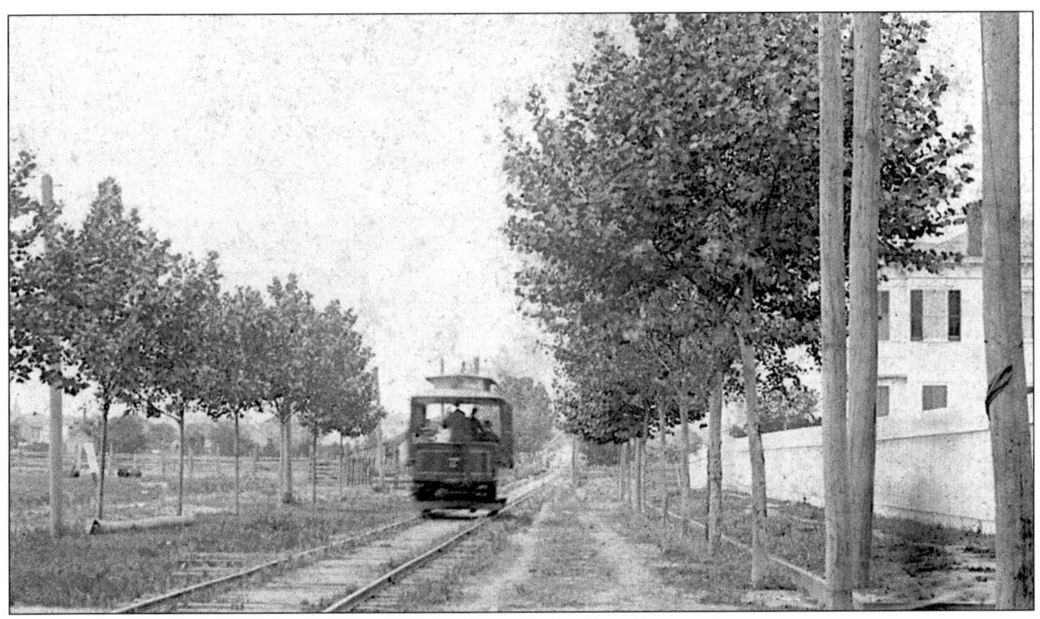

Collinsville was south of Bolton Street and east of Habersham.

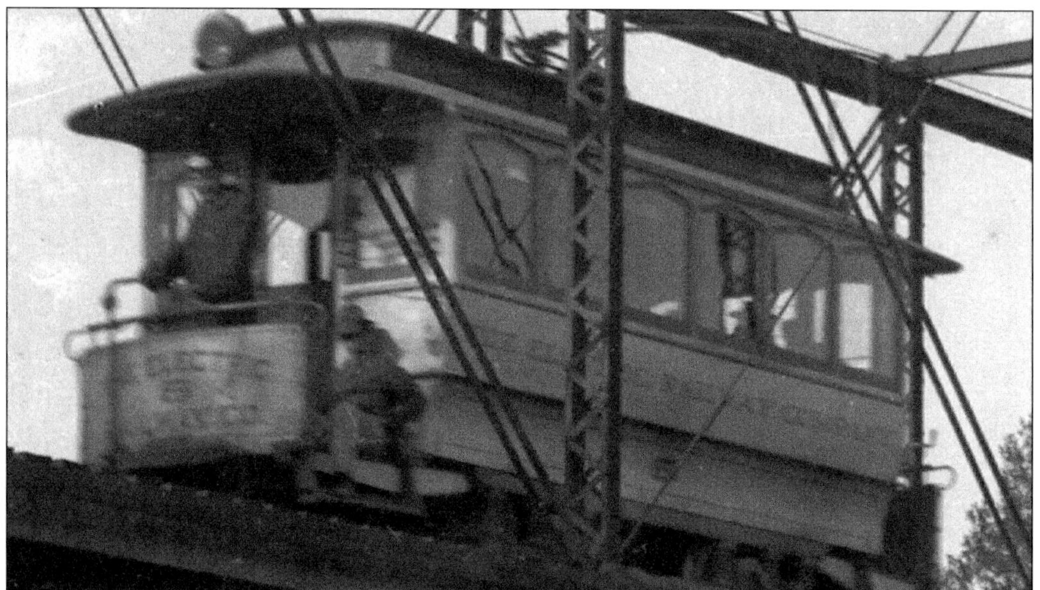

In August 1891, the General Assembly authorized the use of power other than horses on the Coast Line and on the C. & S. Also that month, the ERC formally opened. Later in the year, the S.S. & R.R. was renamed the Savannah Street Railroad.

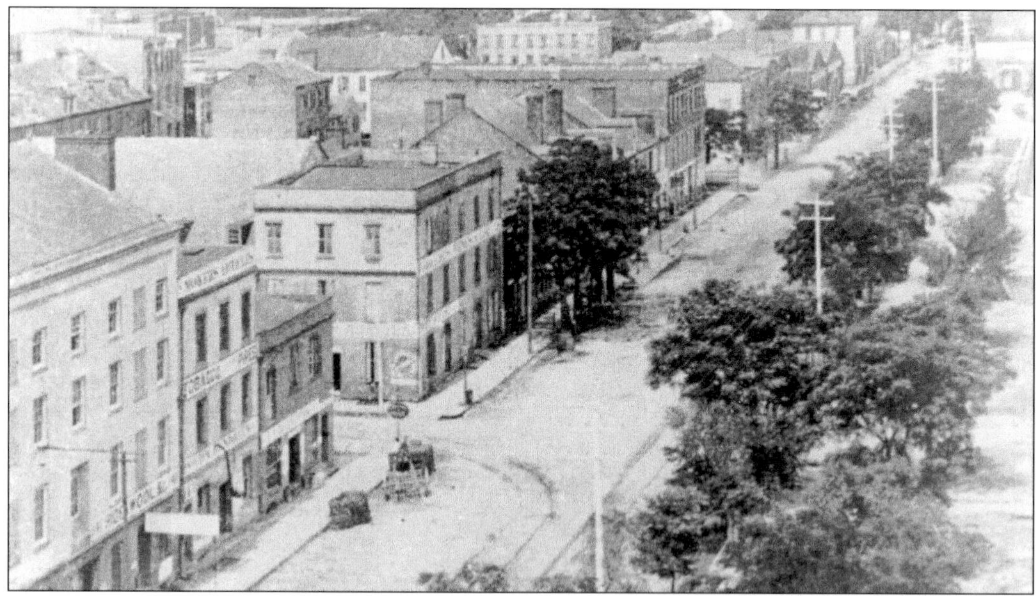

In 1889, amid the creation of many small lines, the Coast Line was experiencing financial troubles. In 1892, it was ordered by Superior Court to be sold at auction. Henry Parsons, brother of George Parsons, bought it for $75,000. Those bidding, Henry Parsons of the C. & S., J. Rowland of the Belt Line, and J.S. Collins of the Electric Railway, represented the three main street railroads in Chatham County. On July 11, 1892, with J.T. Johnston, Edward J. Thomas, and Luke Carson, and using the old Coast Line, Parsons formed the Savannah, Thunderbolt, and Isle of Hope Railroad (S.T. & I.H). By 1901, the Parsons brothers would own or control most of the streetcar companies in Savannah. They created what became known as the Parsons System Street and Suburban Railways. The tracks shown here were part of that network.

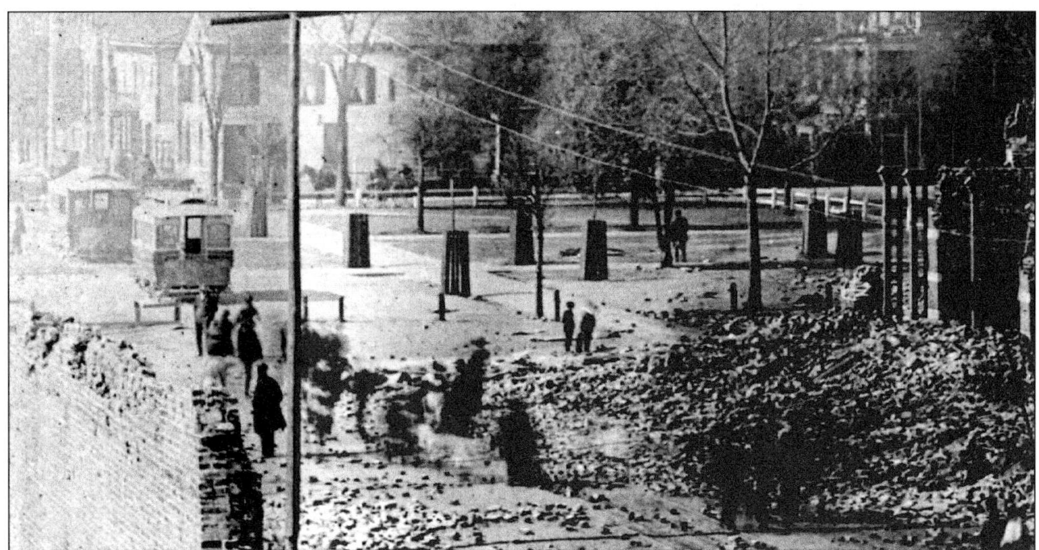

George Parsons was the president of the Coast Line for a number of years, and it was announced at the 1889 C. & S. annual meeting that he had secured controlling interest in that company's stock. That was the same year that one of the great fires swept through Savannah. Cars were stopped on their tracks as mules and horses were driven to safety. Some roads were impassable after the fire.

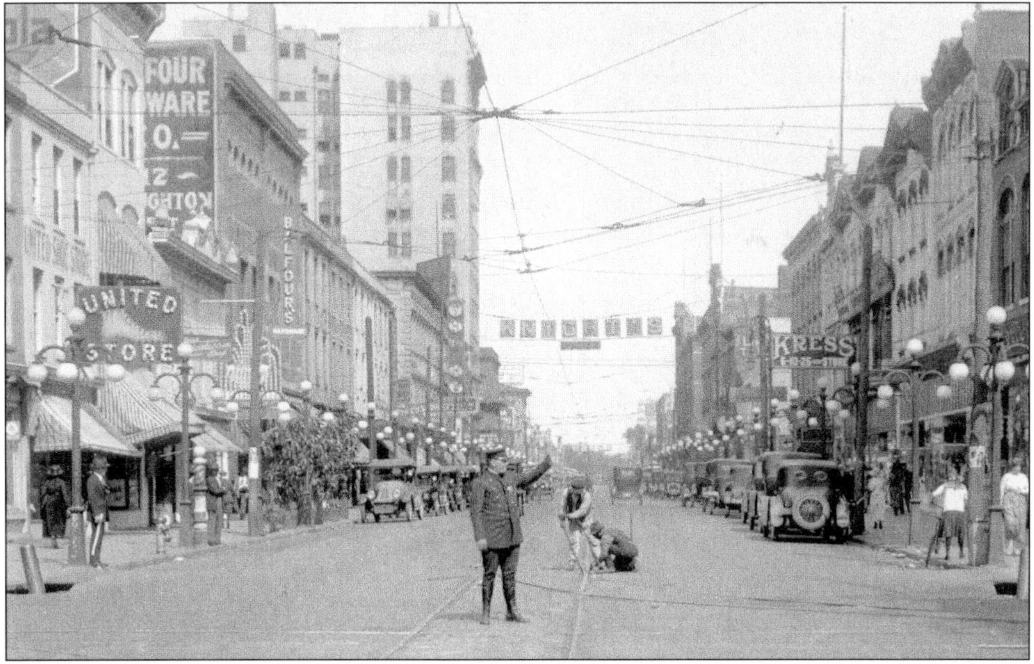

ERC took control of the Belt Line. The impetus for the sale was the Belt Line's inability to pay its bondholders. Repairs and new equipment were needed to allow the company to be competitive enough to turn a profit. The ERC was able to produce enough power at its Gwinnett Street power house and held enough cars to equip both lines. ERC made the purchase with stocks and bonds from both systems, and most of the investors remained involved as owners.

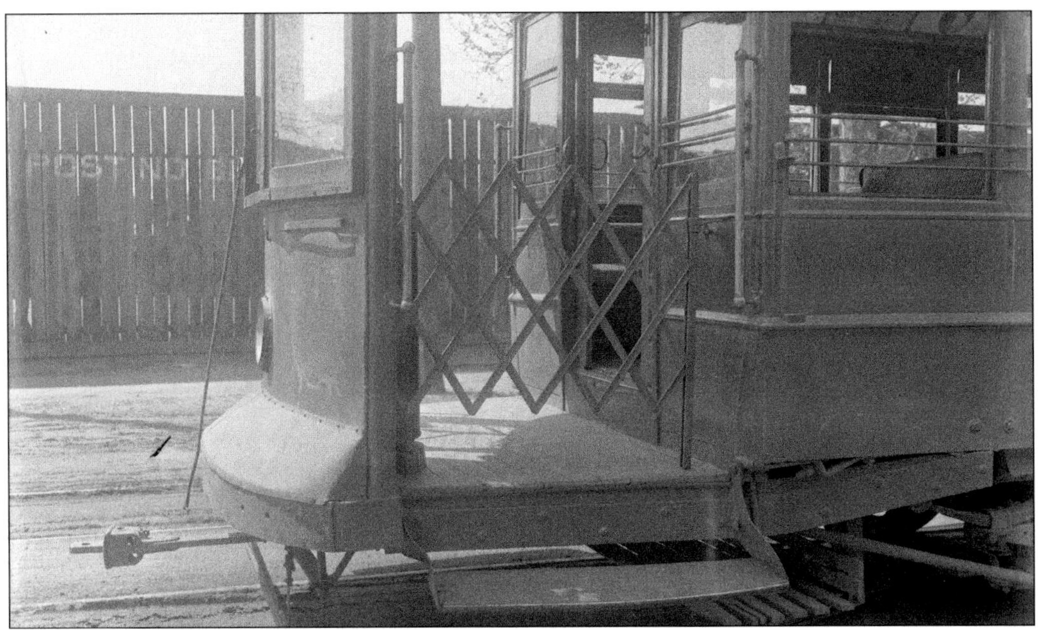

The year 1894 was the year of the streetcar fare wars. The C. & S. and ERC lowered their fares in an attempt to increase business. Maximum fares were initially set in a company's charter. When the C. & S. dropped its fare on its West Broad Street line to 3¢, the director of ERC responded by arguing that his company gave better service. On the ERC, a 5¢ fare allowed a passenger to ride between 4 and 7 miles while the best the C. & S. could do was to offer a 2-mile ride for 3¢. In July of 1894, the C. & S. fare on the Broughton and Habersham line was reduced to 1¢. The director declared, "We were here first, and we intend to keep our patronage at any cost." This made stepping onto a streetcar easier for many people.

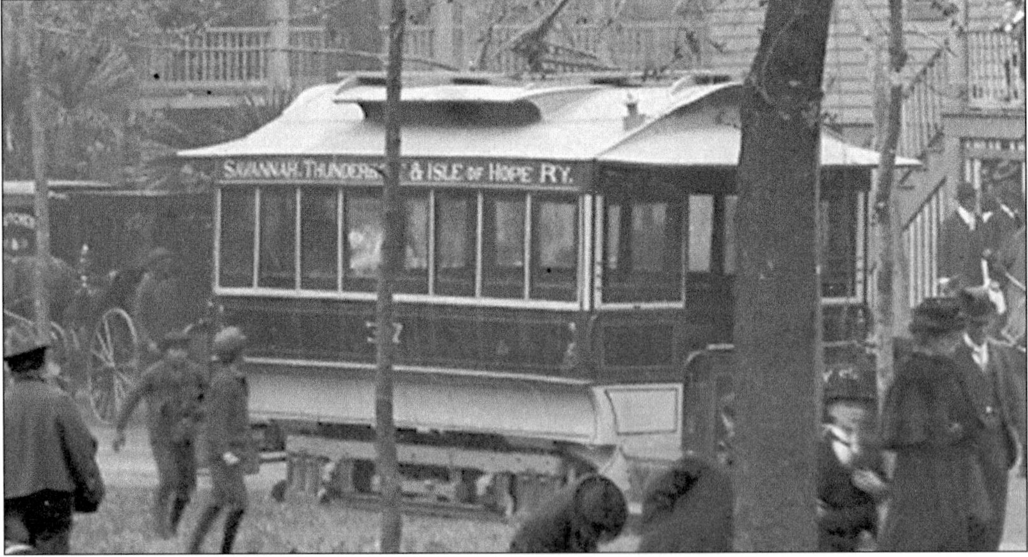

On January 5, 1897, the ERC was bought by Herman Myers and J.H. Fall, who sold it on May 29, 1897, to S.T. & I.H., owned by George Parsons. When S.T. & I.H. bought the Suburban and West End Line for $5,750 in 1901, the Parsons System of Street and Suburban Railway was complete.

Four
LOCAL STOPS

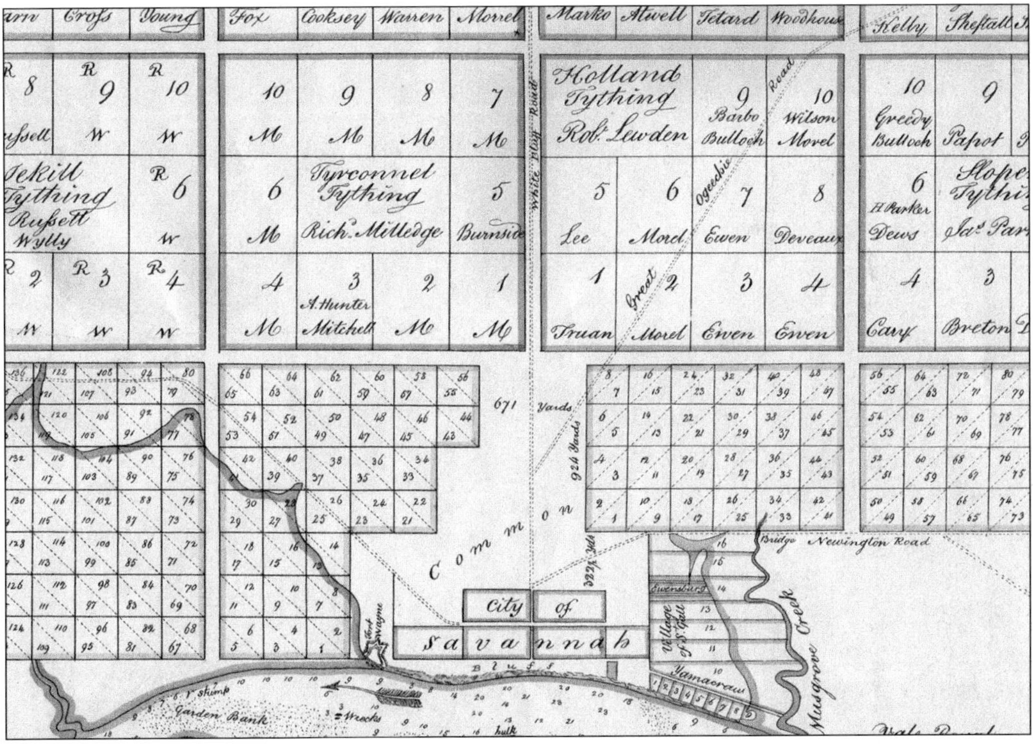

As Savannah was laid out, General James Oglethorpe granted to each free holder a total of 50 acres, composed of a 60-by-90-foot downtown lot, a 5-acre garden lot, and a 44-acre farm lot. This map of Savannah in 1798 shows the division of land.

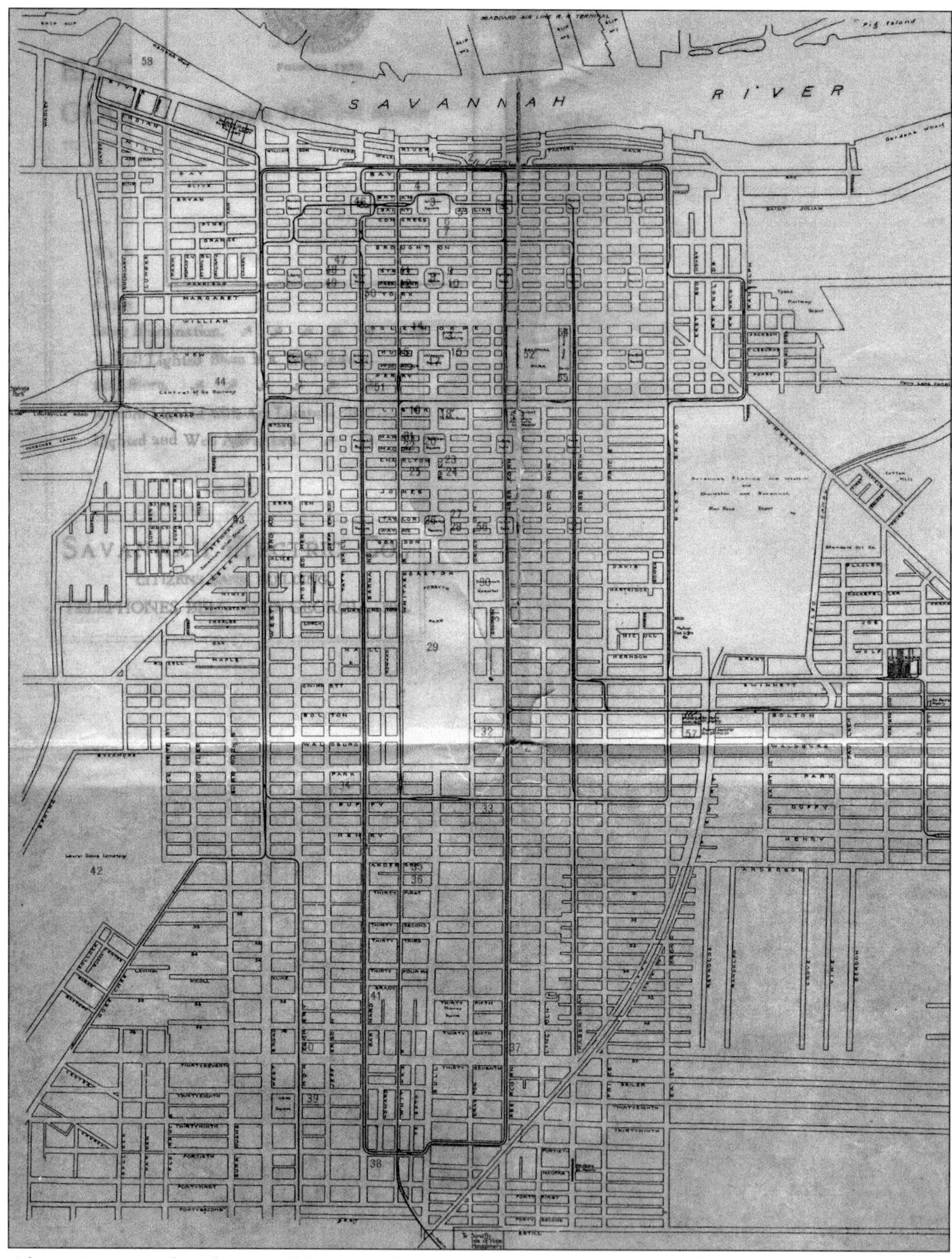

Above is an undated map of Savannah showing streetcar routes and important destinations. Although the first lines were begun as means of transportation to the suburban "resorts" of Savannah, downtown service increased with public demand and official approval.

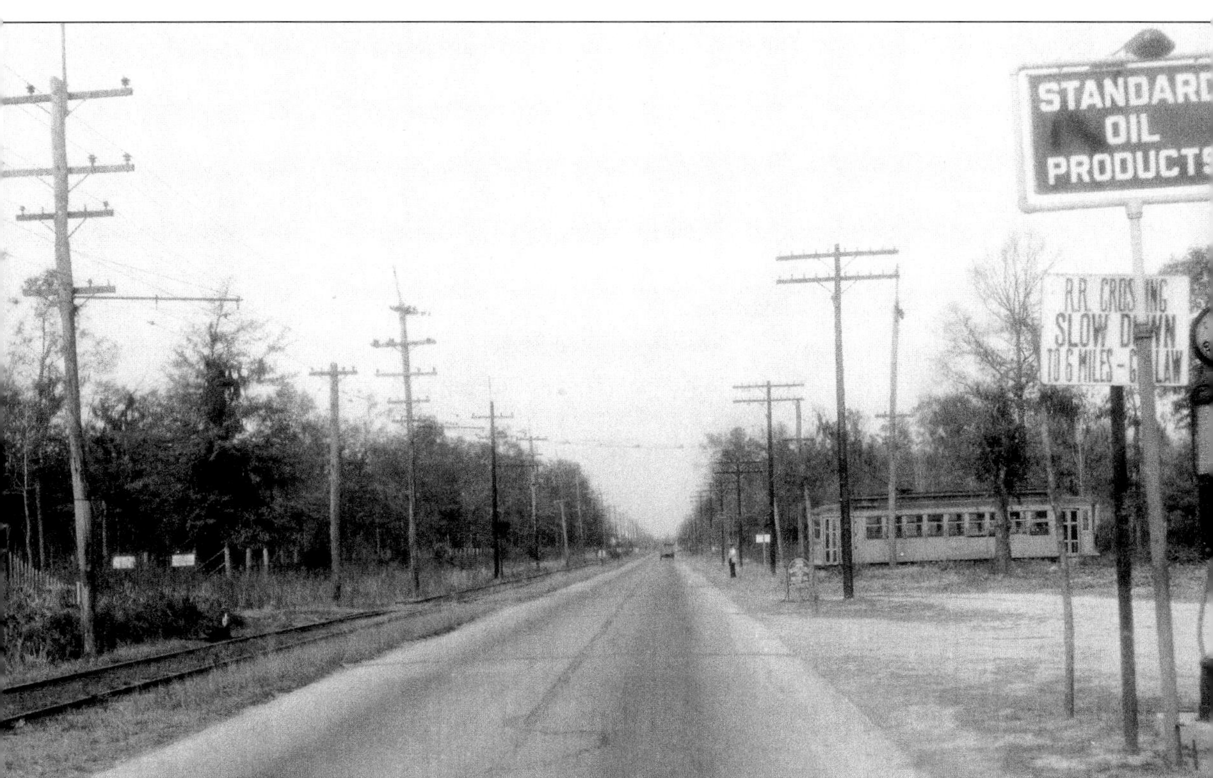

This is an electric streetcar running along Georgia Route 17. Suburban cars passed through sparsely populated areas on the way to their resort destinations. This hastened the development of suburban neighborhoods. Since people now had a reliable mode of transportation, they were free to leave the confines of the city when looking for a place to live.

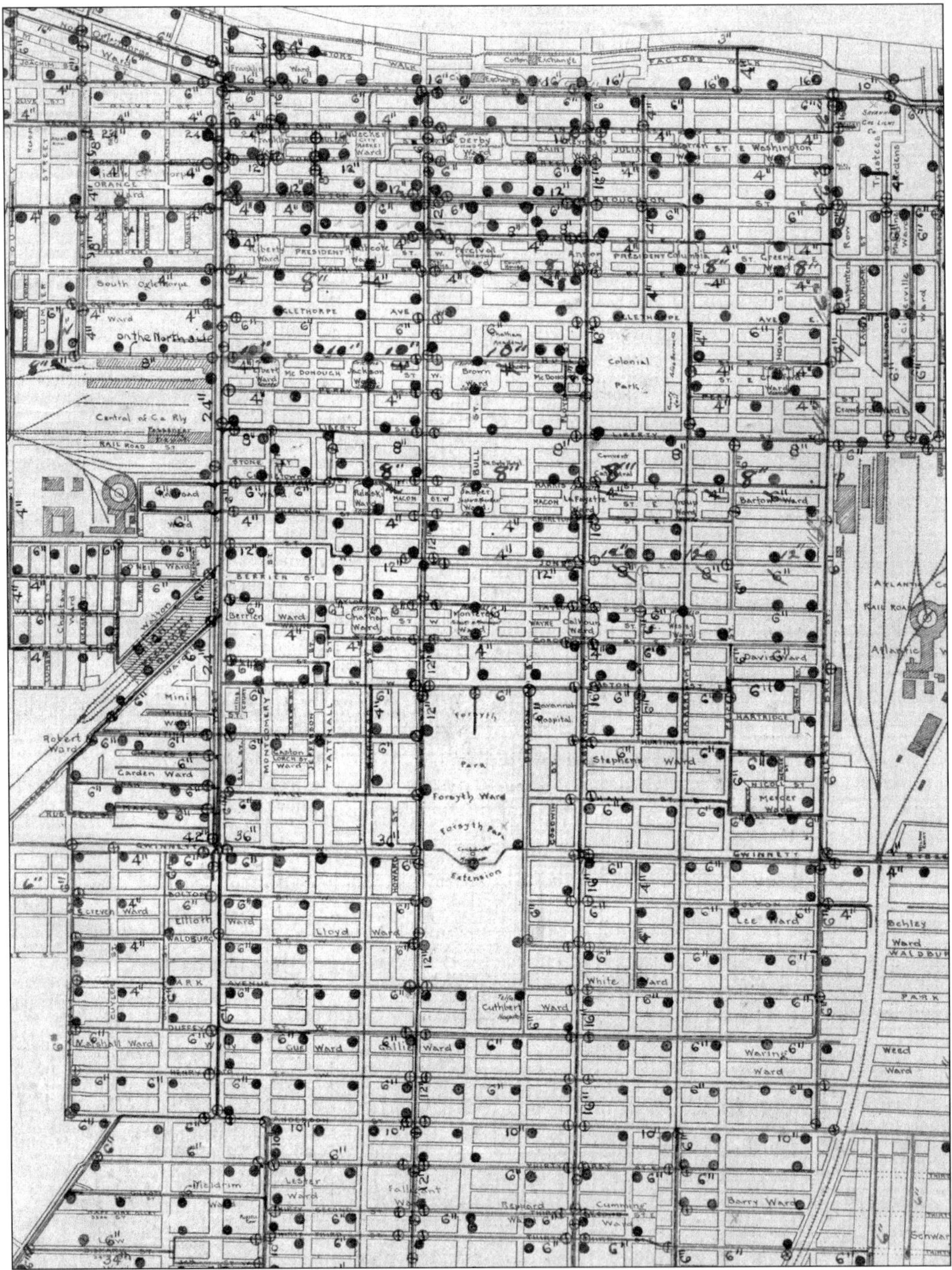

The existence of streetcar lines increased the desirability of a piece of property. In 1889, along with new water mains, public transportation was advertised as an inducement to build homes in certain areas. By 1906, water mains had been extended through much of Savannah, and streetcar service was expanding. This map shows water mains, stop valves, and hydrants.

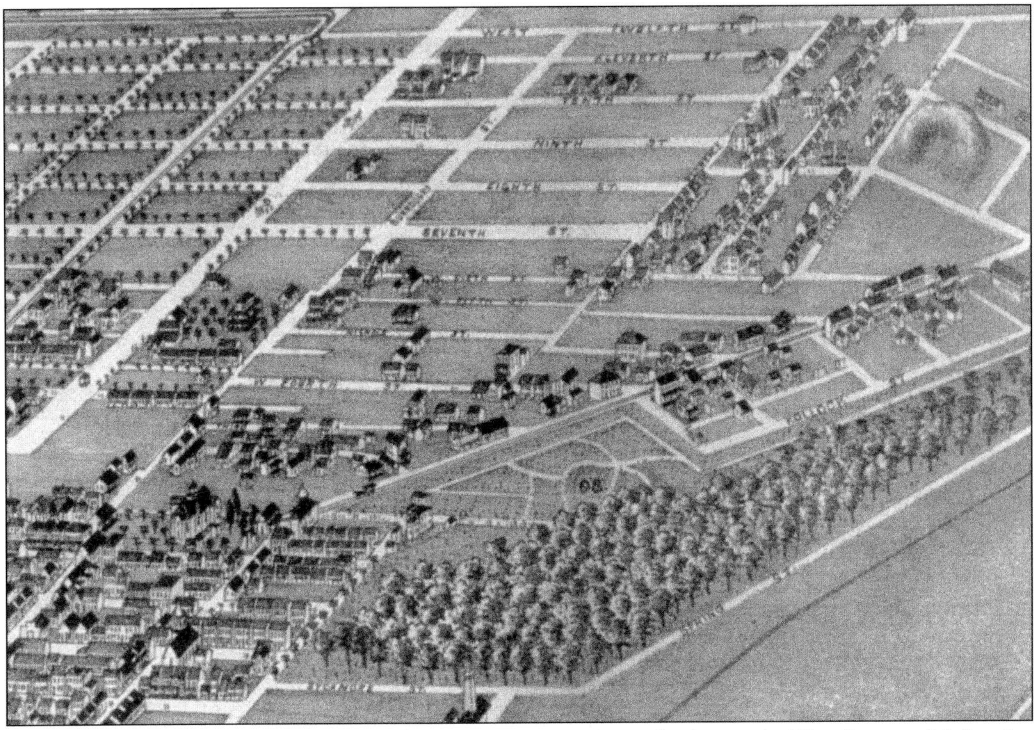

The increased construction Savannah was experiencing made the news. The *Savannah Morning News* carried an article exclaiming how quickly a great number of buildings were going up. "South of Little Jones and west of West Broad is building up rapidly. One hundred tenements are being erected and about that have been finished in the past three months. . . North of Anderson Street and also Cemetery Street is experiencing growth. There are very few vacant lots north of Anderson." This detail of Augustus Koch's 1891 print, *Bird's Eye View of Savannah*, shows the western parts of town around Laurel Grove Cemetery.

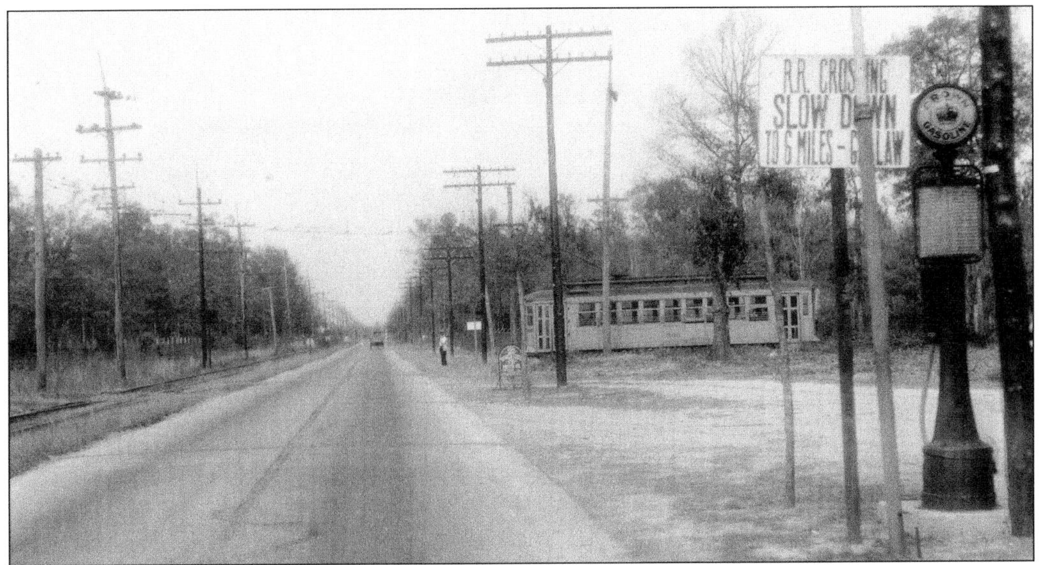

This streetcar crosses Augusta Road as it runs along one of Chatham County's outer routes.

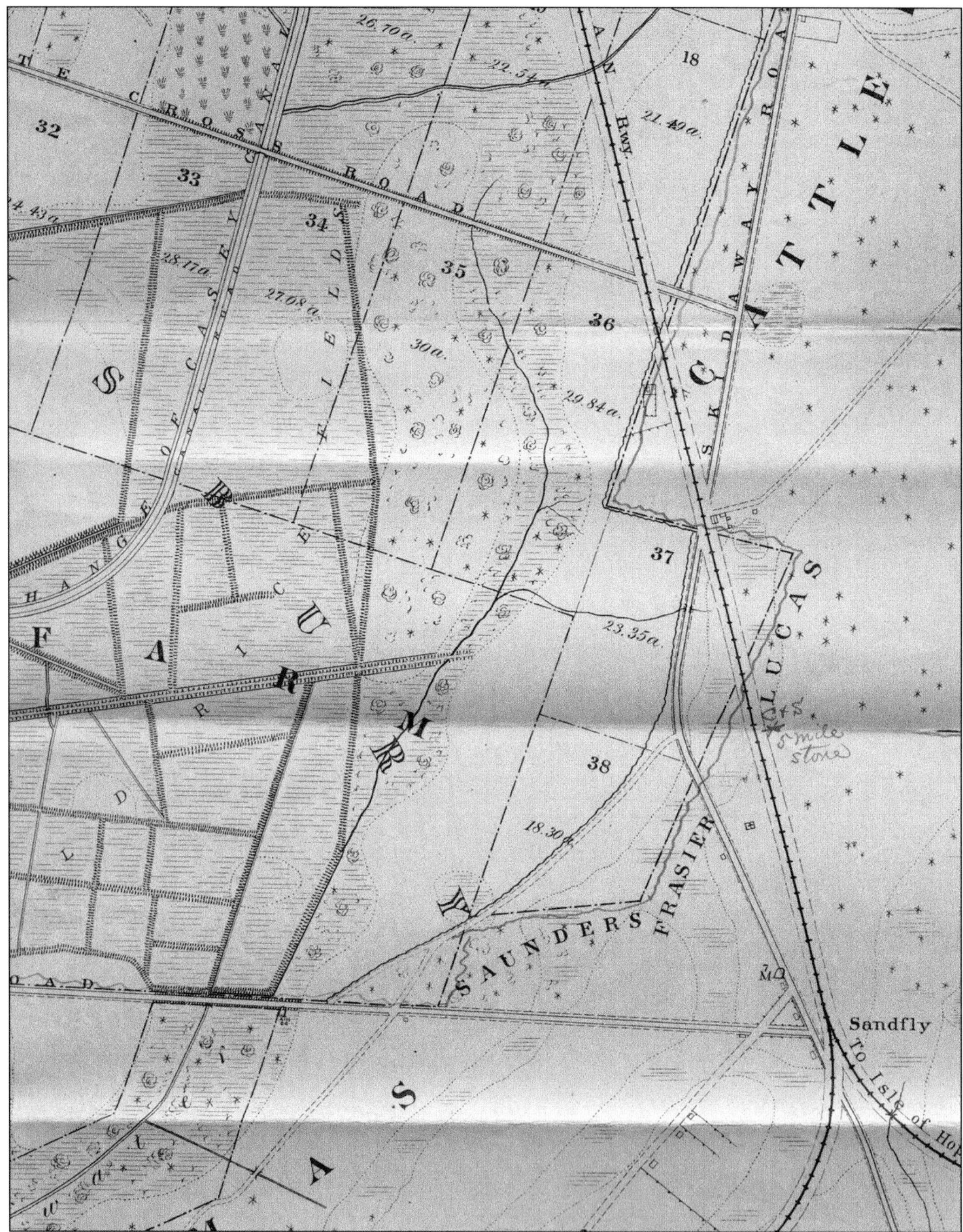

Individually owned residences and businesses followed the paths made by streetcar lines. A more structured growth came in the form of real estate companies. The desire to realize a profit was as strong in the late 1800s as at any other time. Investors saw land as a commodity to divide and sell. This subdivision map shows roads proposed near the C. & S. line, just north of Sand Fly.

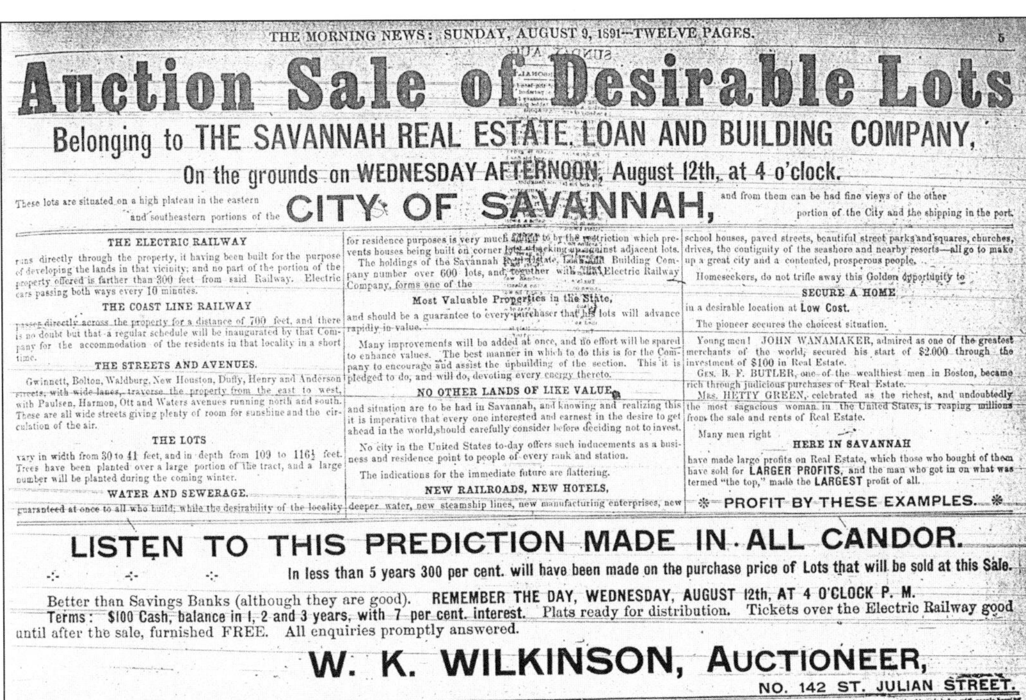

THE MORNING NEWS: SUNDAY, AUGUST 9, 1891—TWELVE PAGES. 5

Auction Sale of Desirable Lots

Belonging to THE SAVANNAH REAL ESTATE, LOAN AND BUILDING COMPANY,

On the grounds on WEDNESDAY AFTERNOON, August 12th, at 4 o'clock.

These lots are situated on a high plateau in the eastern and southeastern portions of the **CITY OF SAVANNAH,** and from them can be had fine views of the other portion of the City and the shipping in the port.

THE ELECTRIC RAILWAY

runs directly through the property, it having been built for the purpose of developing the lands in that vicinity; and no part of the portion of the property offered is farther than 300 feet from said Railway. Electric cars passing both ways every 10 minutes.

THE COAST LINE RAILWAY

passes directly across the property for a distance of 700 feet, and there is no doubt but that a regular schedule will be inaugurated by that Company for the accommodation of the residents in that locality in a short time.

THE STREETS AND AVENUES.

Gwinnett, Bolton, Waldburg, New Houston, Duffy, Henry and Anderson streets, with wide lanes, traverse the property from the east to west, with Paulsen, Harmon, Ott and Waters avenues running north and south. These are all wide streets giving plenty of room for sunshine and the circulation of the air.

THE LOTS

vary in width from 30 to 41 feet, and in depth from 109 to 116½ feet. Trees have been planted over a large portion of the tract, and a large number will be planted during the coming winter.

WATER AND SEWERAGE.

guaranteed at once to all who build; while the desirability of the locality for residence purposes is very much added to by the restriction which prevents houses being built on corner lots backing up against adjacent lots.

The holdings of the Savannah Real Estate, Loan and Building Company number over 600 lots, and, together with the Electric Railway Company, forms one of the

Most Valuable Properties in the State,

and should be a guarantee to every purchaser that his lots will advance rapidly in value.

Many improvements will be added at once, and no effort will be spared to enhance values. The best manner in which to do this is for the Company to encourage and assist the upbuilding of the section. This it is pledged to do, and will do, devoting every energy thereto.

NO OTHER LANDS OF LIKE VALUE

and situation are to be had in Savannah, and knowing and realizing this it is imperative that every one interested and earnest in the desire to get ahead in the world, should carefully consider before deciding not to invest.

No city in the United States to-day offers such inducements as a business and residence point to people of every rank and station.

The indications for the immediate future are flattering.

NEW RAILROADS, NEW HOTELS,

deeper water, new steamship lines, new manufacturing enterprises, new school houses, paved streets, beautiful street parks and squares, churches, drives, the contiguity of the seashore and nearby resorts—all go to make up a great city and a contented, prosperous people.

Homeseekers, do not trifle away this Golden opportunity to

SECURE A HOME

in a desirable location at **Low Cost.**

The pioneer secures the choicest situation.

Young men! JOHN WANAMAKER, admired as one of the greatest merchants of the world, secured his start of $2,000 through the investment of $100 in Real Estate.

GEN. B. F. BUTLER, one of the wealthiest men in Boston, became rich through judicious purchases of Real Estate.

MRS. HETTY GREEN, celebrated as the richest, and undoubtedly the most sagacious woman in the United States, is reaping millions from the sale and rents of Real Estate.

Many men right

HERE IN SAVANNAH

have made large profits on Real Estate, which those who bought of them have sold for **LARGER PROFITS,** and the man who got in on what was termed "the top," made the **LARGEST** profit of all.

❋ PROFIT BY THESE EXAMPLES. ❋

LISTEN TO THIS PREDICTION MADE IN ALL CANDOR.

In less than 5 years 300 per cent. will have been made on the purchase price of Lots that will be sold at this Sale.

Better than Savings Banks (although they are good). **REMEMBER THE DAY, WEDNESDAY, AUGUST 12th, AT 4 O'CLOCK P. M.**

Terms: $100 Cash, balance in 1, 2 and 3 years, with 7 per cent. interest. Plats ready for distribution. Tickets over the Electric Railway good until after the sale, furnished FREE. All enquiries promptly answered.

W. K. WILKINSON, AUCTIONEER,

NO. 142 ST. JULIAN STREET.

The Savannah Real Estate, Loan, and Building Company auctioned lots southeast of Forsyth Park in August of 1891. Above is a newspaper advertisement placed on August 9. Among those who bought lots were J.S. Collins, J.R. Anderson, and Thomas Nugent.

In addition to private home building, companies were formed to buy large tracts of land in order to subdivide them for resale. The Savannah Real Estate, Loan, and Building Company was organized by a number of men involved with the streetcar companies. They include the following: J.S. Collins, W.F. McCauley, W.K. Wilkinson, Jacob Paulson, Jefferson Randolph Anderson, R.M. Hicks, T. Nugent, and H. Logan. At right is a photograph of Anderson. In addition to practicing law, he was involved in the incorporation of the Electric Railway Company. He was a founder of the Savannah Electric Company (SEC) and was involved with the evolution of this company for over 55 years. He also served in the Georgia Legislature and as a state senator.

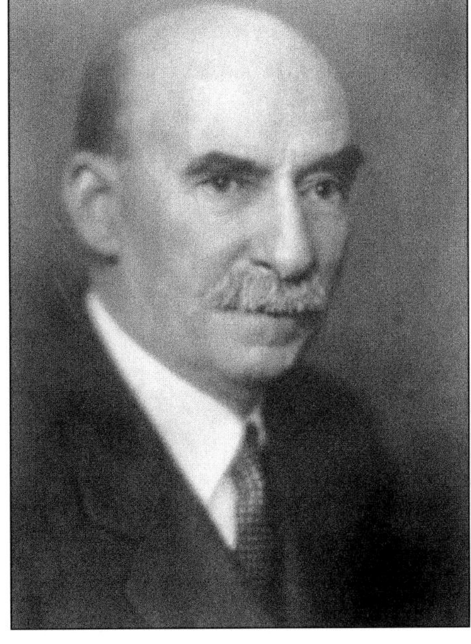

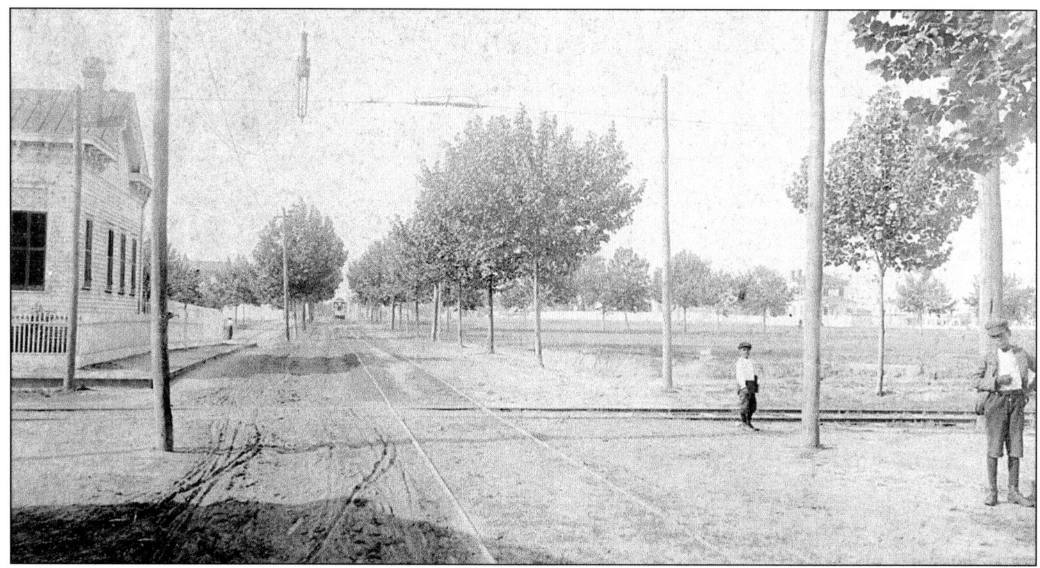

Collinsville is an early example of a neighborhood affected by streetcar lines. Located between Bolton and Anderson Streets, east of the S.F. & W. tracks to Waters Avenue, Collinsville was a development in the 1880s and 1890s. The owners incorporated the People's Line and ran cars on a circuit from the neighborhood to the City Market and Laurel Grove Cemetery. Transportation to services and recreation increased the attractiveness of any potential home. These images, *c.* 1890, demonstrate the open space that would later be covered by houses.

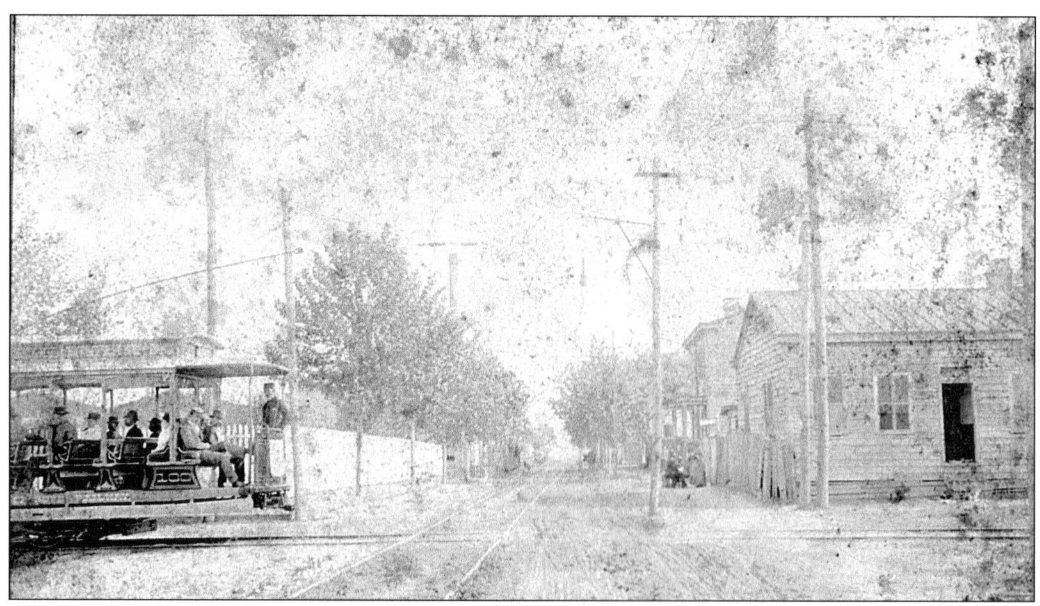

This car ran through Collinsville on its way to Isle of Hope.

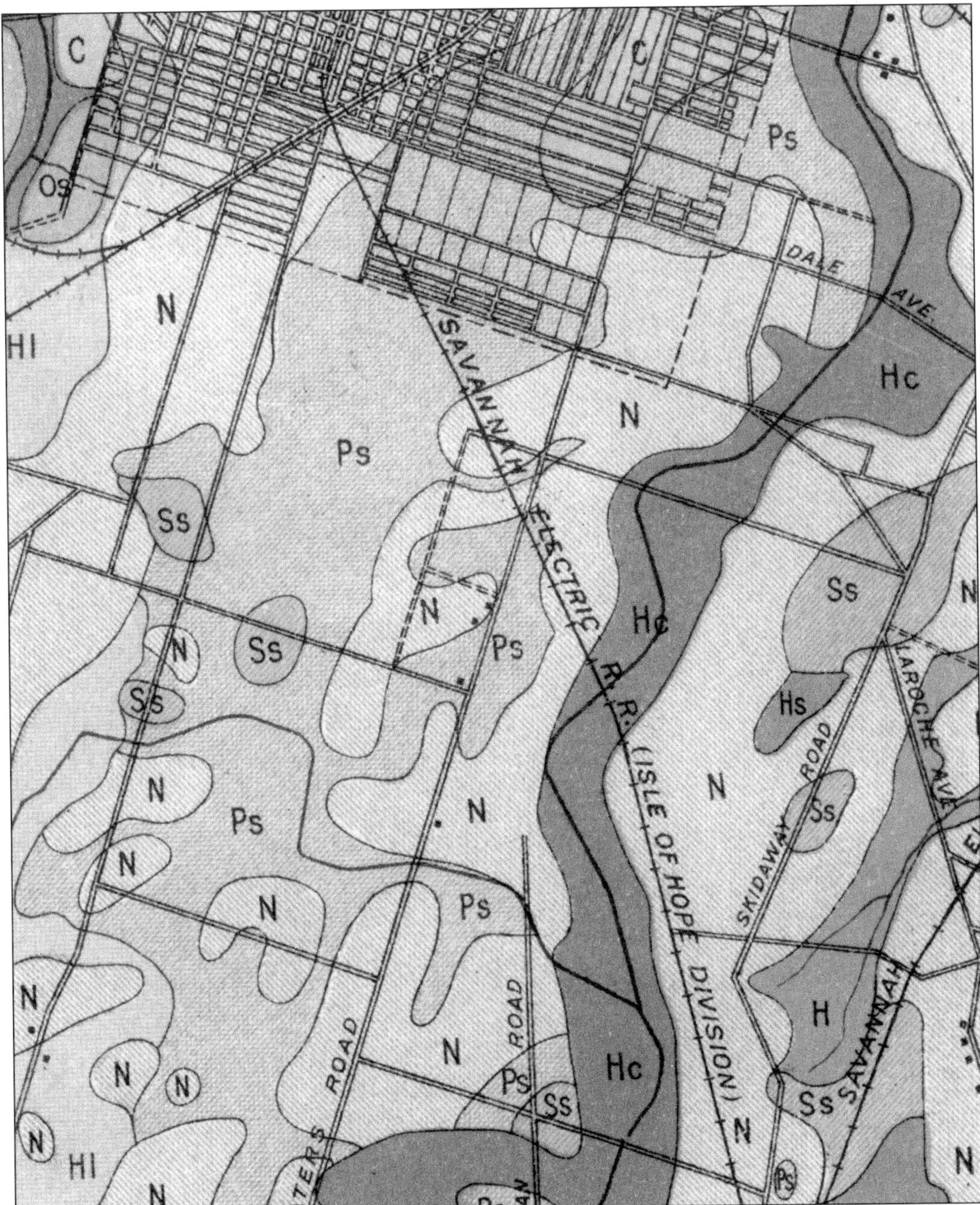

A new station house was built about 2 miles from Savannah, along the S.S. & S. line. It was in an area called Thomasville in honor of E.J. Thomas, superintendent of that line. He previously served in the same capacity for the Coast Line. The *Savannah Morning News* noted, "The county in the vicinity is becoming thickly settled, and this station was the result of the petition of a number of the colored residents who are engaged in truck farming." This is a later map of the county illustrating soil type in the area in question.

ORDER OF INCORPORATION.

....

IN THE SUPERIOR COURT OF CHATHAM COUNTY GEORGIA, MARCH TERM 1890.

....

In the matter of the incorporation of the

CITY AND SUBURBAN IMPROVEMENT COMPANY.

....

Upon reading and considering the petition of Charles H.Dorsett,Charlton H.Way,John C.Rowland,Charles H.Olmstead,Daniel G.Purse,Charles R. Herron,Andreas E.Moynelo,Thomas F.Stubbs,Andrew Hanley,Charles A. Shearson, E.G.Cabaniss and J.J.Gaudry for the incorporation of themselves and such other persons as may be associated with them into a private corporation to be known as the CITY AND SUBURBAN IMPROVEMENT COMPANY: And the Court being satisfied that the application of said petitioners is legitimately within the purview and intention of the laws of Georgia: and it appearing that said petition has been filed, recorded and published as the law requires, and that the petitioners have complied with all the requirements of the law in such cases provided, It is therefore upon motion of Mess.Denmark,Adams & Adams,Attorneys for the said petitioners,considered and ordered that said petition be, and the same is hereby granted, and that the said petitioners their associates and successors be, and they are hereby, incorporated and made a body politic in accordance with the laws of Georgia for the term of twenty (20) years, with the privilege of renewing their charter at the expiration of said term, under and by the said corporate name of the CITY AND SUBURBAN IMPROVEMENT COMPANY:

That the said corporation be, and it is hereby, authorized and empowered to deal in real and personal property, to buy,sell,lease,rent, grant,mortgage,encumber,improve and otherwise hold,use,enjoy,dispose of, and deal in real and personal property; to subscribe for,purchase,

City and Suburban Improvement Co. was granted a 20-year charter by the Superior Court of Chatham County for the purpose of buying and improving real estate with the intention of resale. Involved in this enterprise were C.H. Dorsett, C.H. Olmstead, and Daniel G. Purse.

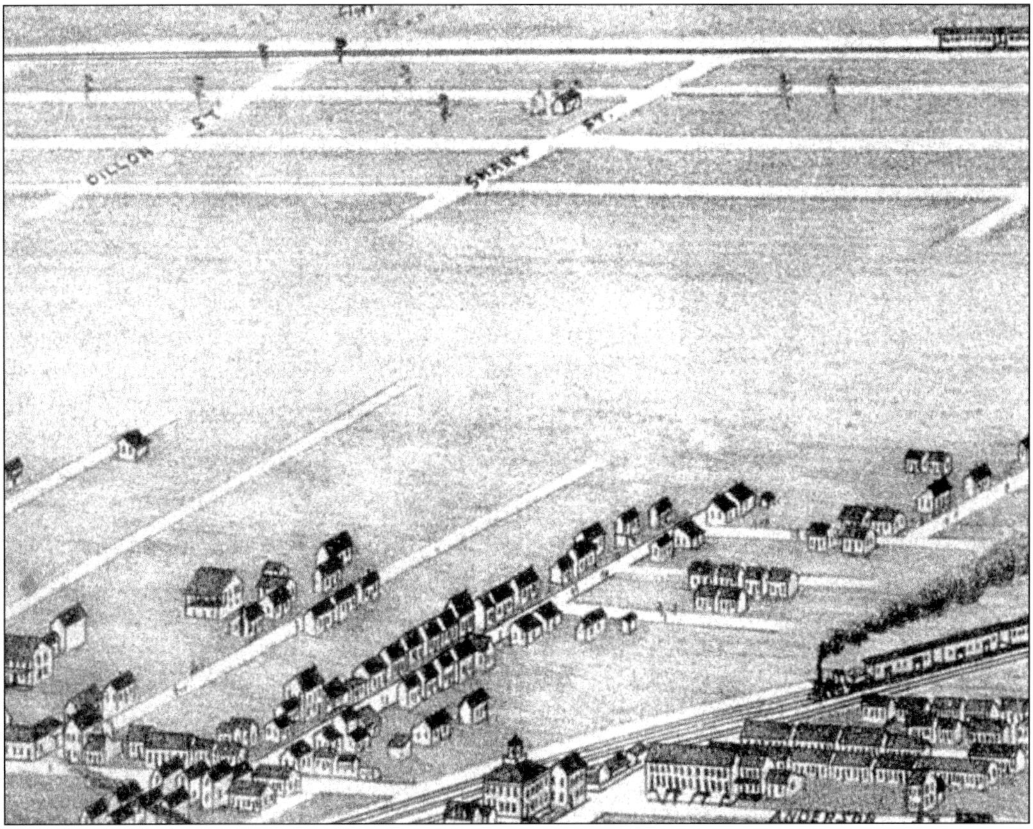

The effects of the combination of the streetcar lines and real estate companies caused the *Morning News* to note on August 21, 1891, "a few years ago the improvement boom was southwest, then southward. Now with new electric street lines and the building of the Savannah and Isle of Hope railway, the greatest development yet known in the city appears to be in the southeastern section." The lands southeast of Savannah from Lovers Lane to Estill Avenue (now Victory Drive) and southeast from the S.F. & W. tracks were held by a number of syndicates and associations that gradually sold tracts to those who then sold off the land by the lot to builders. This detail shows the land around Anderson Street.

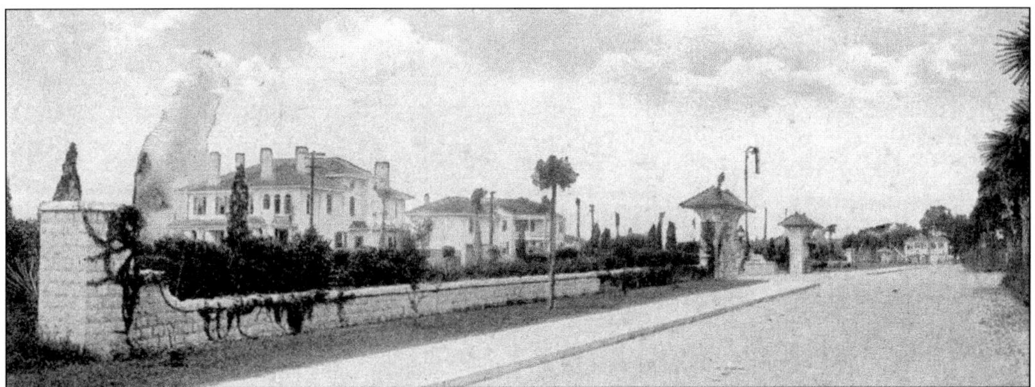

Ardsley Park and Chatham Crescent are two of Savannah's planned suburban neighborhoods. Ardsley Park lies between Bull and Habersham Streets and was bounded by Estill on the north. Some promotional material was aimed directly at doctors, attorneys, and bankers.

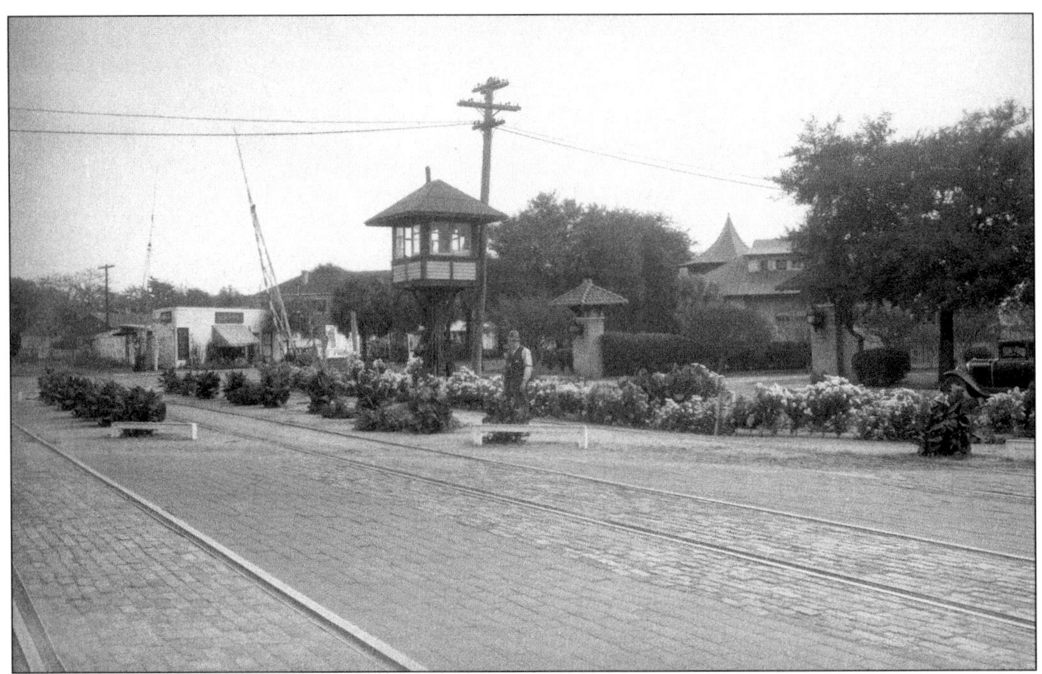

This is the intersection of Estill and Bull Streets with the streetcar tracks and the Atlantic Coast Line tracks.

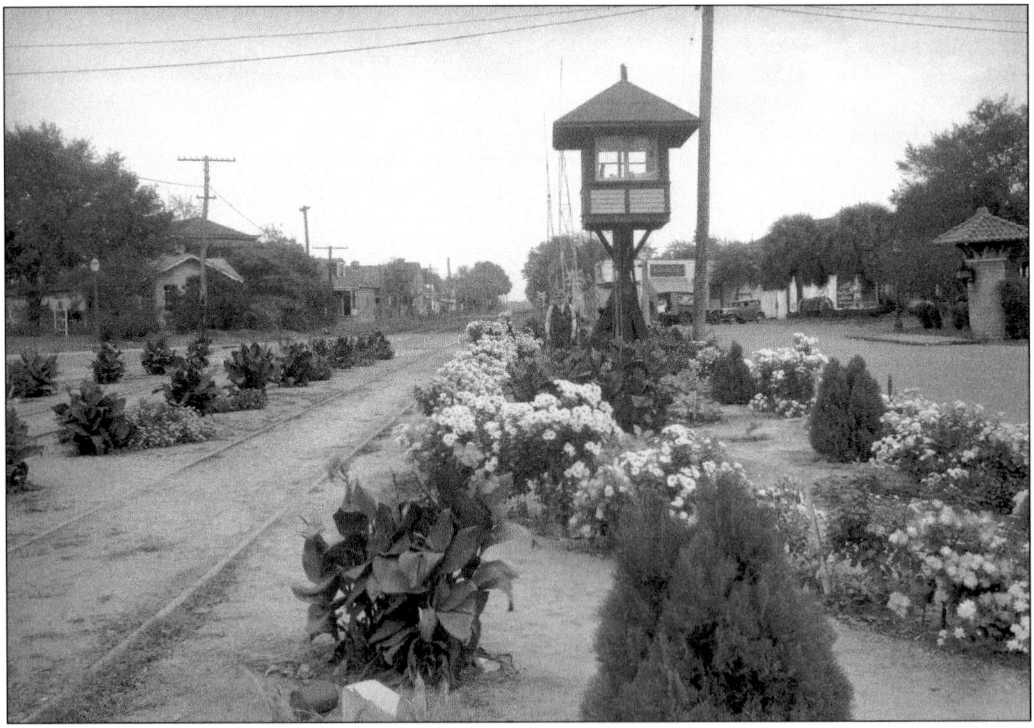

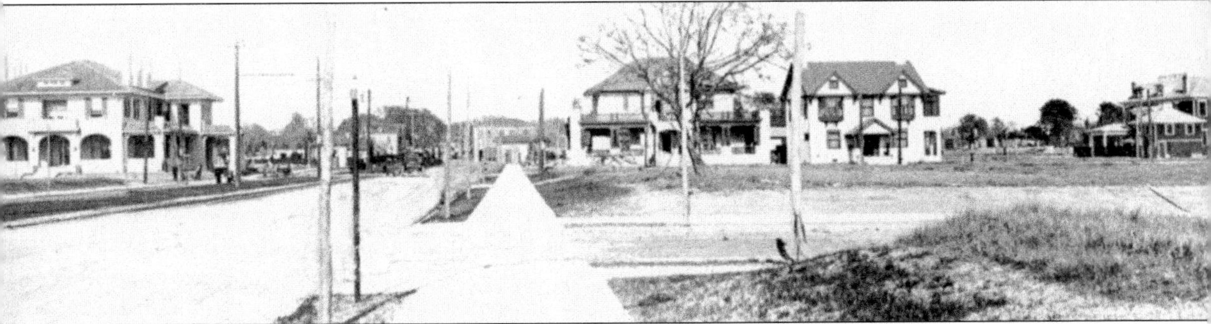

Homes in Ardsley Park were designed to be as secluded as "private estates." Building codes called for lot sizes that would allow for broad lawns and gardens. Stores and apartment houses were not permitted. By preventing the natural occurrence of commercial enterprise within a neighborhood, transportation to the business, civic, and social centers was required. Streetcar lines helped fill this need. This is a view near Estill and Forty-fourth Street.

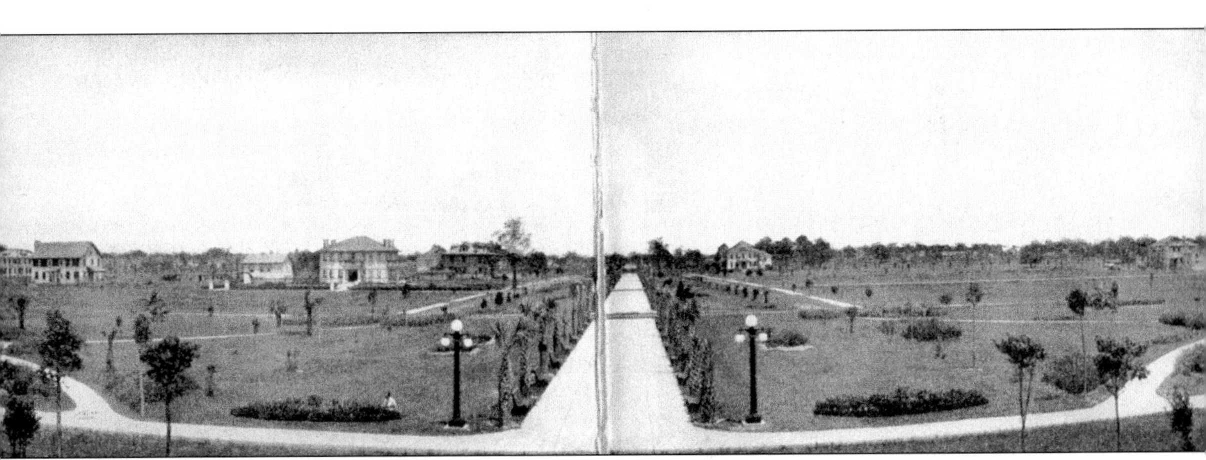

Chatham Crescent stretches east from Ardsley Park to Waters Avenue. In 1915, Chatham Land and Hotel Company ran an advertisement stating, "We want it understood that a person of moderate means can own a home in Chatham Crescent as well as the person who has money." This neighborhood was planned with goals similar to those of Ardsley Park. Another advertisement stated that "intelligent restrictions eliminate the disagreeable features so common to the older sections of the city." Only homes were allowed.

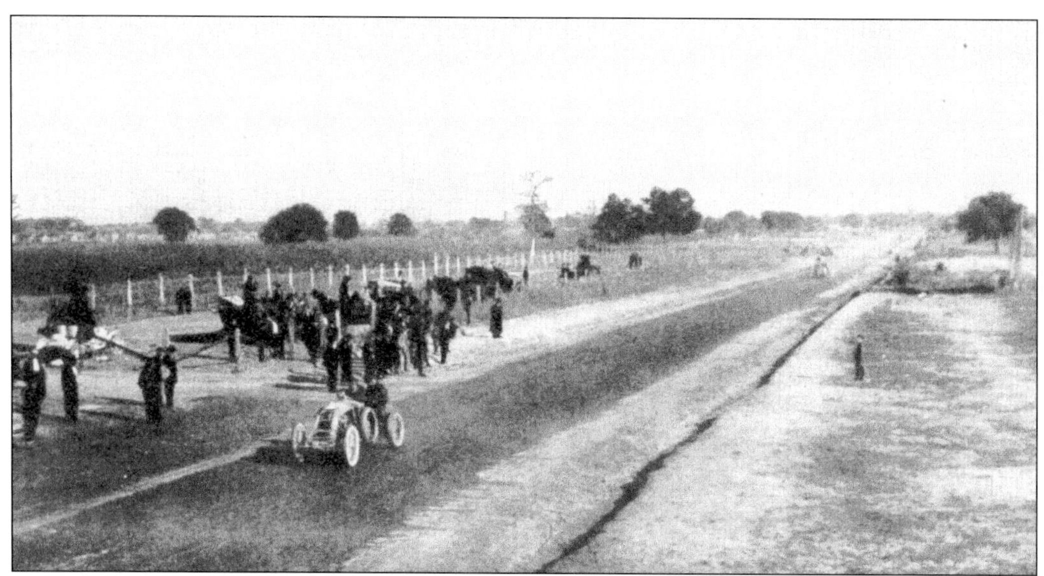

These images were taken two years apart and demonstrate the growth in Chatham Crescent.

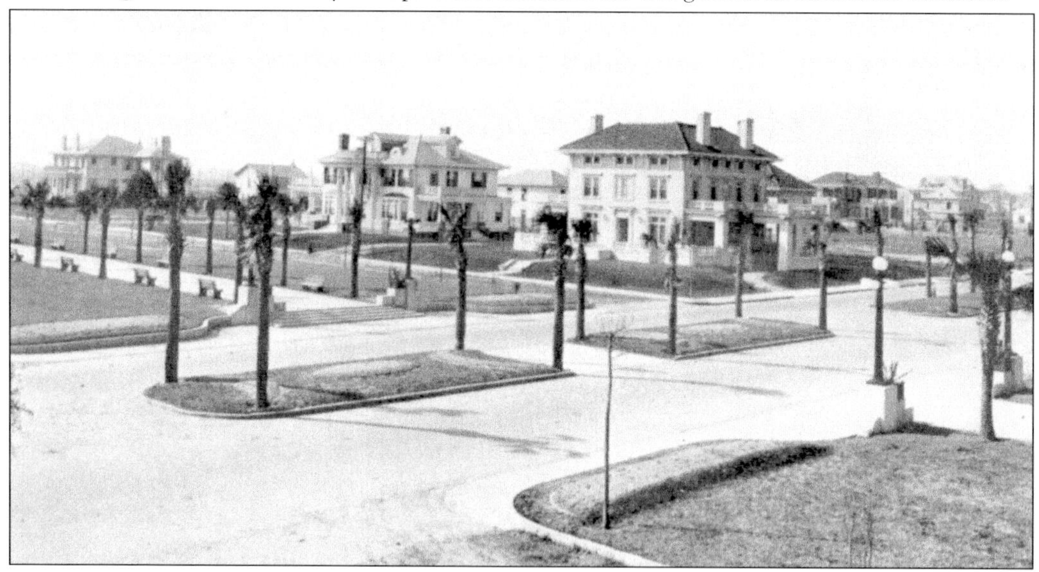

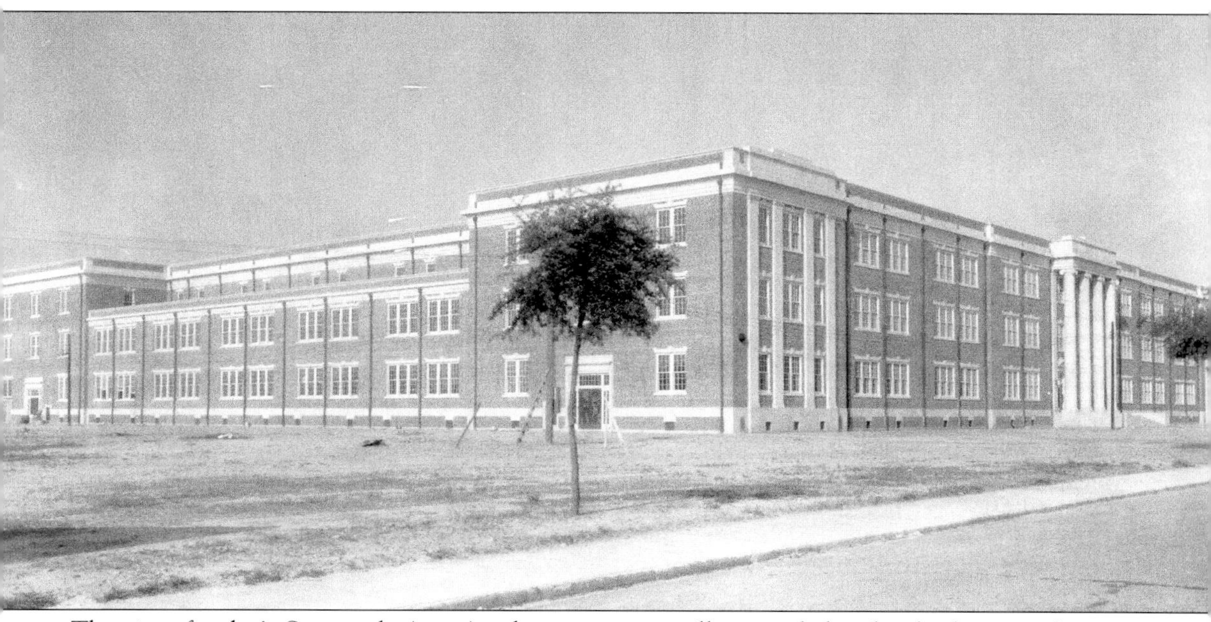

The site of today's Savannah Arts Academy was originally intended to be the location for a grand hotel to serve the guests of Chatham Crescent residents. The hotel was not built, but in 1937, Savannah High School was constructed.

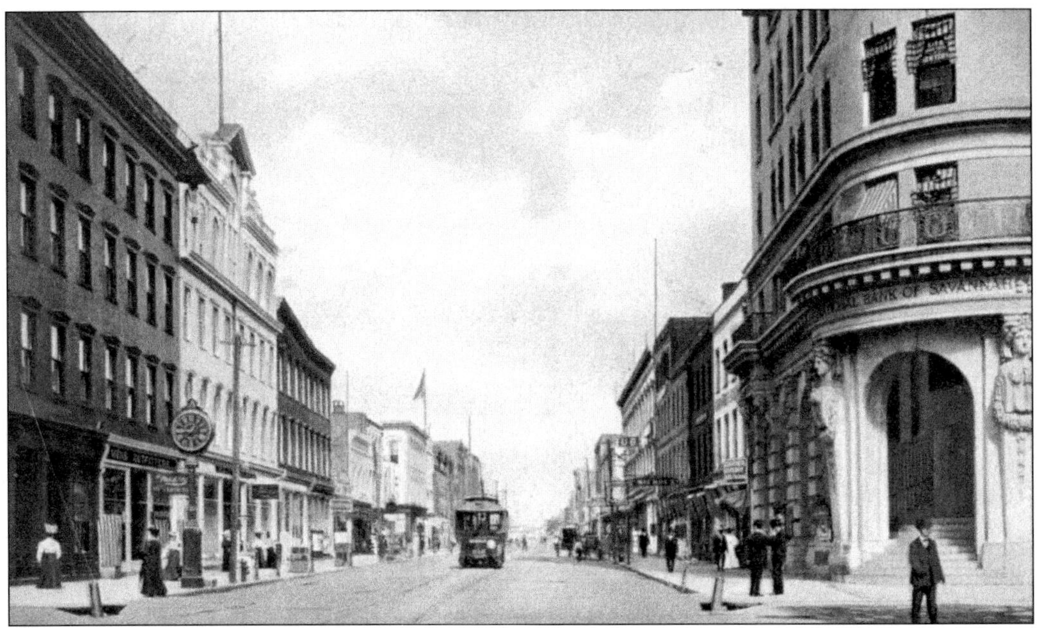

Broughton Street was traditionally one of Savannah's main commercial districts. This view is west toward the intersection with Bull Street. The prominent building on the right housed the National Bank of Savannah, which moved to this location in 1906.

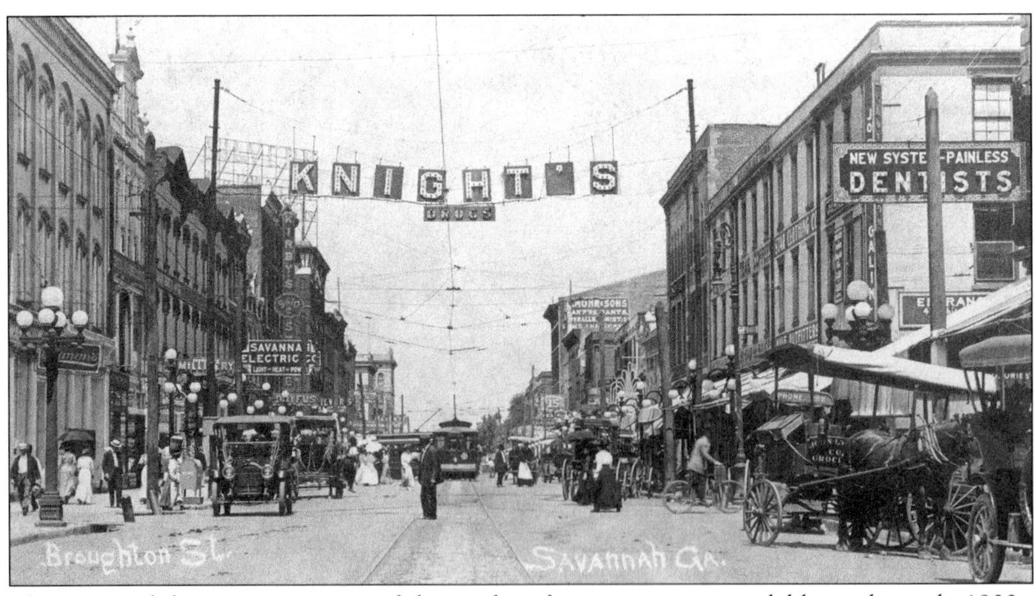

This postcard demonstrates some of the modes of transportation available in the early 1900s. Besides foot and bicycle power, horse-drawn carriages were in use. Personal automobiles were gaining in popularity and accessibility. Streetcars were a reliable, inexpensive, and convenient way to travel from home to business district. Note the north-bound streetcar, behind the group of women with their parasols.

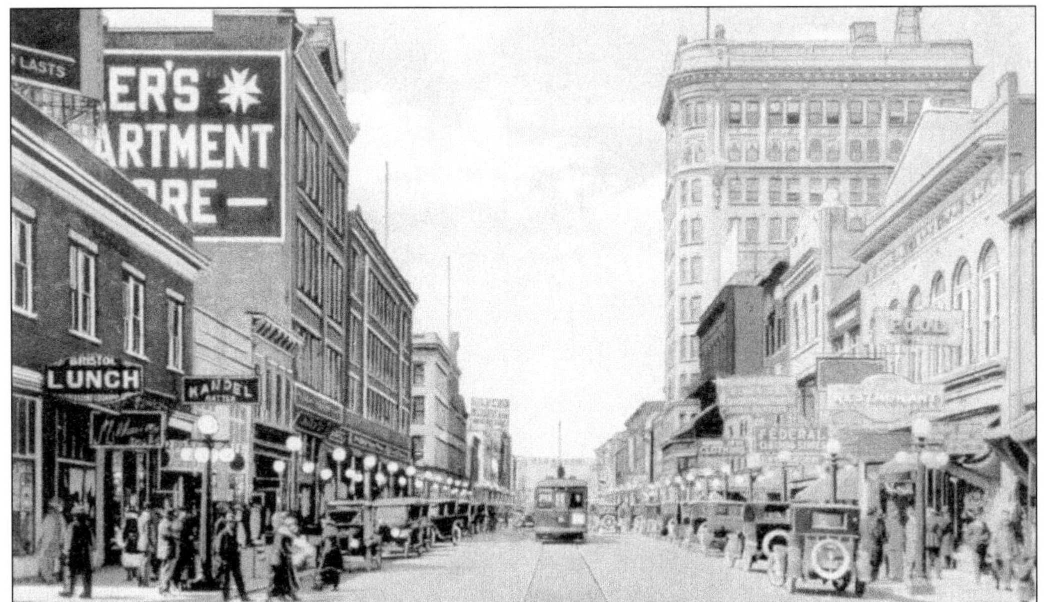

This postcard shows some of the reasons Broughton Street was a busy district. The pedestrians could take advantage of the restaurant or pool hall, the hatter, clothing stores, or Adler's Department Store. The streetcars ran the length of commercial Broughton Street, so after a day out, a shopper could easily find a car on which to return home.

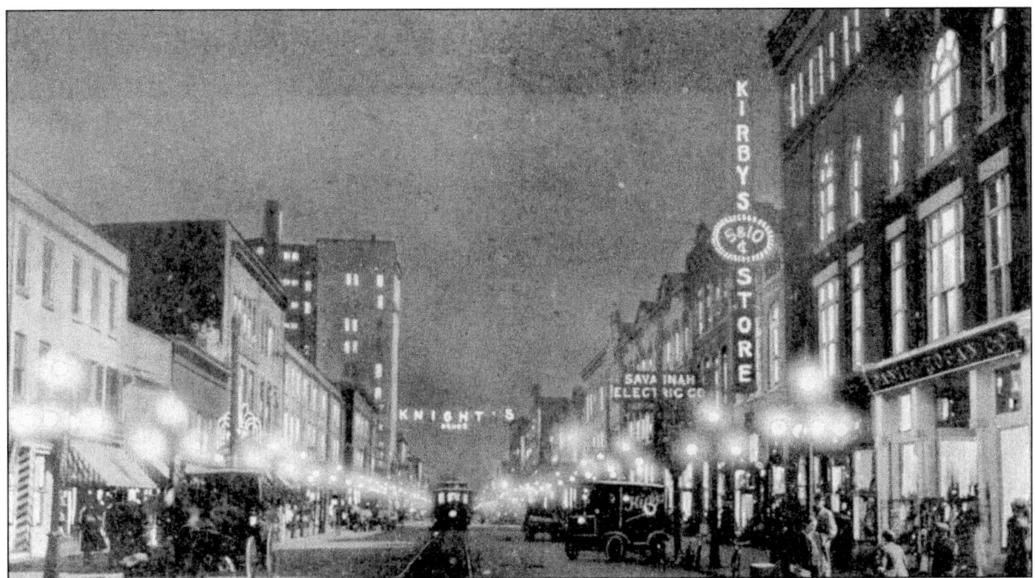

Evening on Broughton Street could be exciting. The street was still filled with people as this postcard shows. The SEC probably powered the signs for Knight's Pharmacy and Kirby's Five and Ten as well its own.

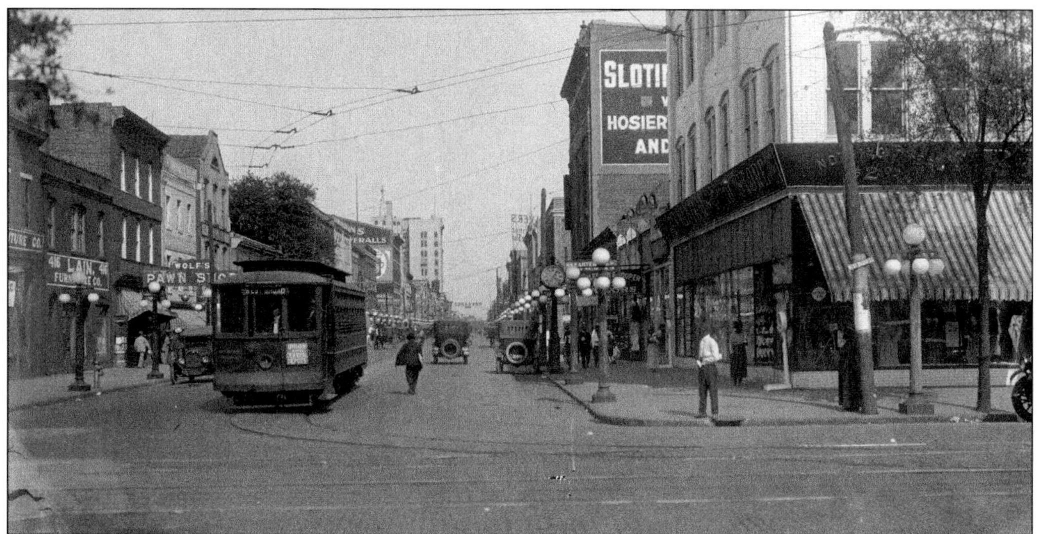

This photograph, taken by Edward H. Girard, shows a streetcar turning south onto West Broad Street (now Martin Luther King Jr. Boulevard) from Broughton. The car is heading to the depots of Central of Georgia's Railroad Company and Union Station. However, the passengers might be getting off to shop at one of the many stores on West Broad.

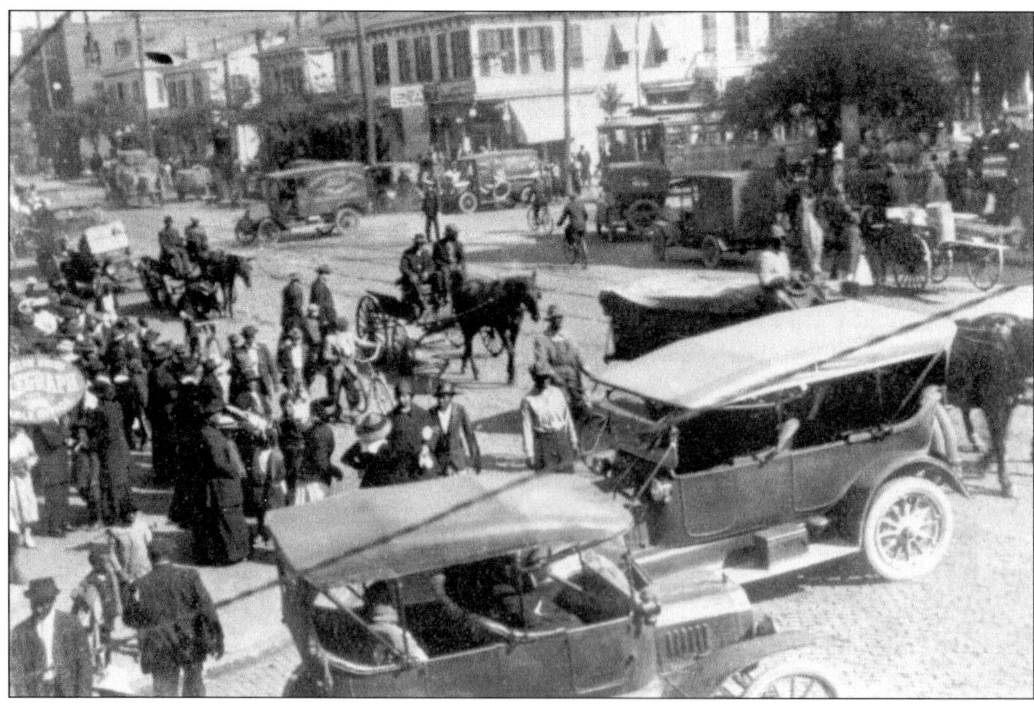

This is a picture of a very busy West Broad at Louisville Road. The streetcar is entering from Liberty Street.

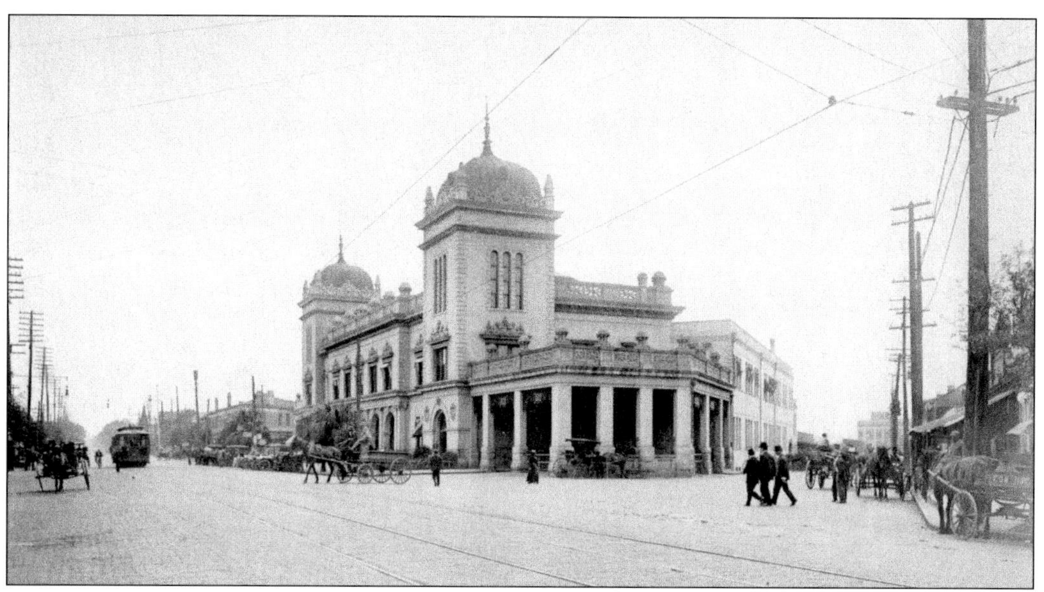

Streetcars offered the convenience of connecting the passenger train depot on the west side of town with Union Station on the east. The station was built in 1902 and demolished in 1962, to make way for the on and off ramps for Interstate 16. Below is a photograph taken in 1912, looking north from the station.

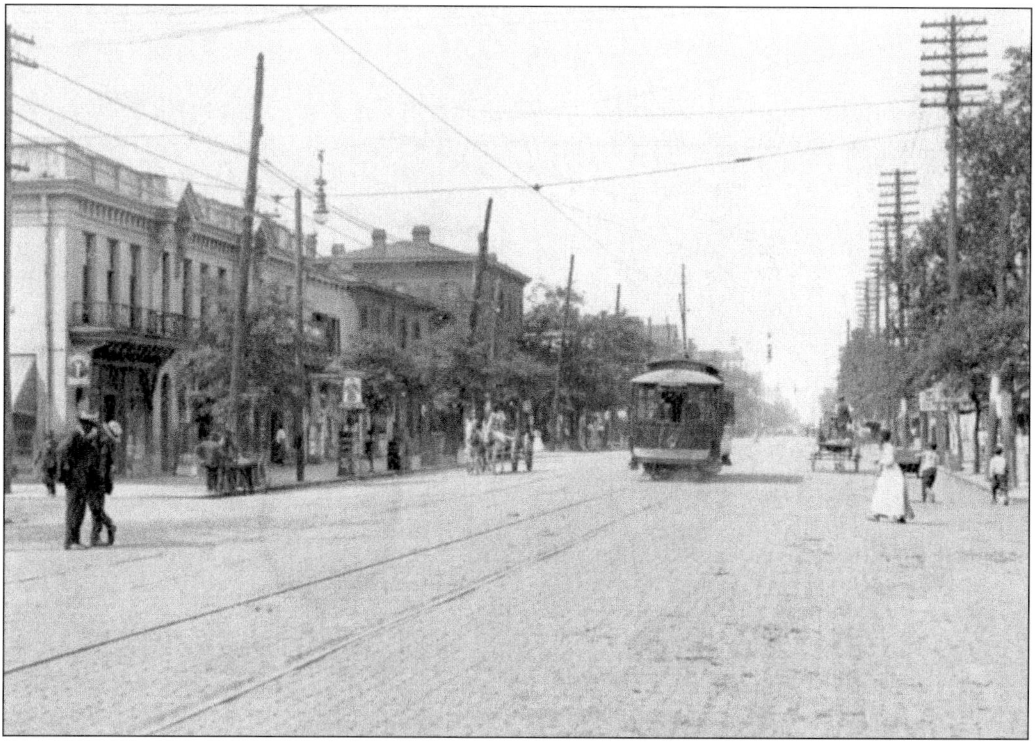

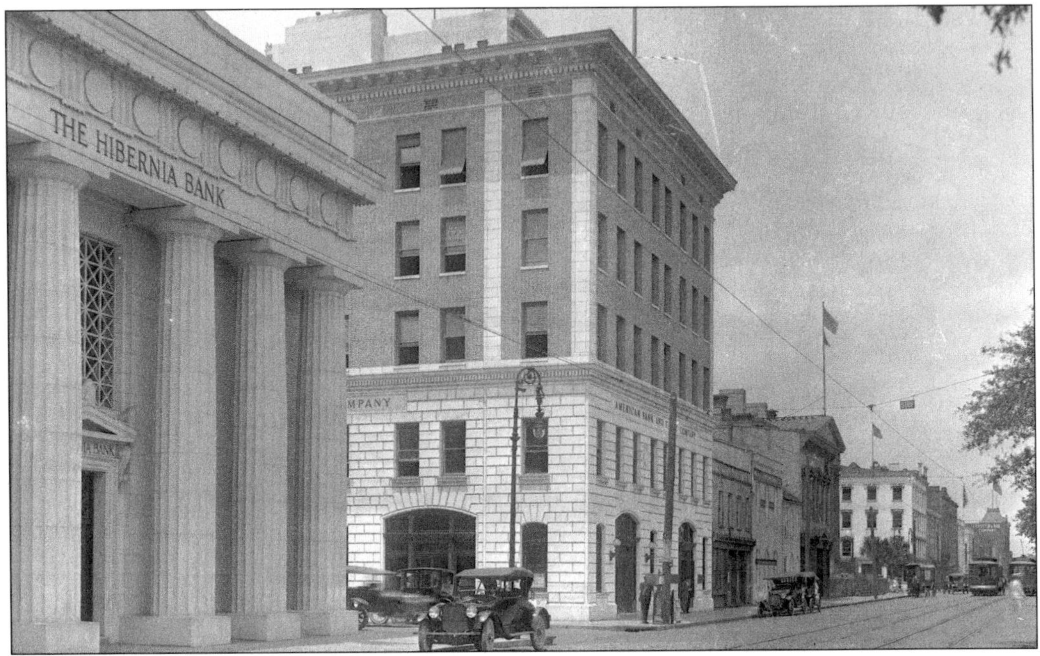

The Hibernian Bank at 29 East Bay Street was accessible by streetcar. This photograph, c. 1917, is a view looking west that shows the Hibernian Bank and the American Bank and Trust Company.

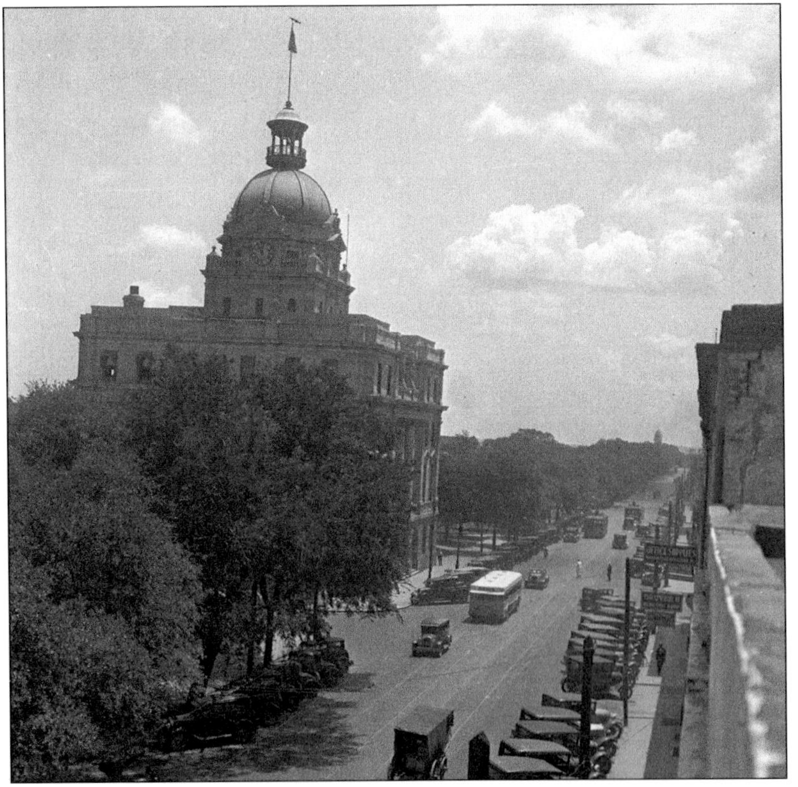

Streetcars made access to city and county services convenient. The same car that brought a Thunderbolt resident into town to shop could then take him or her to City Hall, the Cotton Exchange, and the Customs House. This photograph, taken in 1912, shows City Hall on Bay Street.

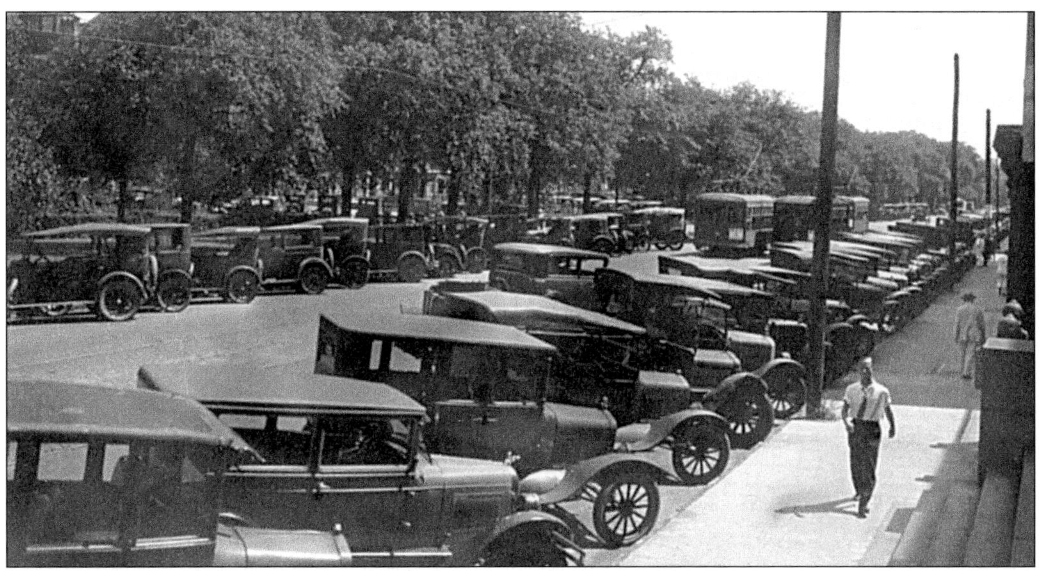

In this undated photograph, the number of parked automobiles indicates the popularity of personal transportation. The fact that there are also three streetcars shows that these cars were heavily used.

Savannah's City Exchange was built in 1799 and replaced by the current city hall in 1904. The exchange was the seat of city government and public activities. A bell was installed in 1804, and, in addition to other uses, it rang to signal the close of business at 9 p.m. (from March 31 to September 22), and at 8 p.m. during the remainder of the year. In 1903, due to the needs of a growing town, Mayor Herman Myers requested that City Council study the feasibility of a new municipal building. The recommendation was made to construct a new building on the same site. Demolition of the City Exchange began the following March, and the cornerstone was laid for the new city hall in August.

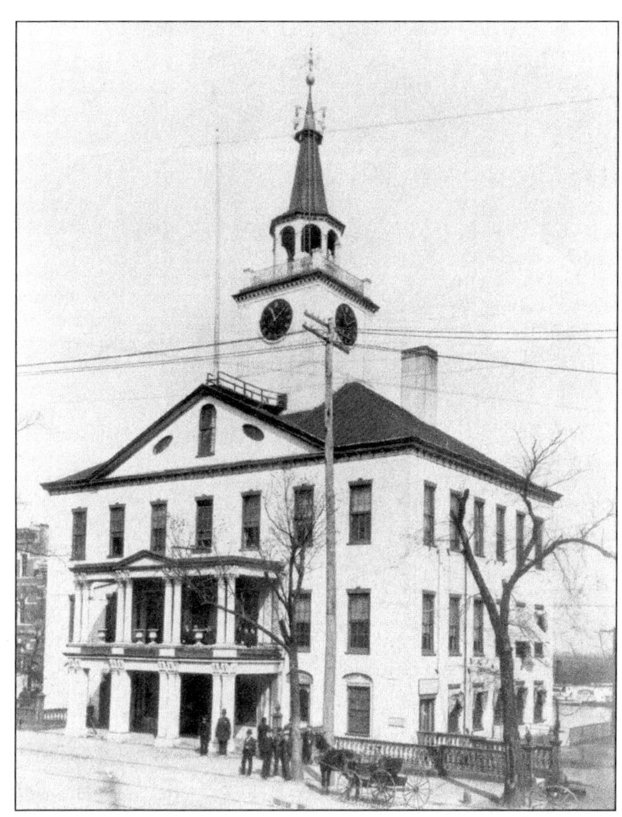

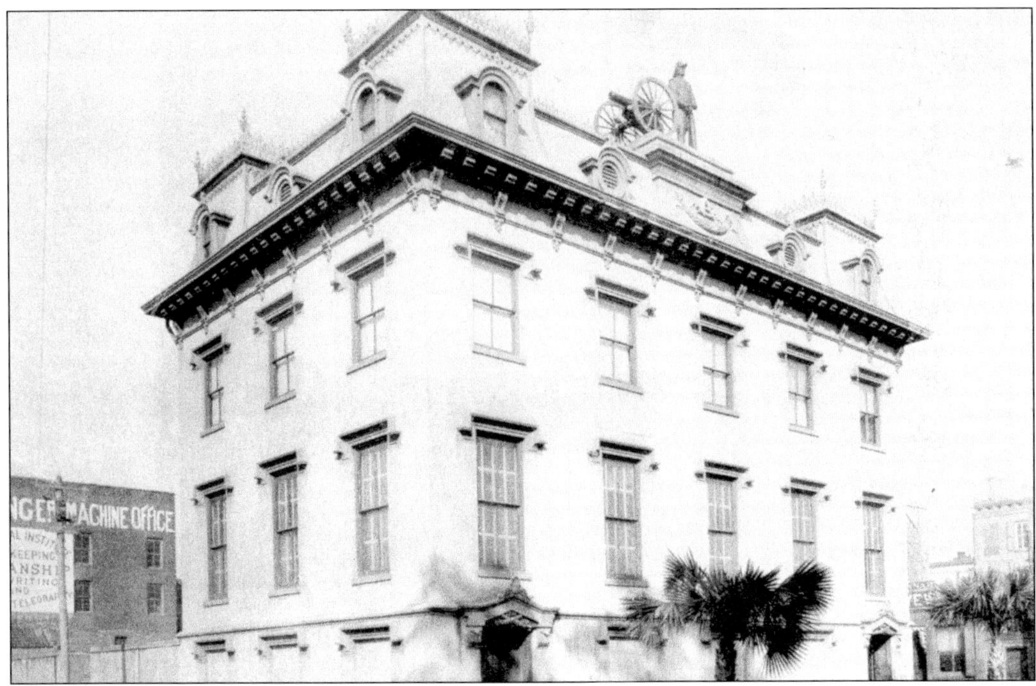

Surrounding Wright Square at various times were the Chatham Artillery Armory, the Federal Building, the old Chatham County Court House, and the current Court House. The Armory was built in the 1840s, and the Federal Building was erected in two phases. Above is a picture of the Armory. The picture below shows the original Federal Building. The left side of the construction site is the spot where the Armory stood.

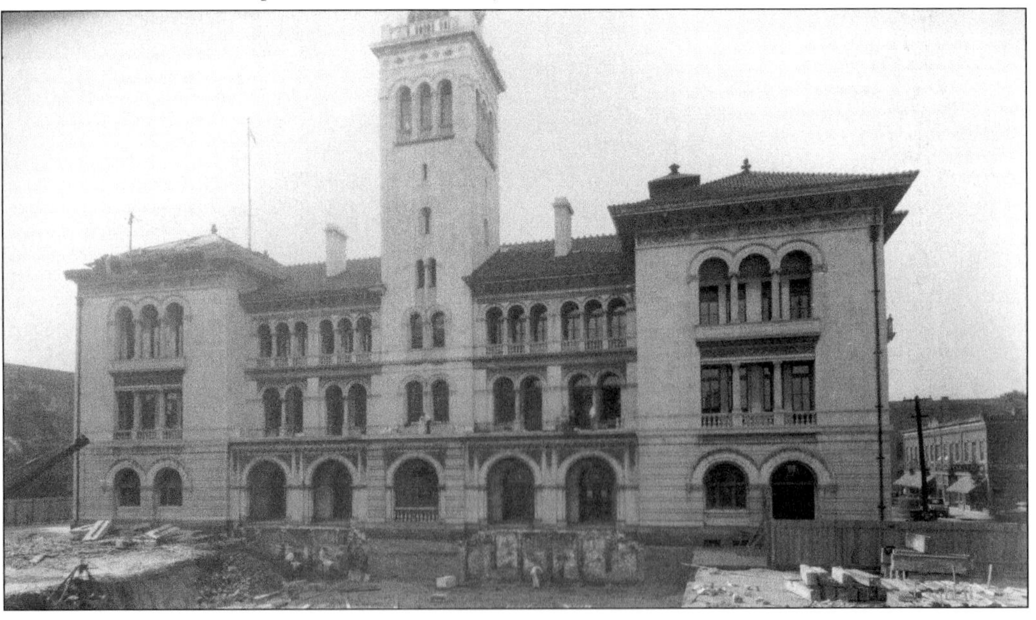

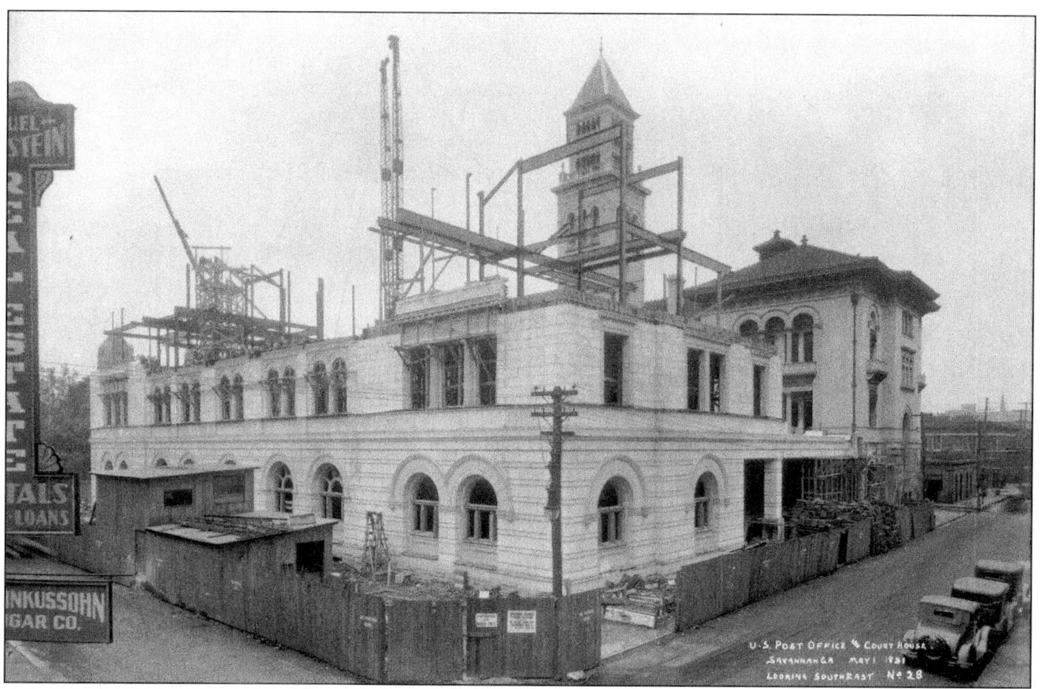

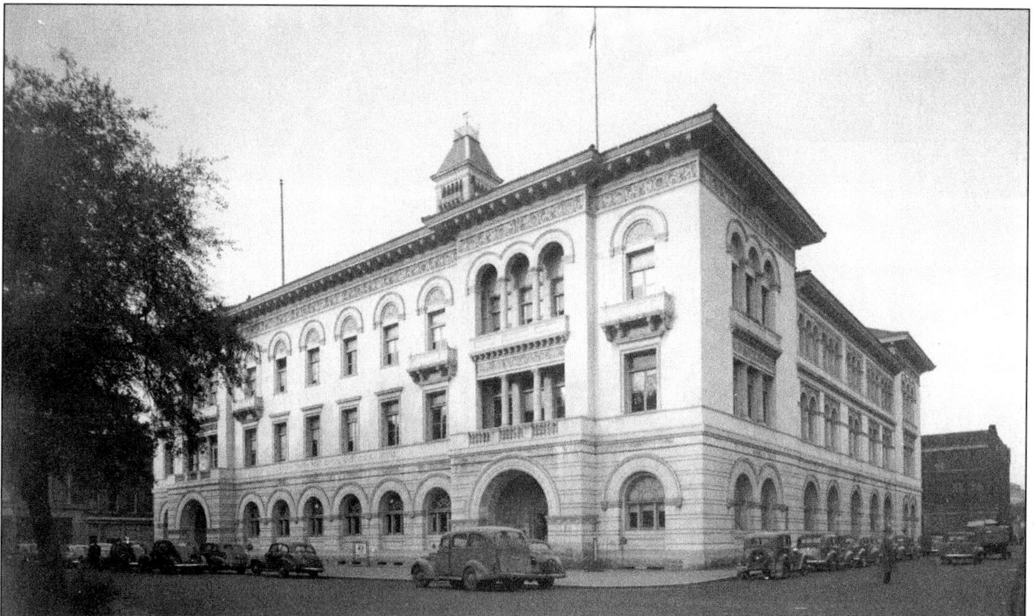

This series of three photographs (two above and the bottom of p. 96) documents the growth of the Federal Building. In 1899, a building was erected facing President Street. The first image shows the north facade. In 1930, the northern portion of the building was added, closing off President Street and occupying the Chatham Artillery site.

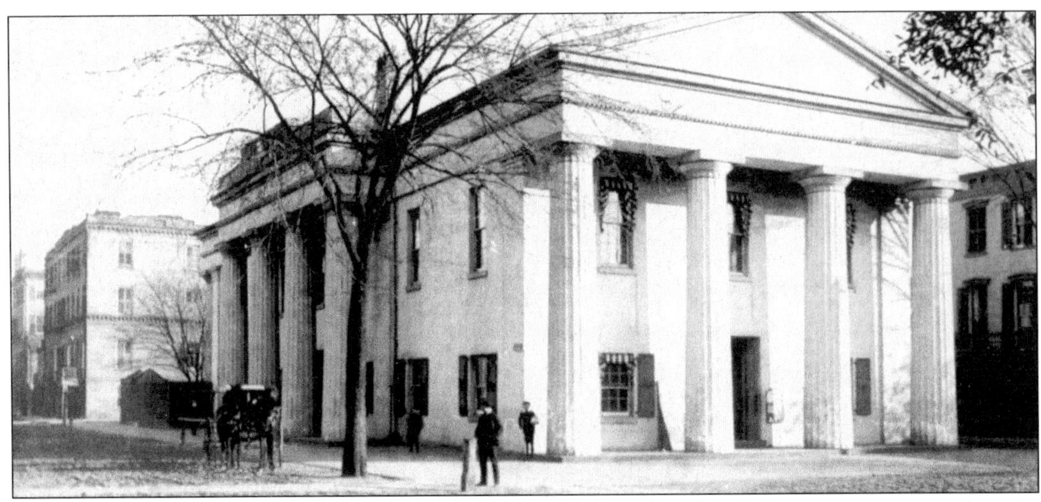

Above is the old courthouse that stood between 1833 and 1889. Below is a picture taken in 1930 of the existing courthouse.

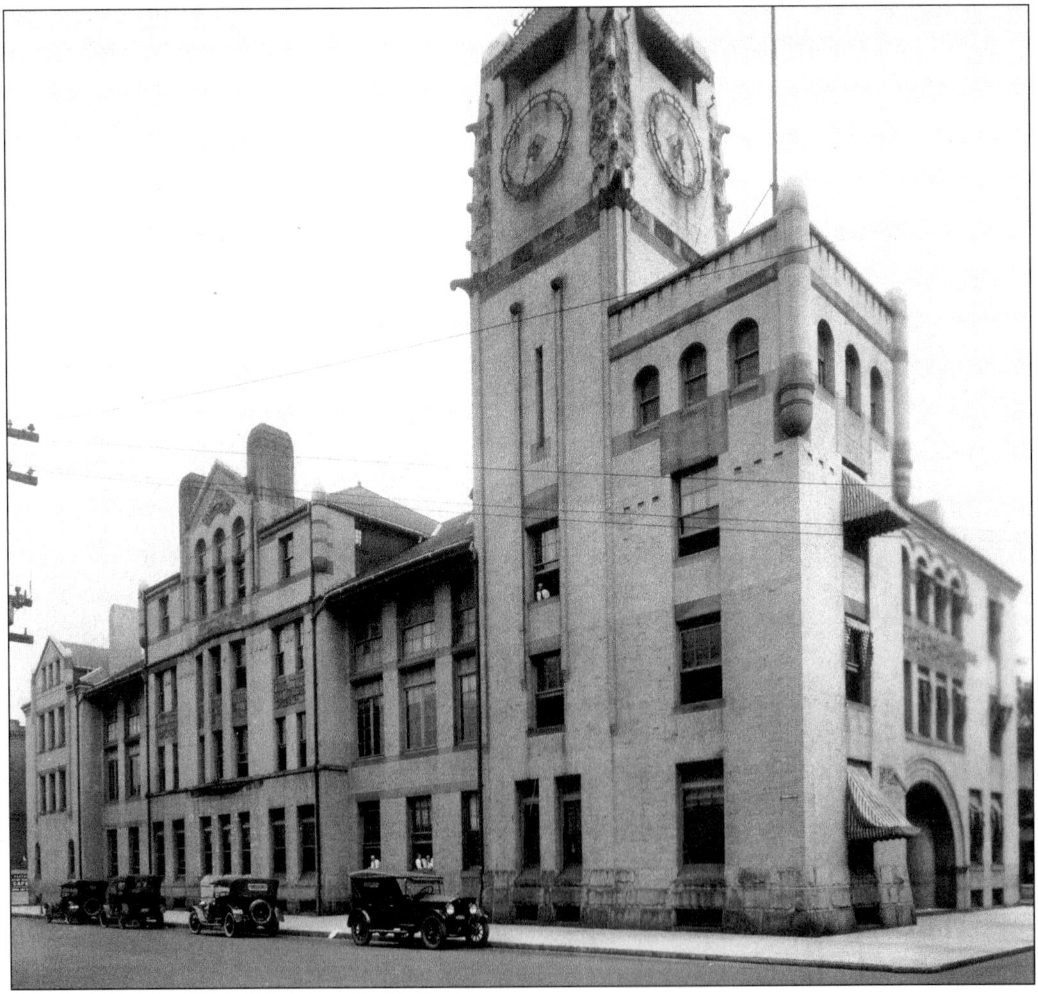

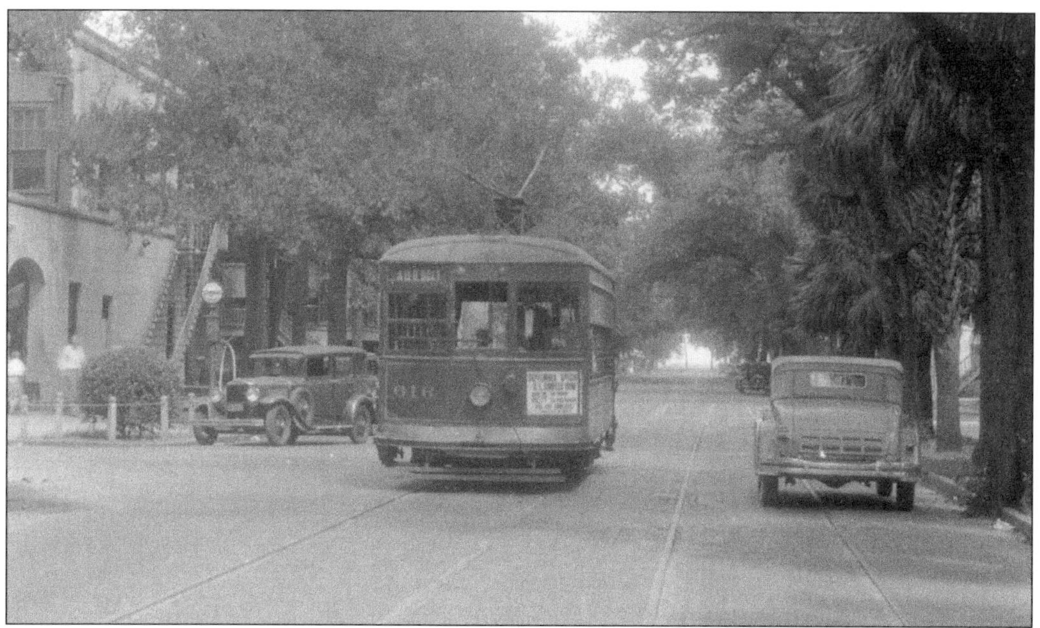

Theater-goers wanted after-theater cars run. In September of 1889, C. & S. requested the use of McDonough Street, from Abercorn to Whitaker Streets, to fulfill this need. The car pictured above is on Abercorn Street, at the intersection of McDonough. The Savannah Theater, which would have been served by a line down McDonough, was on Chippewa Square. The car pictured below provided transportation to the theater as well as an advertisement spot. The streetcar companies benefited by the popularity of theater and other types of entertainment in Savannah and were quick to offer service that would increase their ridership.

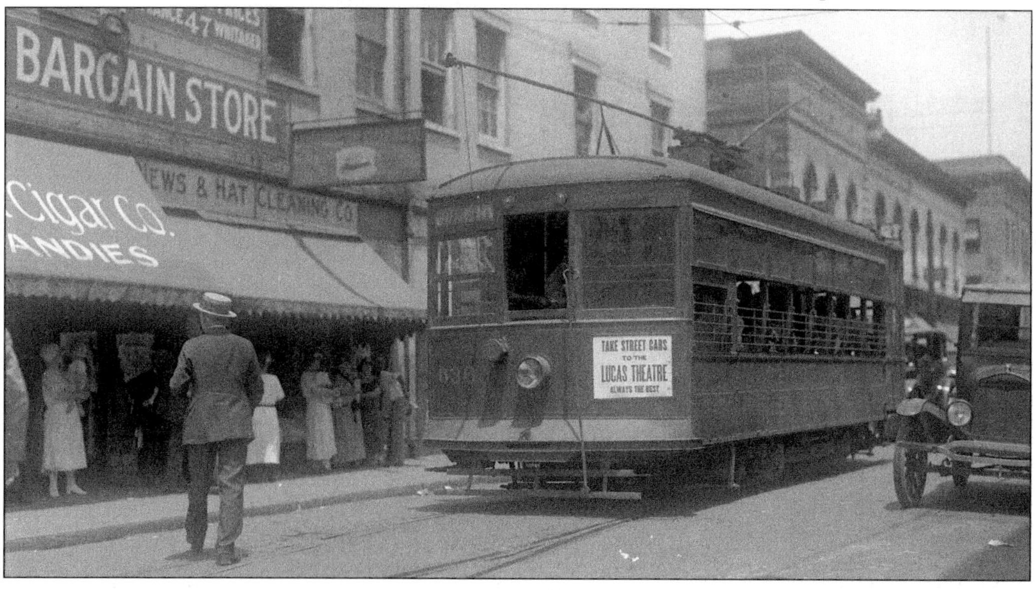

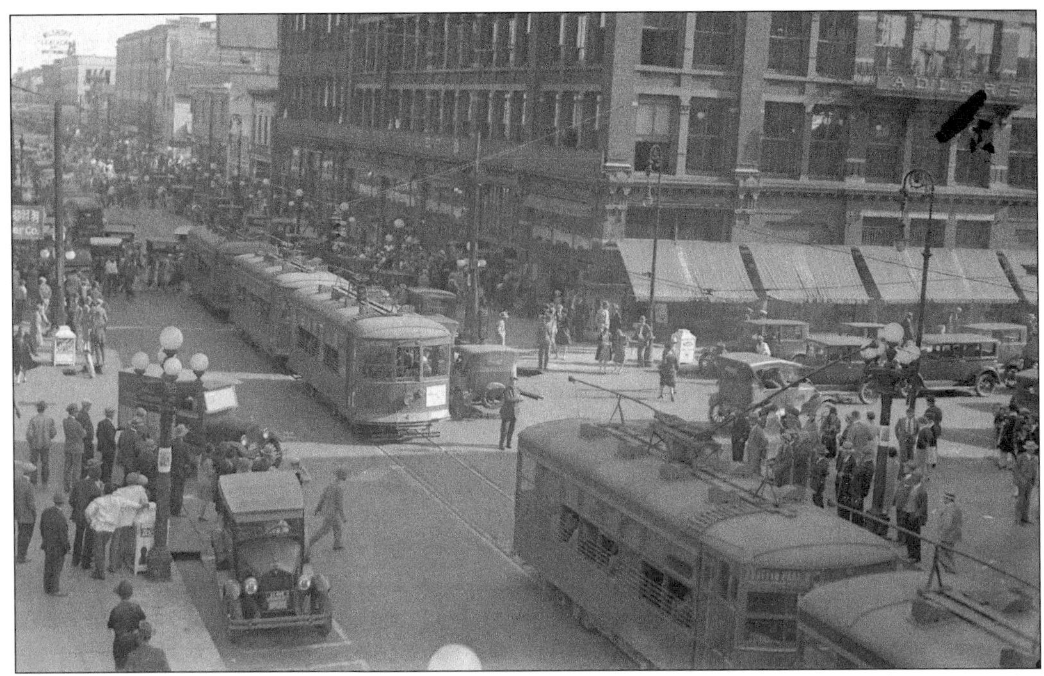
Streetcars on Broughton Street are shown taking part in an unidentified parade. Notice the destination placard that reads "Daffin Park."

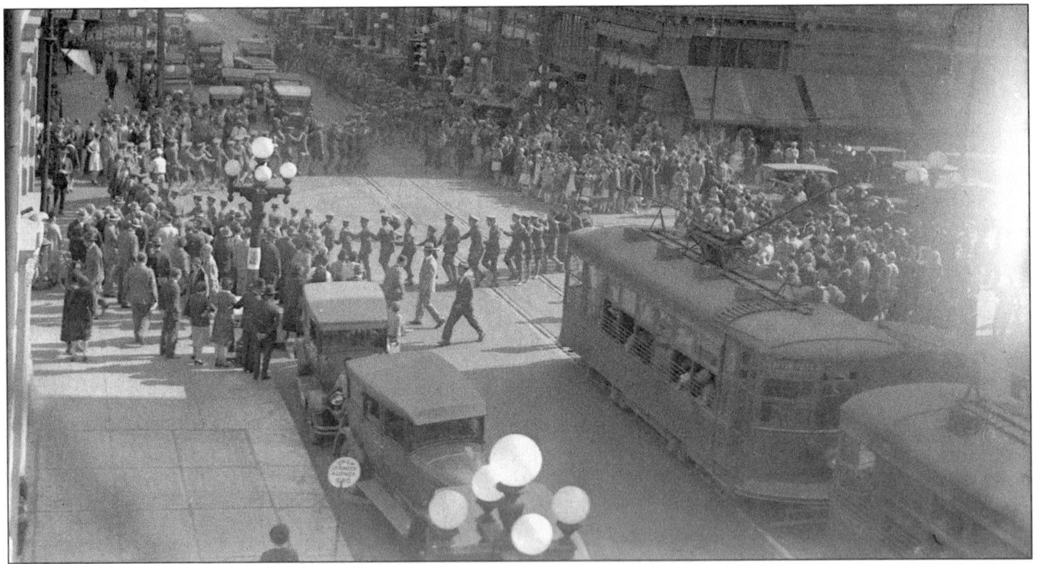

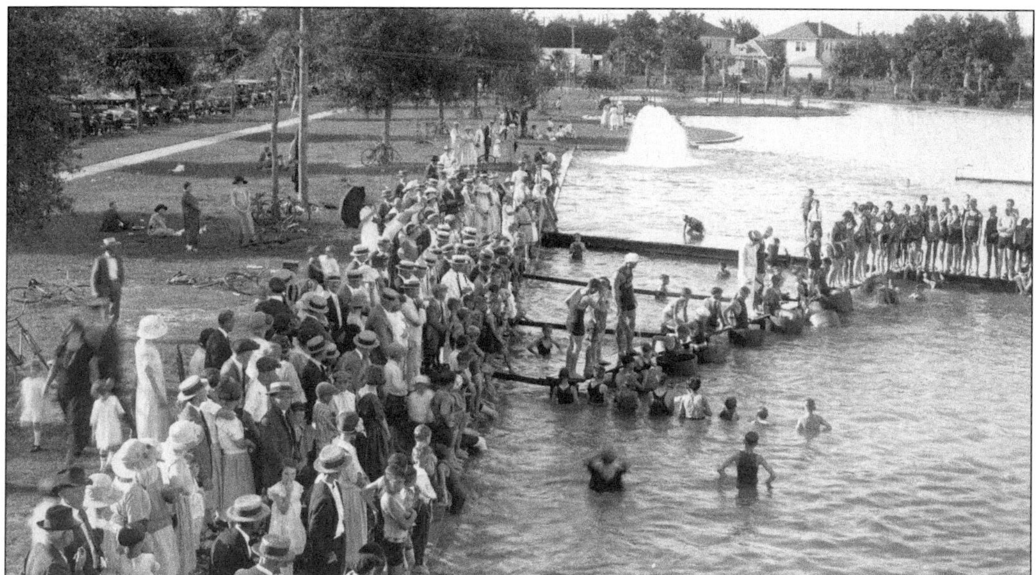

With its swimming pool and pavilion, Daffin Park provided a welcome respite from the summer heat. These images show swimmers and spectators enjoying the facilities. The park also included a tennis court and a municipal stadium.

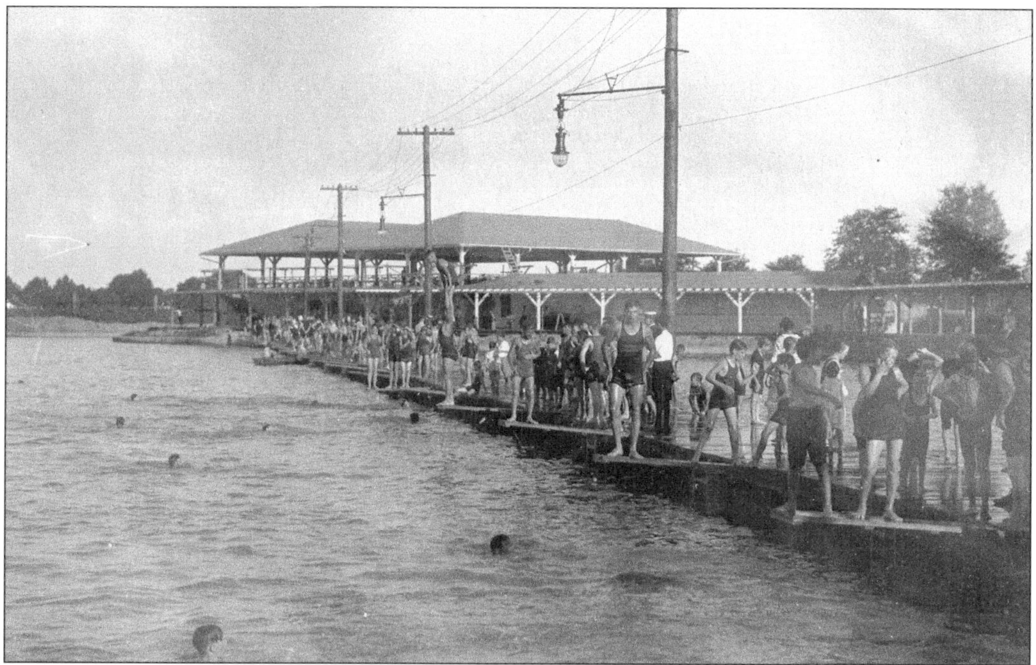

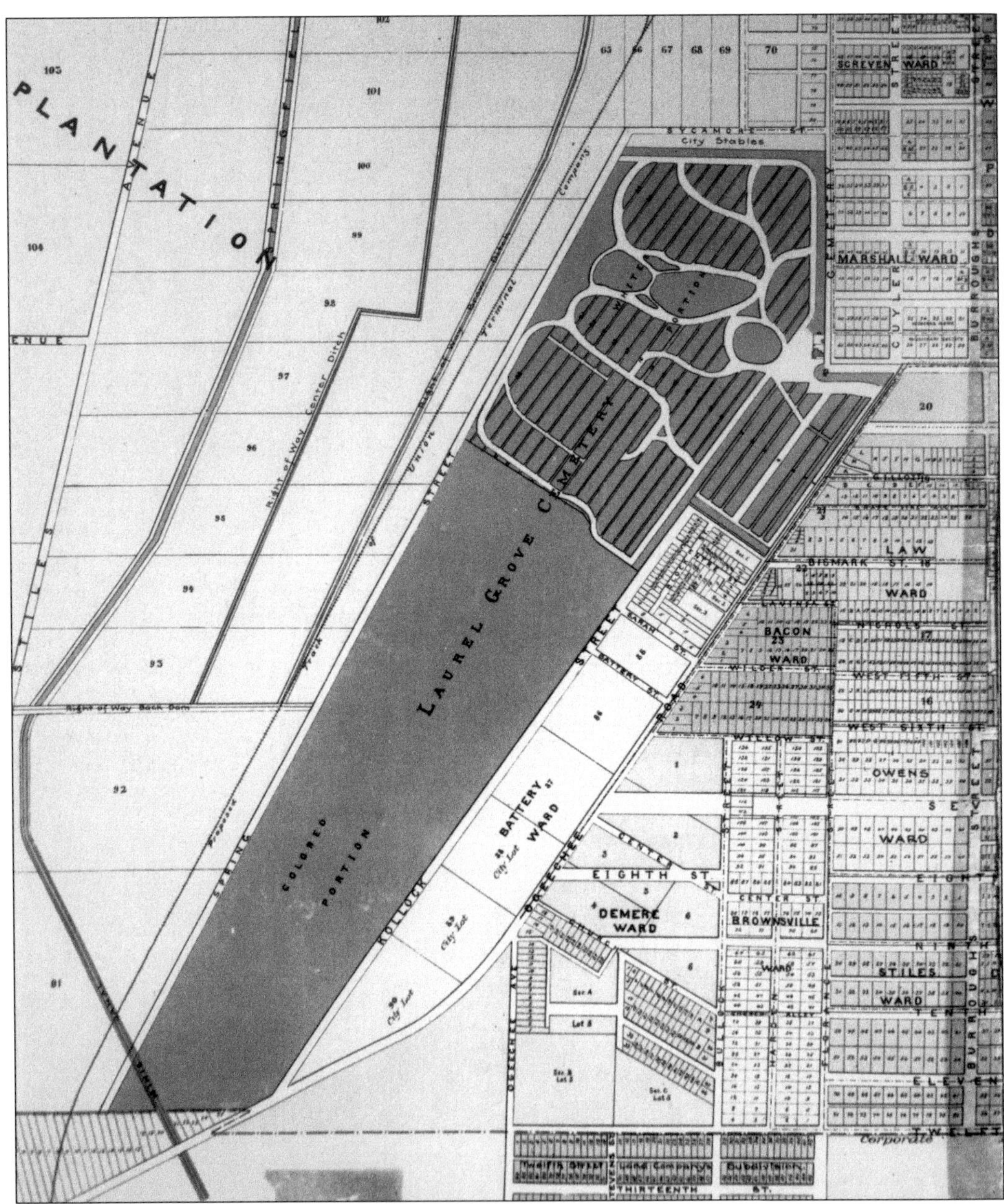

City Council adopted an ordinance in June of 1852 that carved Laurel Grove Cemetery from part of Springfield Plantation. The plan for the plots, roads, and walks was laid out by James O. Morse. Dedicated in November 1852, the first interment had taken place the previous month.

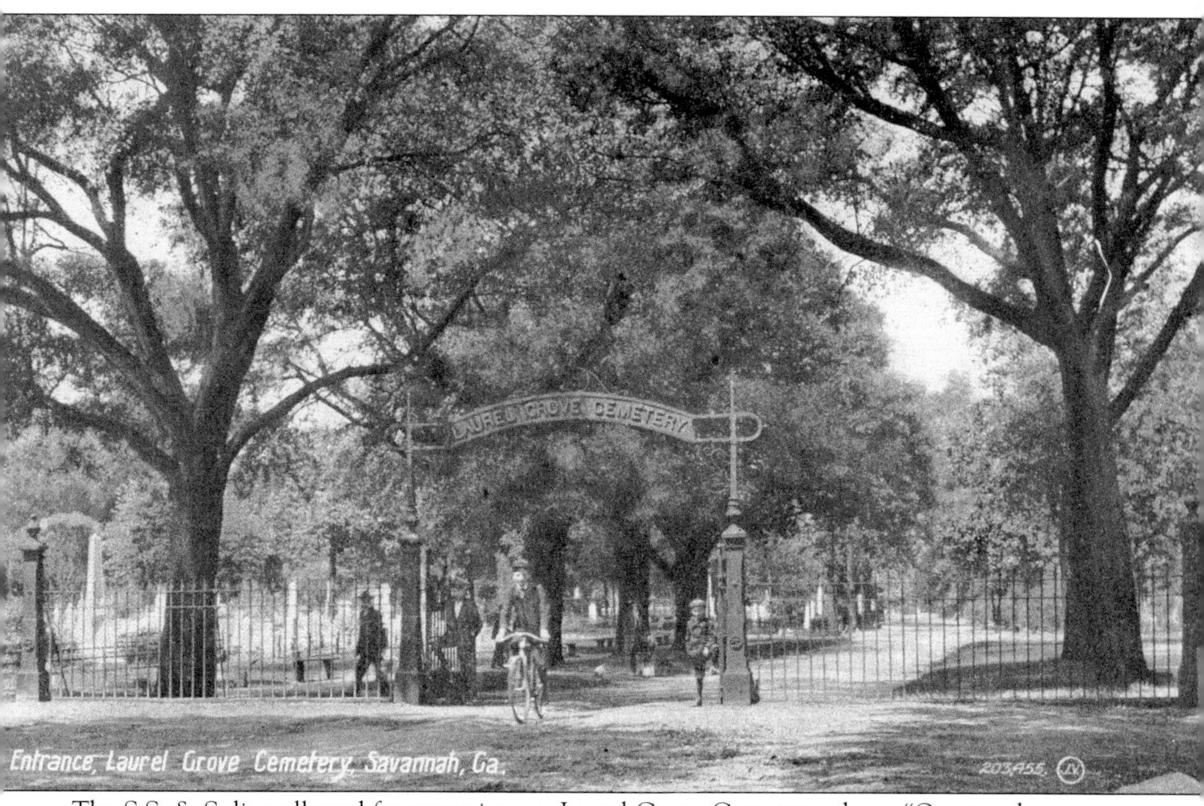

The S.S. & S. line allowed for excursions to Laurel Grove Cemetery where, "Our people may pass the sultry hours of summer afternoons in roaming through the shaded walks of the place or sitting beneath the trees." This is a photograph of such a scene.

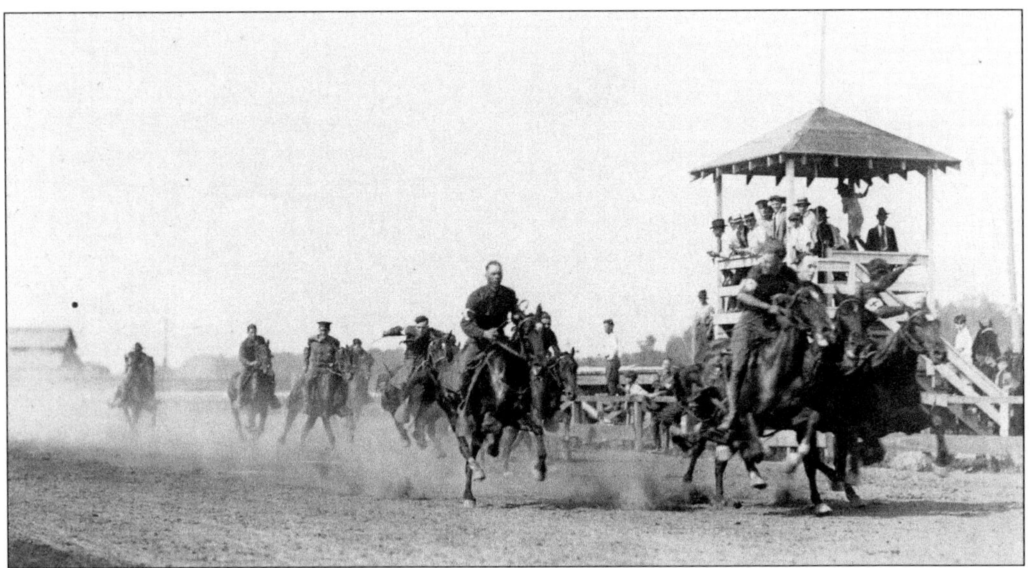

The Ten Broeck Race Course was a 1-mile-long, horse-racing track at the fairgrounds of the Agricultural and Mechanical Association of Georgia, located 2.5 miles west of Savannah on the Augusta Road. Events such as those pictured here were held at Ten Broeck as well as the tracks at Thunderbolt and Vernonburg.

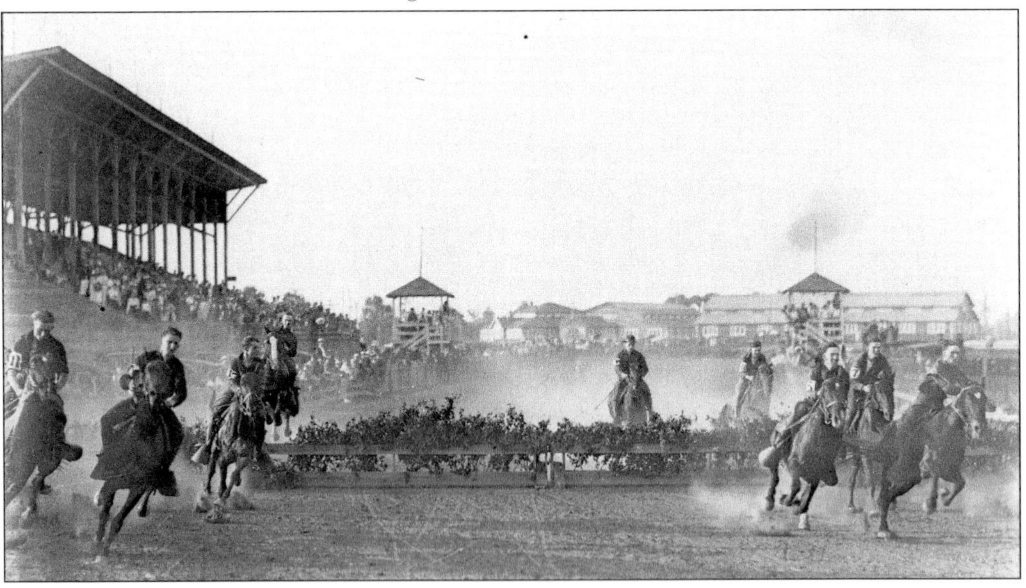

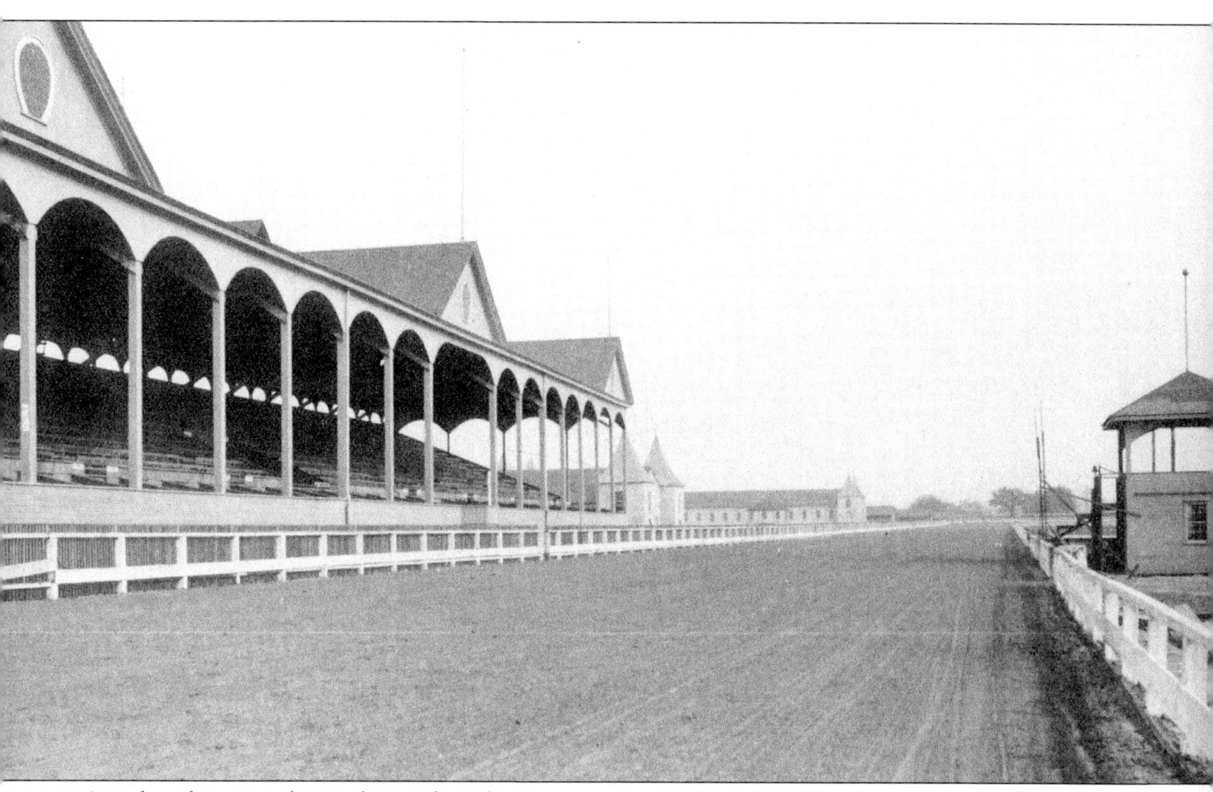

Another fairgrounds was located at the intersection of Ogeechee Road and Victory Drive. In the 1890s, when this picture was taken, it was served by the C. & S.

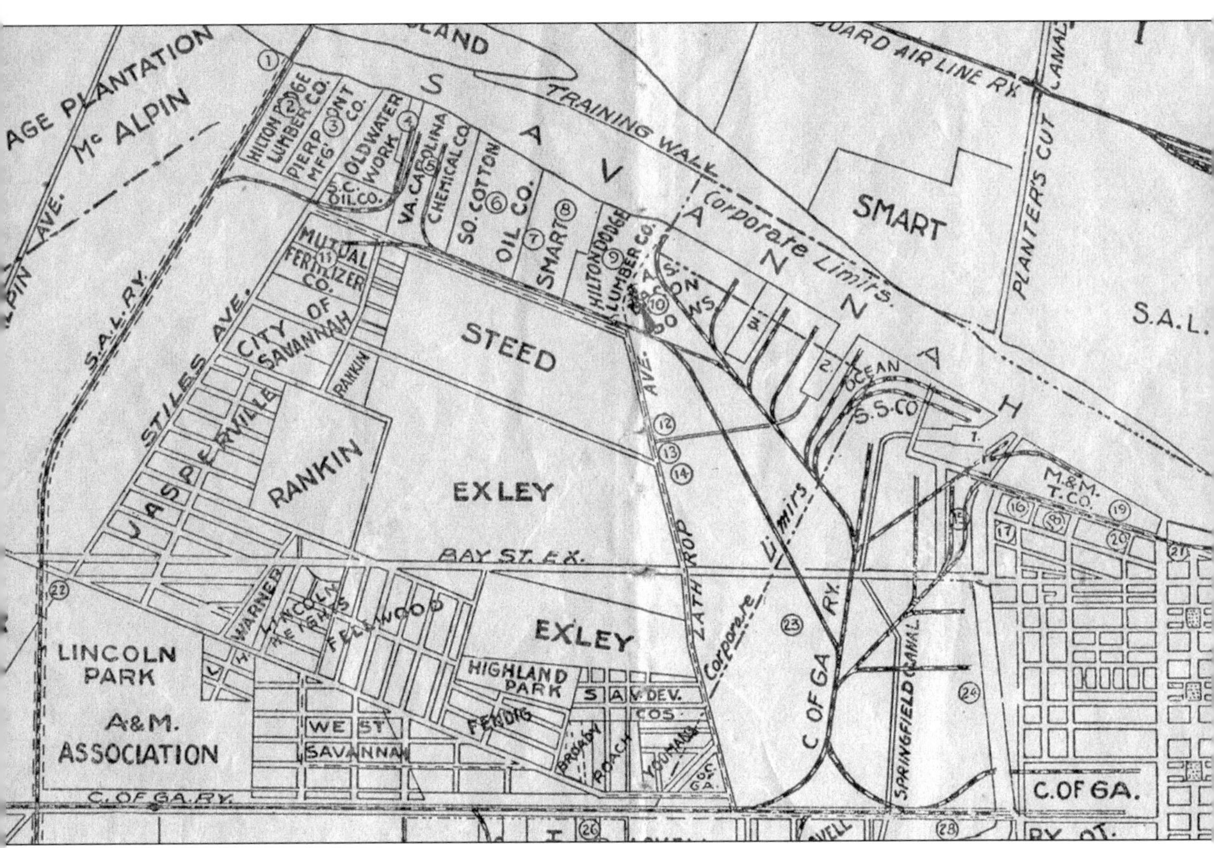

The end of World War I saw an increase in traffic to the suburb of Port Wentworth, located about 8 miles northwest of Savannah. To fill the need, the Chatham County Traction Company was incorporated. After construction in 1918, the line was leased to Savannah Electric Company. Running in the same direction, the Mill Haven Line served the factory district on the west end of Bay Street. This detail of a map, drawn in 1910, shows the industries that were clustered along the Savannah River, immediately west of Savannah.

Five
The Electric Companies

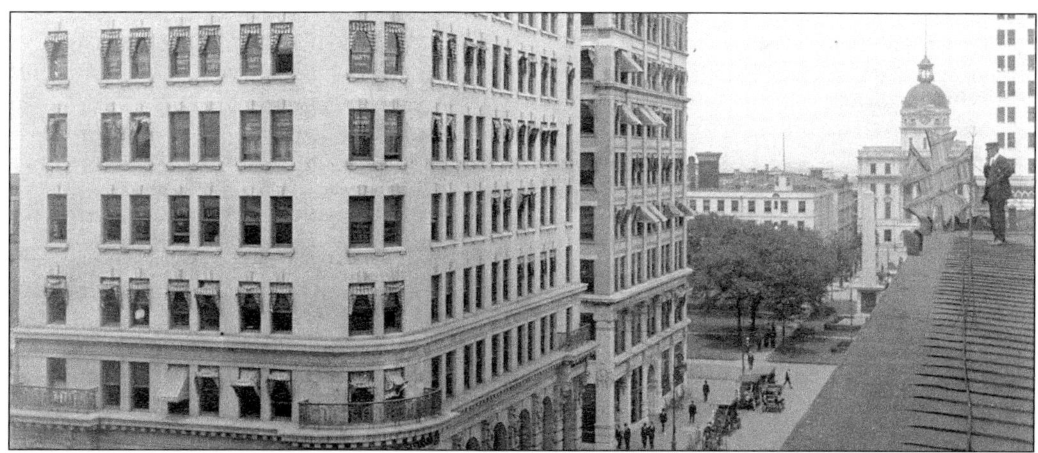

At the turn of the century, Savannah's streetcar lines and power companies were independent, though inter-related. On January 15, 1902, SEC purchased Savannah and Isle of Hope Railway Company, C. & S., S.T. & I., and Edison Electric Company. On October 28, 1928, SEC and Chatham County Traction Company were sold to Savannah Electric and Power Company (SEPCO). In 1923, with the purchase of Savannah Lighting, SEPCO owned and operated all the streetcar lines and electric companies in town.

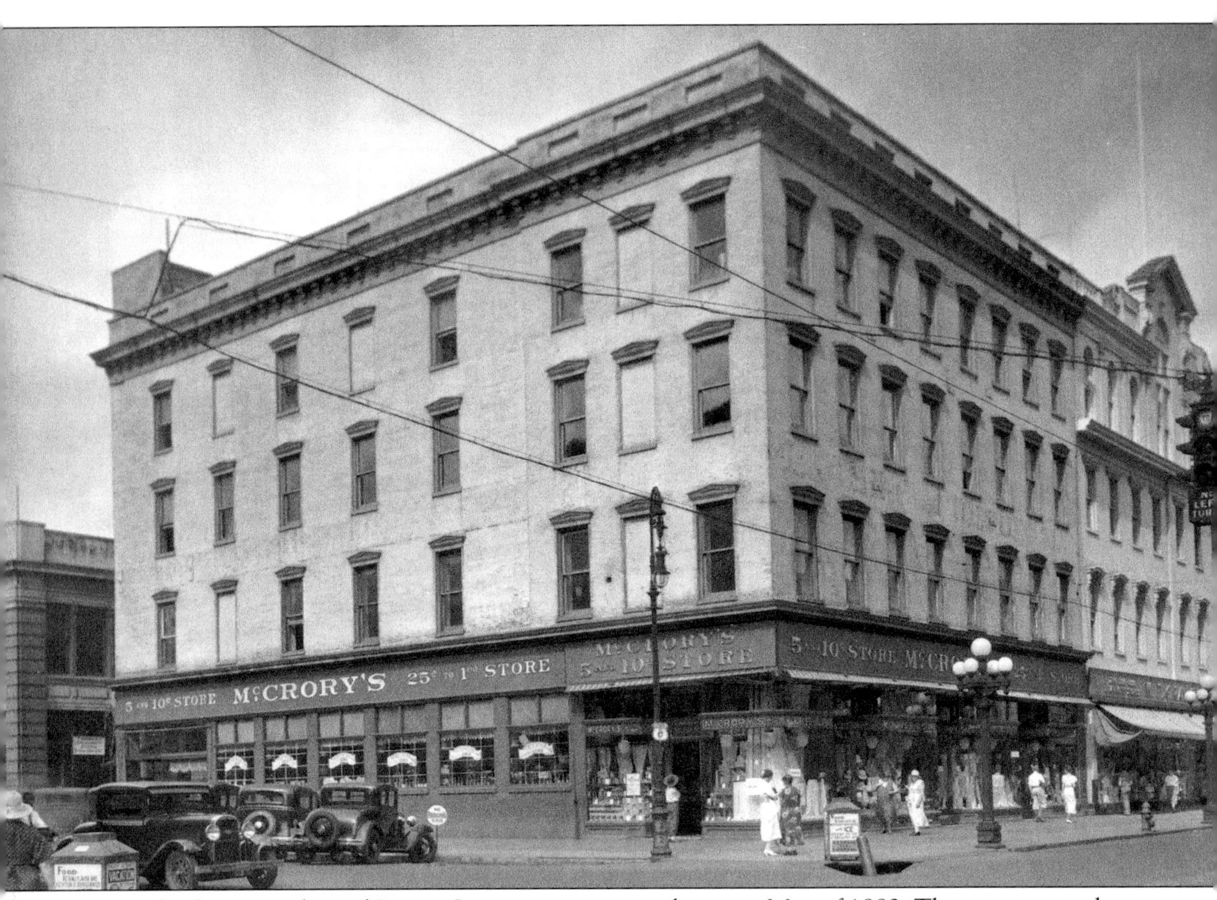

Brush Electric Light and Power Company came into being in May of 1882. The name was taken from Brush Electric Company of Cleveland, Ohio, from whom the first "dynamo machine" or generator was purchased. C.F. Brush was an engineer at Edison's Electric Works who developed the first successful generator. The Savannah company was started by D.G. Purse, J.H. Estill, and George Walker, among others. Brush's first office was located at 125 Broughton Street, now 1 West Broughton. This photograph shows that address in 1933.

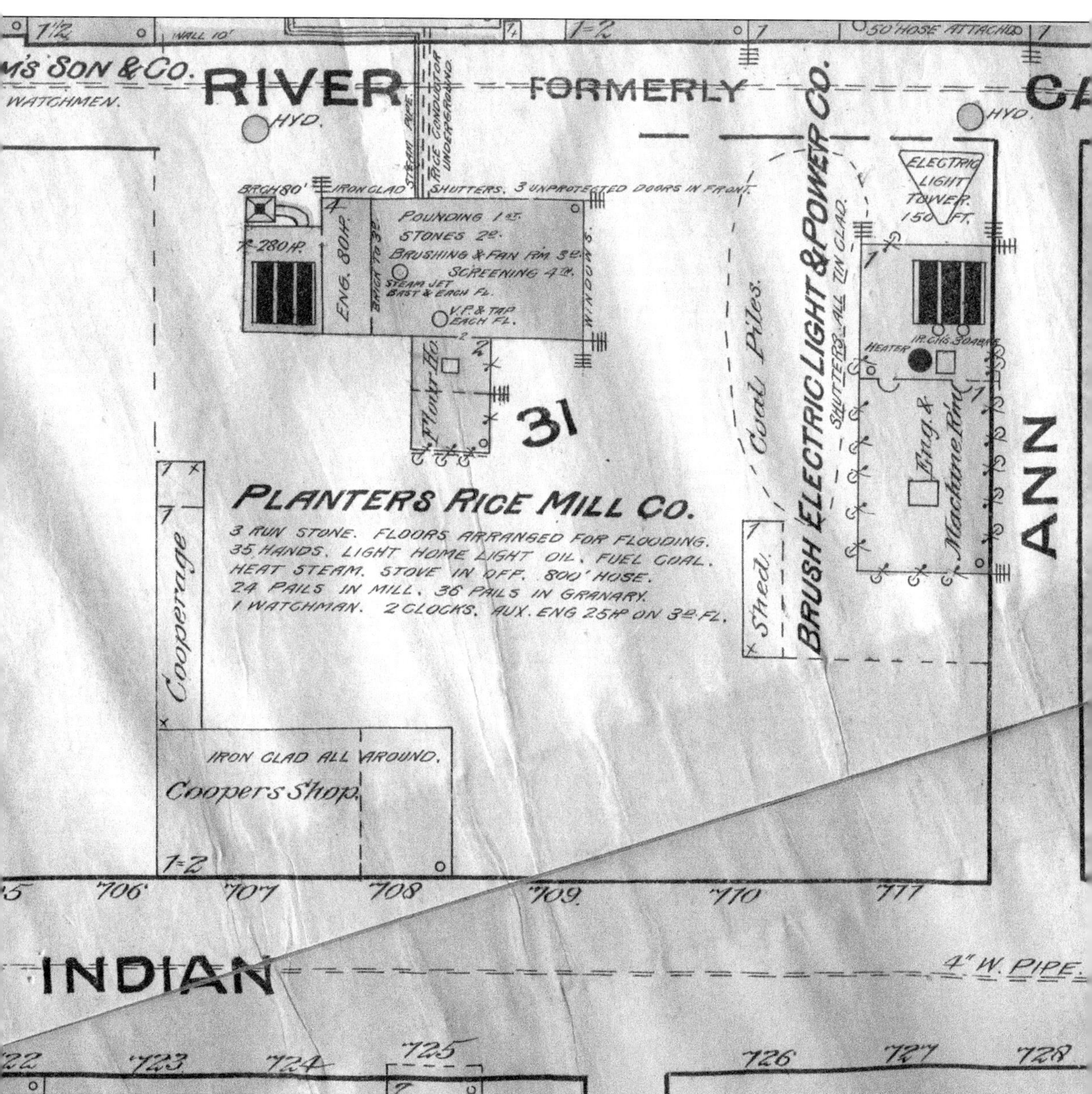

In 1882, a site between Indian and River Streets was purchased as the location for the power plant.

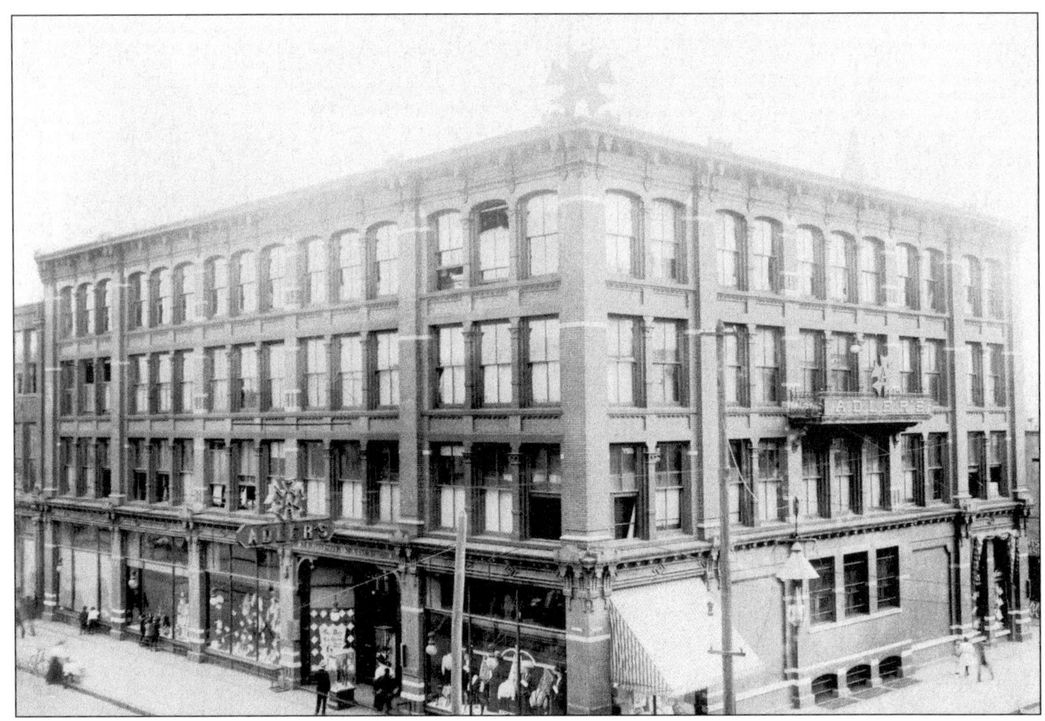

Savannah was first electrified on September 23, 1882. Crowds turned out to witness the spectacle. In all, 12 buildings received power for the night. According to newspaper accounts, "A.R. Altmayer was particularly brilliant . . . There were two lights in this commodious establishment and the illumination was very fine." Two nights later, power was turned on again, this time for uninterrupted nighttime service. These are images of Adler's Department Store, which had been Altmayer's.

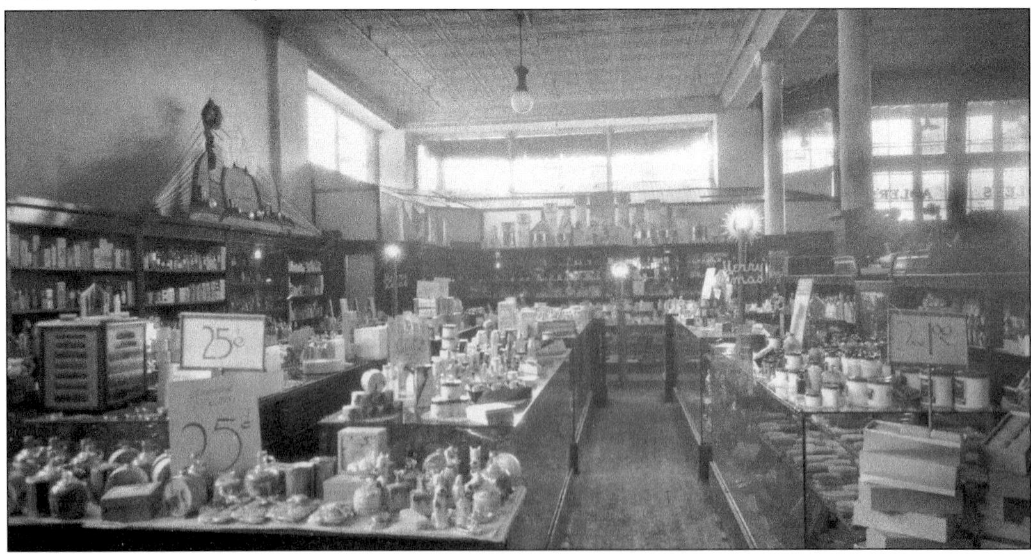

A committee, assigned to study the possibility of lighting the city market, recommended that Brush be given a contract to light the city each night from sunset to broad daylight, except nights before and after a full moon. Brush would be paid $1,500 a month. The contract for electric light on the streets called for the brightness to be equivalent to the moon in its third quarter.

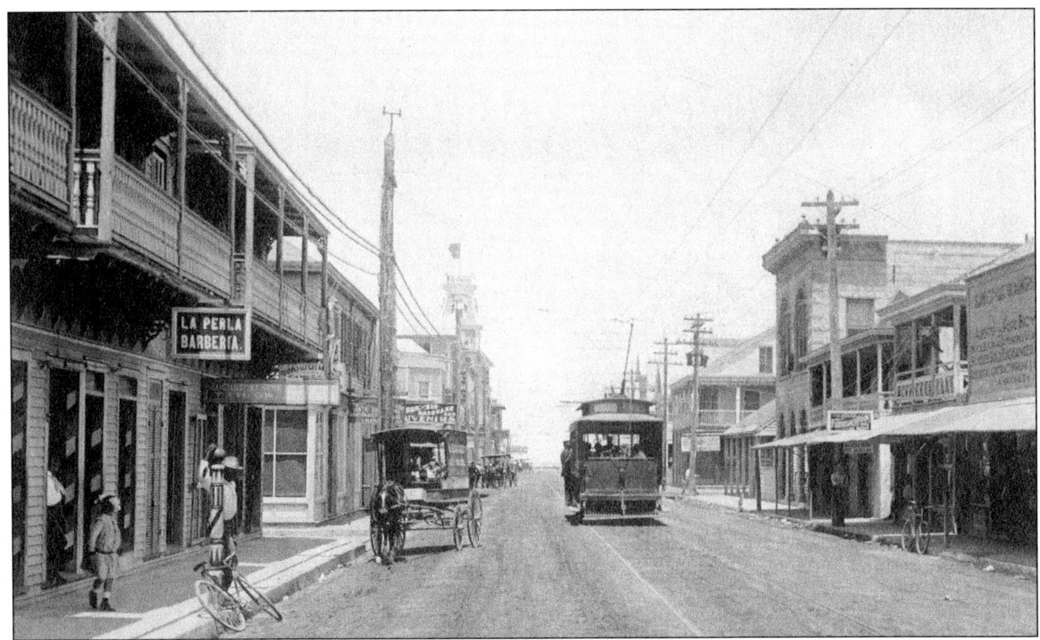

Edison Electric was begun by Charles Stone, Edwin S. Webster, and George J. Baldwin. Stone & Webster, a Boston based company, owned streetcar companies all along the east coast. This photo from an album, marked "Stone and Webster Southeastern Properties," is of lower Duval Street in Key West, Florida.

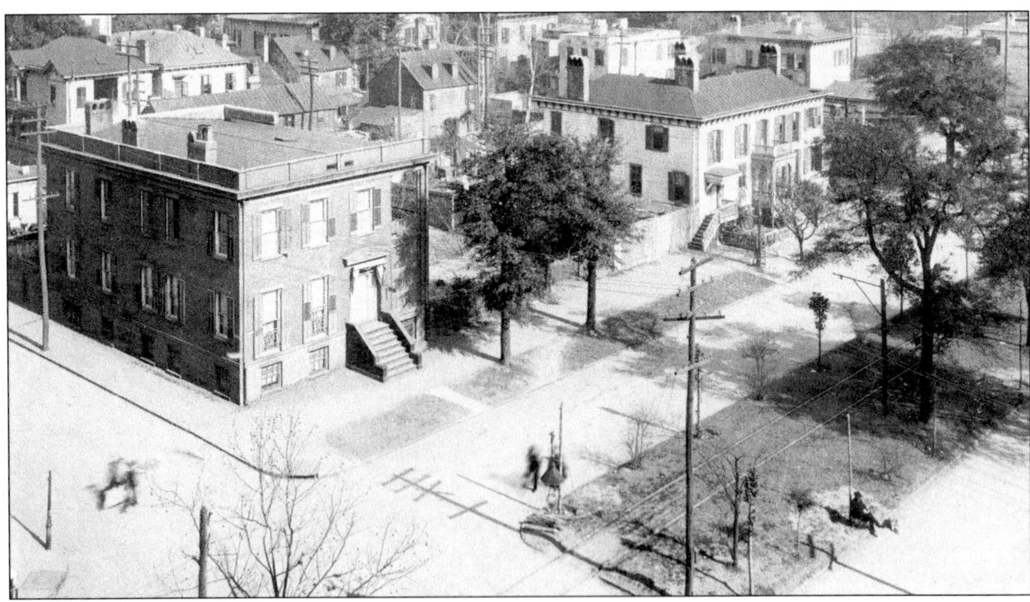

The city of Savannah approved an underground right-of-way and the use of poles for electricity. Areas of service were assigned to each company. Brush was granted the area from Bay to State streets and Abercorn to West Broad streets. Edison Electric received River to Broughton Streets and Montgomery to Lincoln Streets. They were ordered to share poles whenever possible. This view of Liberty Street shows tracks and poles.

GEO. J. BALDWIN, PRESIDENT, A. L. DRUM, RESIDENT MANAGER. A. MINIS, SECRETARY.
G. E. TRIPP, VICE-PRESIDENT. T. P KECK, SUPERINTENDENT. W. CAMERON FORBES, TREASURER.
STONE & WEBSTER, CONSULTING ENGINEERS.

EDISON ELECTRIC ILLUMINATING COMPANY OF SAVANNAH.

Electric Light, Heat and Power.

New Enclosed Arc Lights Recently Introduced for Inside Lighting.

A Light Clear as Crystal.

Cheap, Ornamental and Cool.

FOR SALE.

500-Volt Motors, all sizes, as good as new.

VERY LOW RATES FOR POWER FOR MOTORS.

CITIZENS BANK BUILDING,

FIFTH FLOOR.

By the spring of 1899, having come to the conclusion that competition was mutually disadvantageous, the two companies decided to merge into the Edison Electric Illuminating Company of Savannah. This is the advertisement that ran in the 1901 *City Directory*.

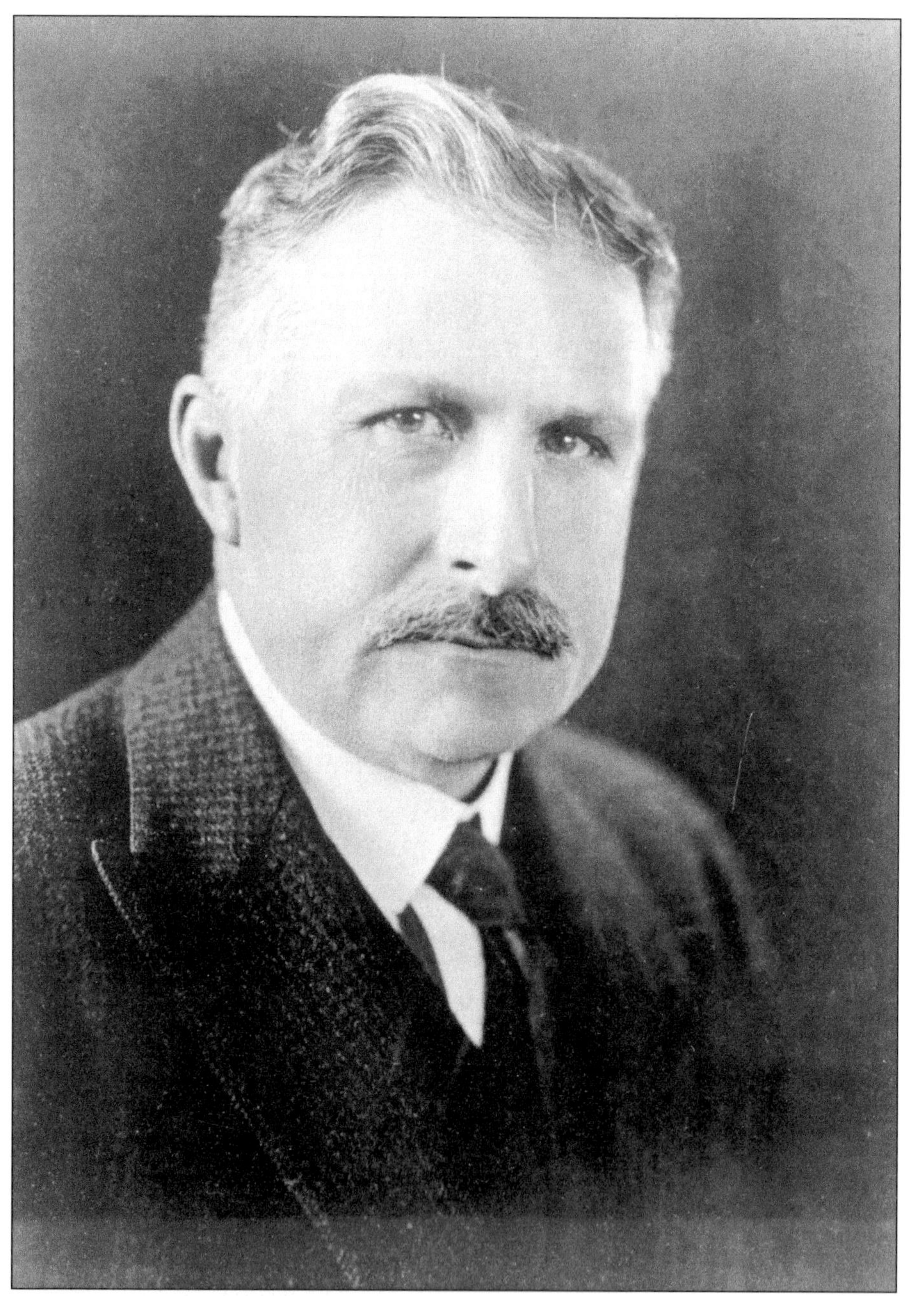

The Secretary of State granted a certificate of incorporation to SEC on December 27, 1901. The company was to build, own, and operate street railroads in Chatham County. It was permitted to run freight or parcel cars and to own and operate electric power plants. Incorporators were George J. Baldwin (pictured above), W.M. Mackall Jr., J.R. Anderson, Abram Minis, W.V. Davis, A. Leopold Alexander, C.B. Kidder, L.H. Baggs, and H.L. Purse.

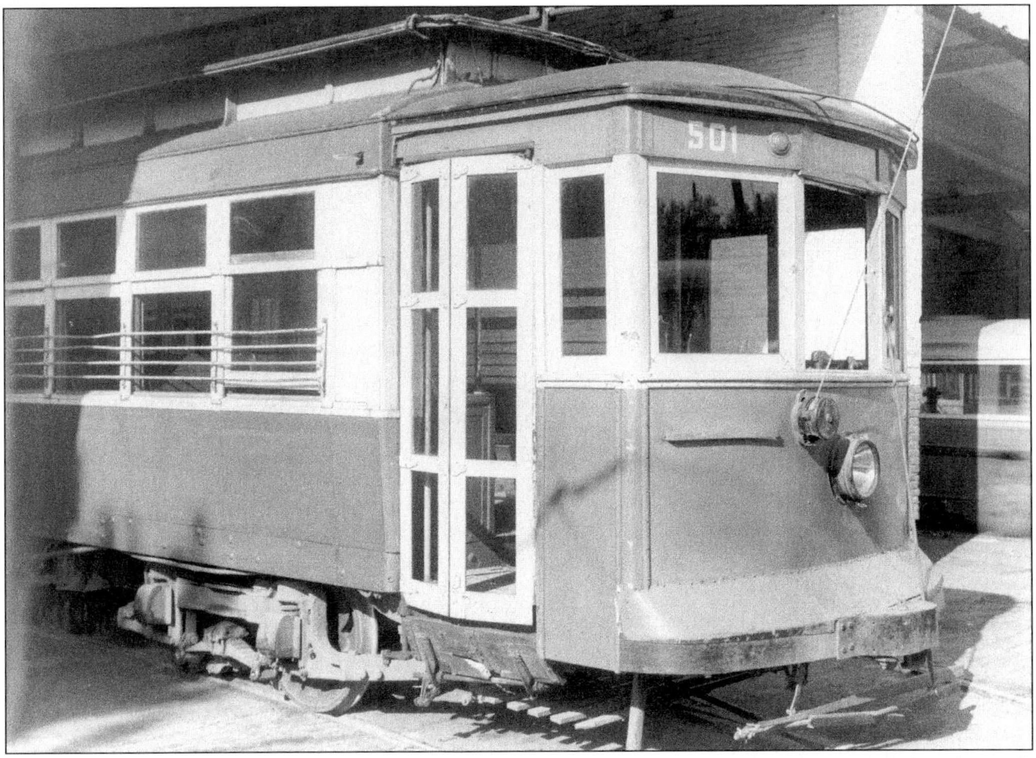

The stockholders of SEC were presented with an offer on January 15, 1902. Through the offer, SEC bought from George and Henry Parsons and J.H. Fall three streetcar lines, the S.T. & I., the S. & I., and the C. & S., as well as the property and franchises of Edison Electric Illuminating.

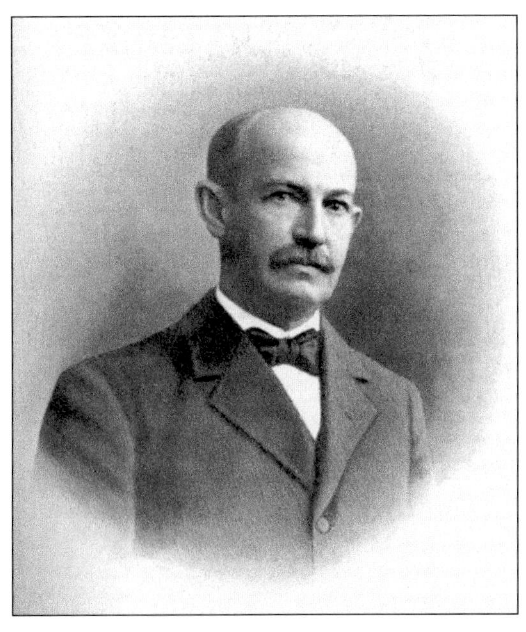

Savannah Lighting Company received a franchise for an electric light and power business in 1905. Savannah Power Company was granted its charter in 1912. Incorporators included G.J. Baldwin, Jacob Paulson, John A.G. Carson (pictured at right), and Bierne Gordon. In 1918, the Chatham County Traction Company received its charter to run electric streetcars to Port Wentworth. SEC leased the line, and, in 1928, SEPCO bought the line outright.

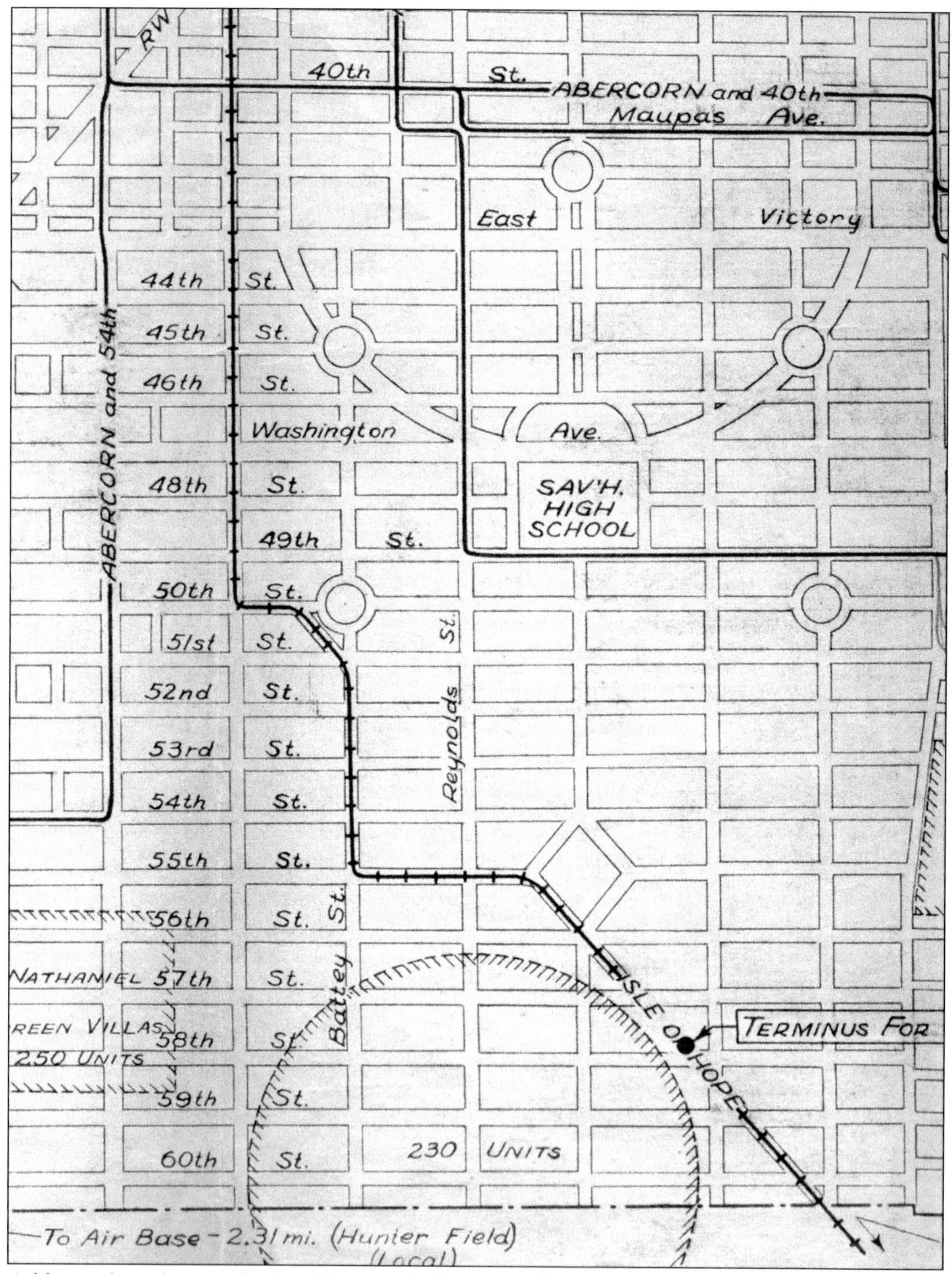

Additional tracks were laid to Forty-sixth Street, and in November of 1917, the tracks were extended again.

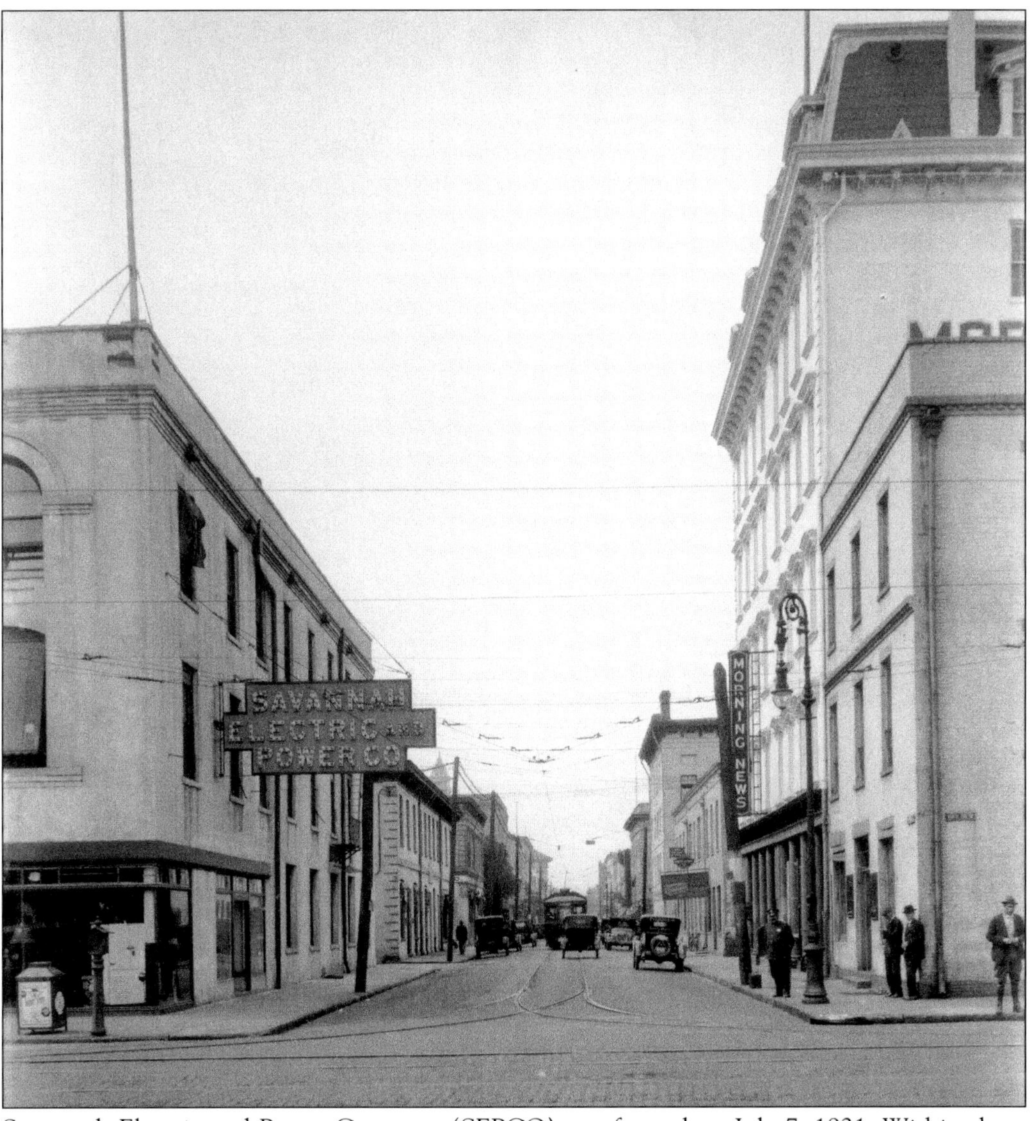

Savannah Electric and Power Company (SEPCO) was formed on July 7, 1921. Within three months, it received an offer to buy SEC and Chatham County Traction. With the acceptance of this offer, SEPCO became Savannah's primary source for streetcar service and electrical power. Savannah Lighting Company would be purchased in 1923. This is the intersection of Bay and Whitaker Streets in 1930.

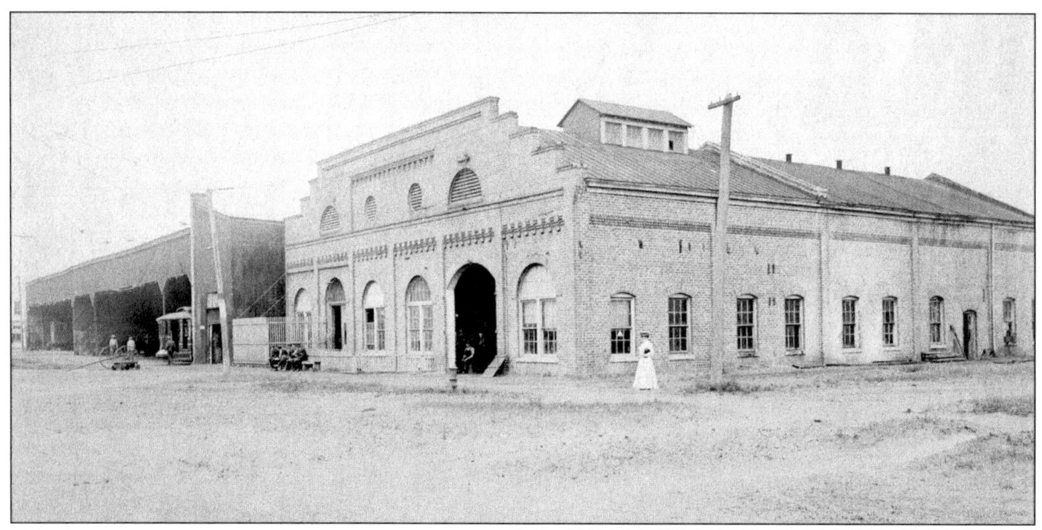

SEPCO's transportation department managed the streetcar lines. The top photograph, taken in 1912, shows SEPCO car barns on Gwinnett Street at Ott. Below is a photograph of the powerhouse near the Savannah River.

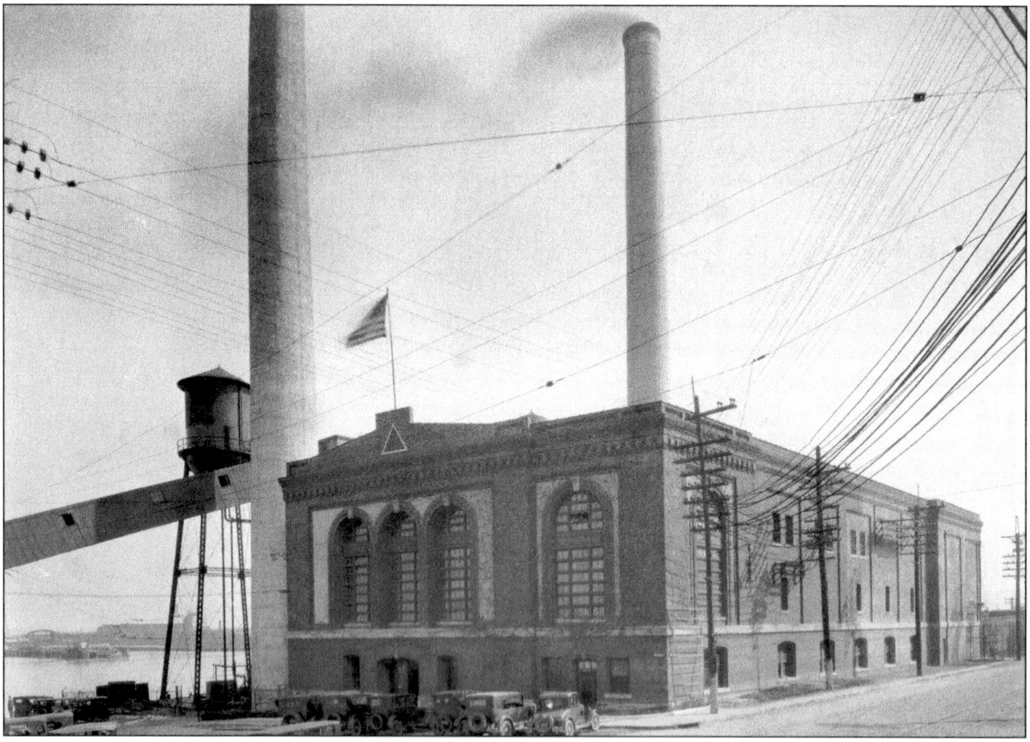

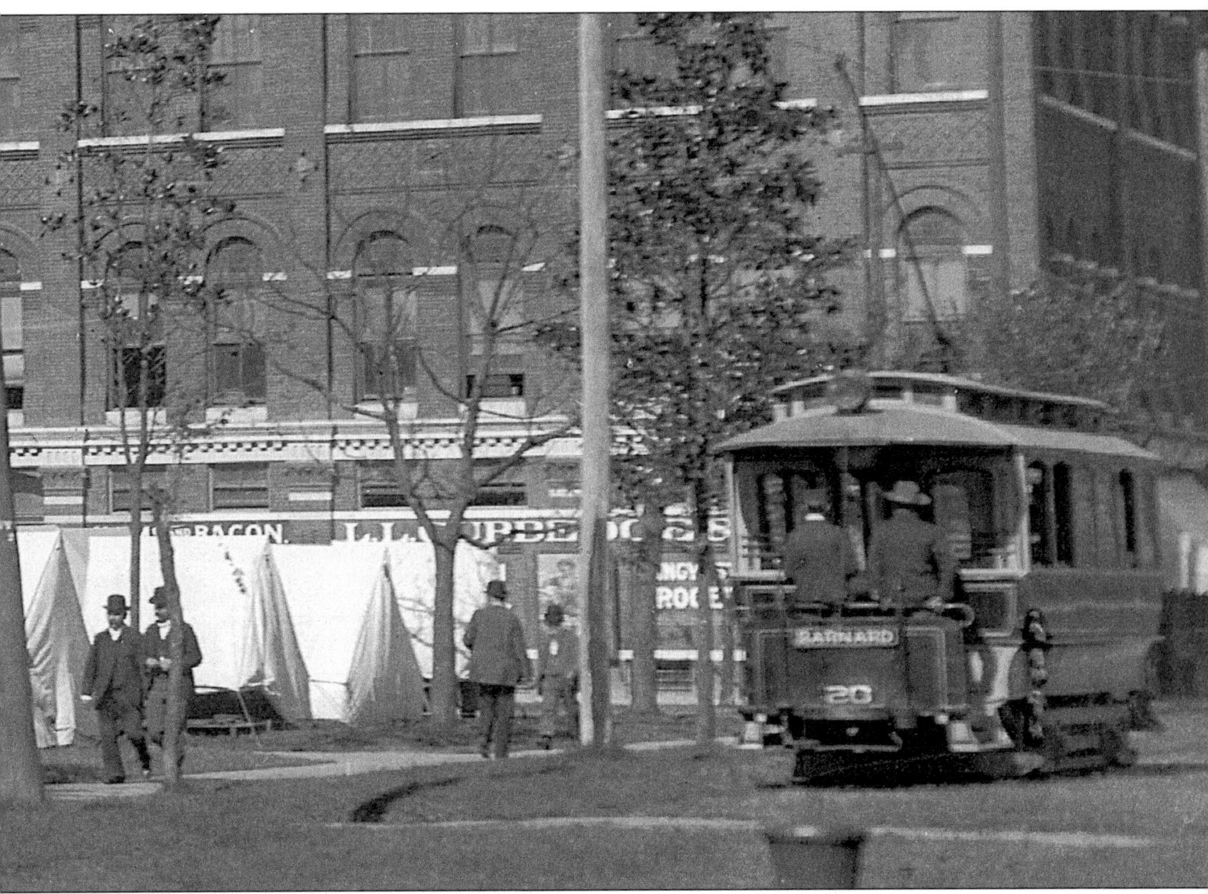

The *American Journal of Commerce* commented in 1903 that "Savannah has one of the most modern and thoroughly equipped electric street railway systems in the South." All sections of the city were connected, and lines operated to the suburban communities, with a total of 54 miles of tracks.

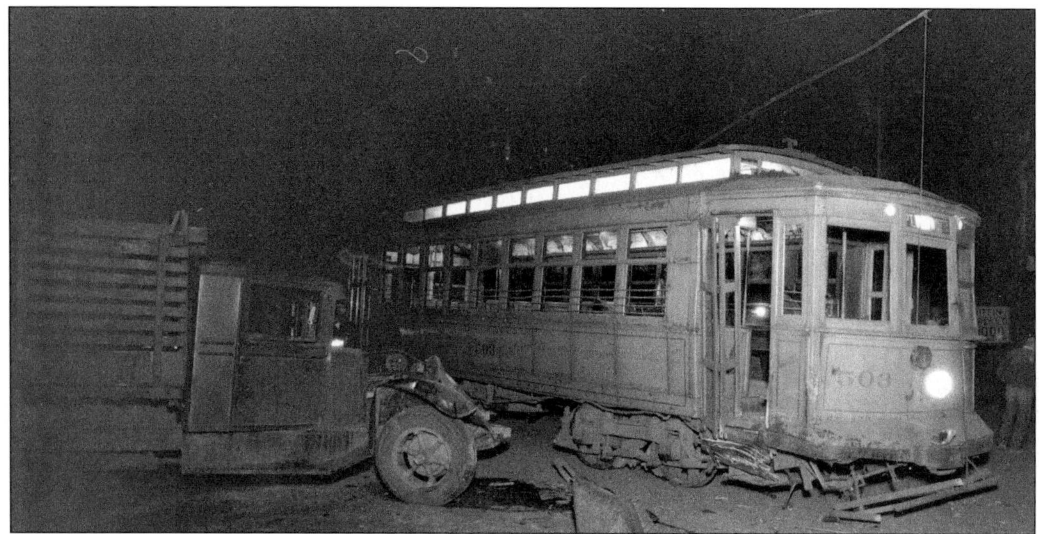

This photograph, taken at the intersection of West Boundary Street and Louisville Road, shows the aftermath of a collision between car #503 and a truck. The first streetcar conductors dealt with horses who bolted, collapsed, and sometimes, died. Heat-related injuries and death were not unheard of in the summertime. Later, conductors had different sorts of challenges as personal automobiles became more common.

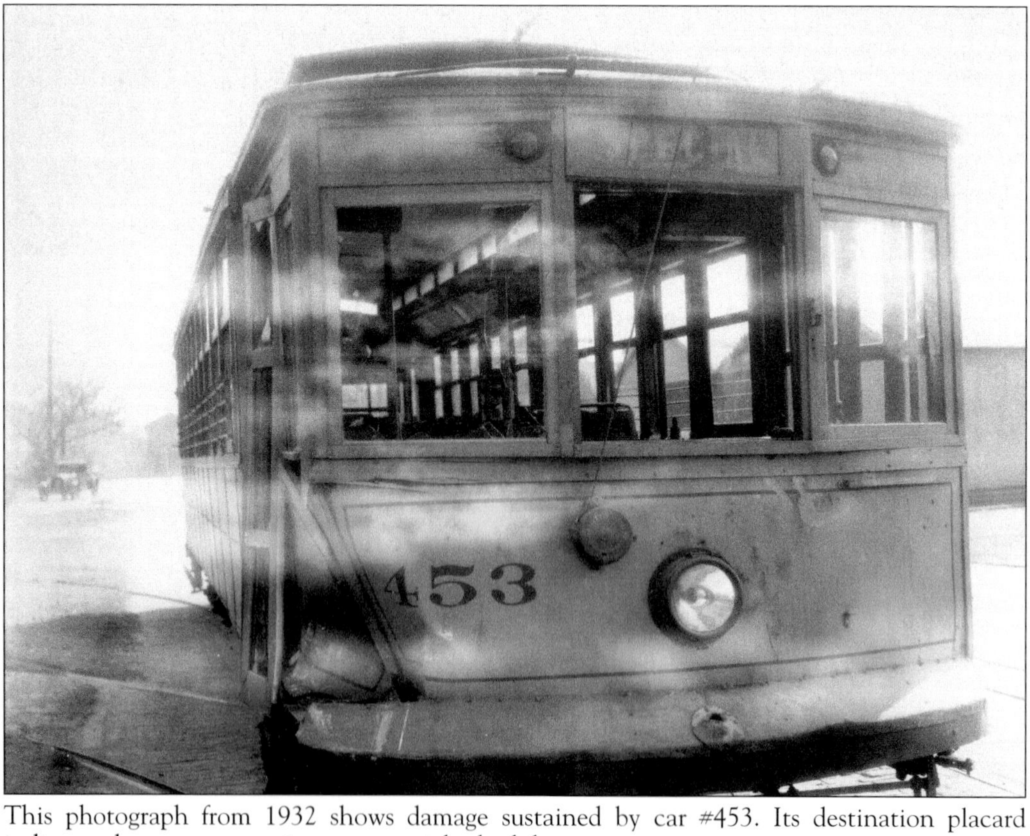

This photograph from 1932 shows damage sustained by car #453. Its destination placard indicates the car was running on a special schedule.

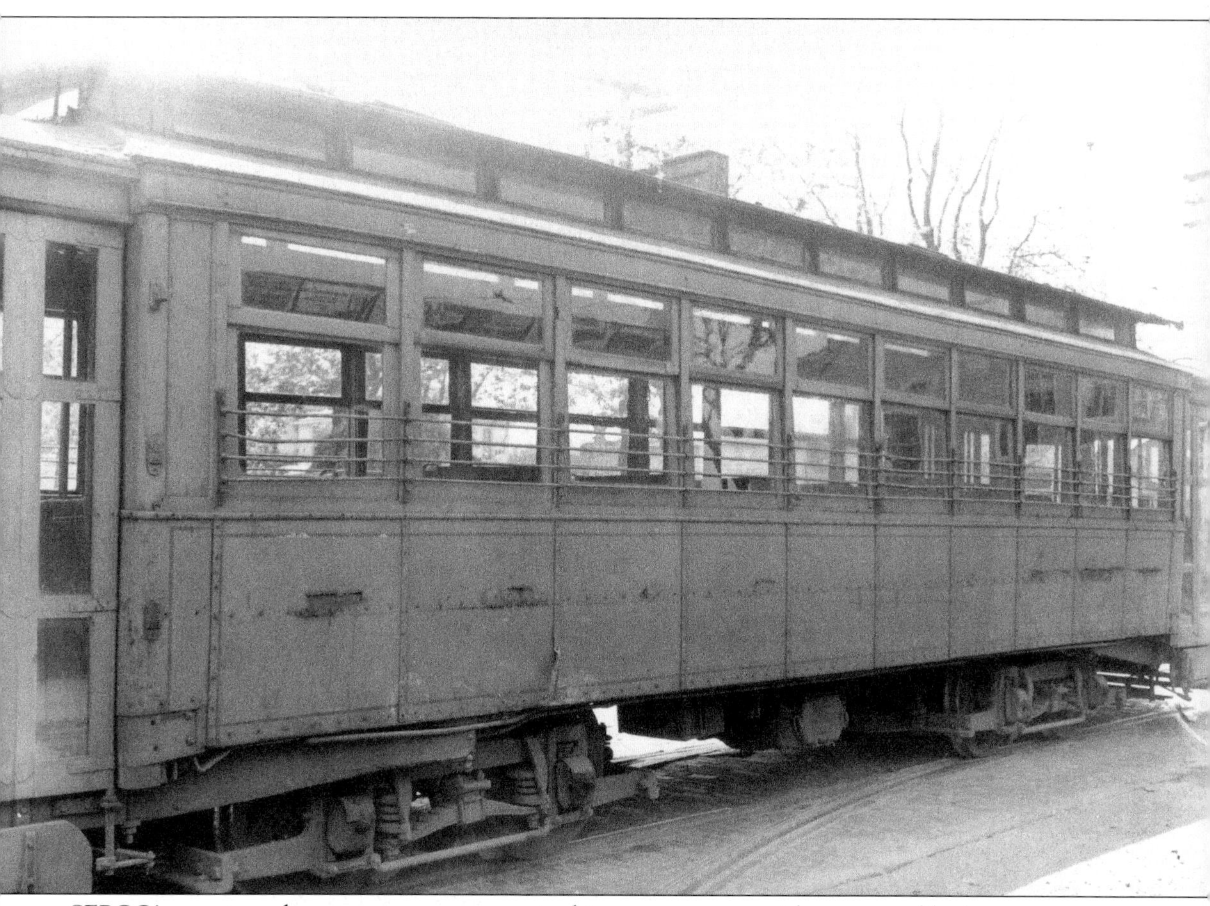

SEPCO's streetcar department was reorganized in response to accidents caused by human error and faulty equipment.

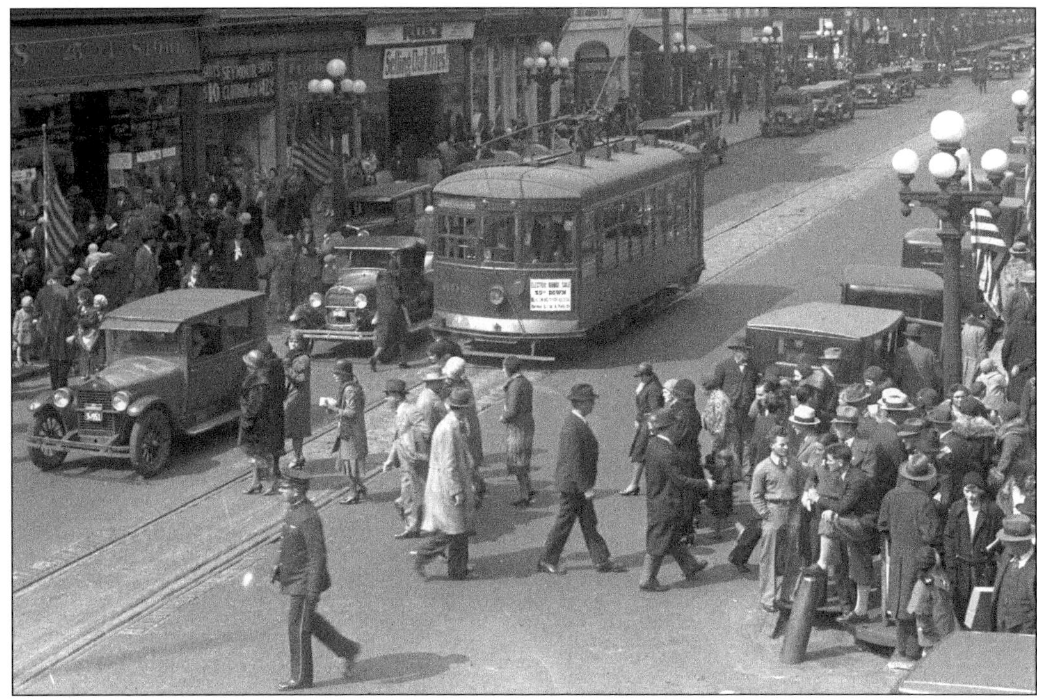

Thirty new cars were ordered by SEPCO. Each car could be operated by a single person and was considered safer than the older cars. The company invited the mayor and city council members for a tour of the power plant and served them lunch in the boiler room. The lunch was well received. Test drives of the new cars were given, and the mayor was offered a chance to operate the car.

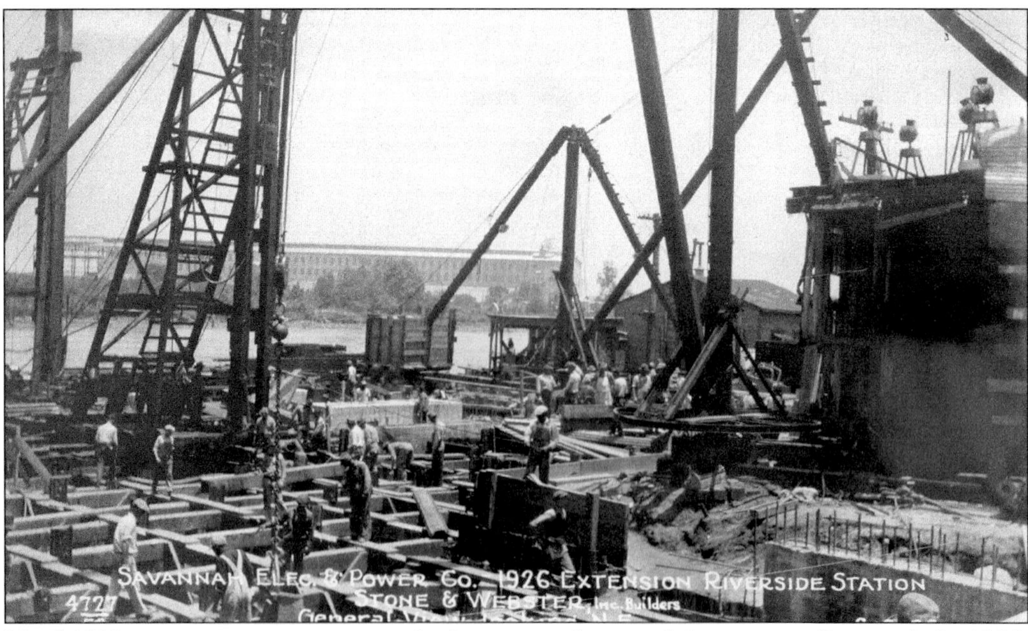

Until 1921, streetcar companies were the largest purchasers of electricity in Savannah. In 1926, SEPCO enlarged its Riverside Plant.

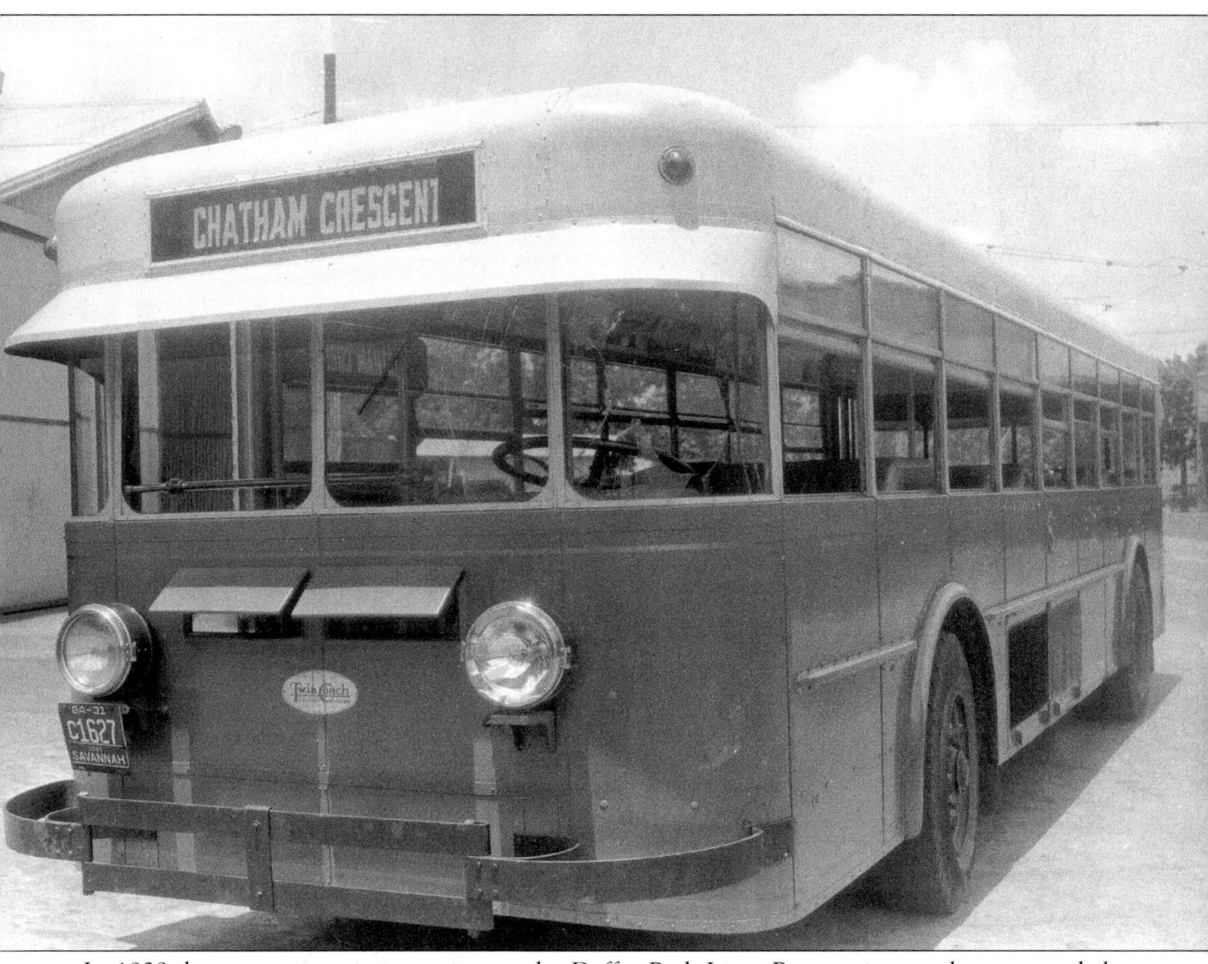

In 1929, buses were put into service on the Daffin Park Line. Bus service was later expanded down the Habersham Street Line and to Chatham Crescent.

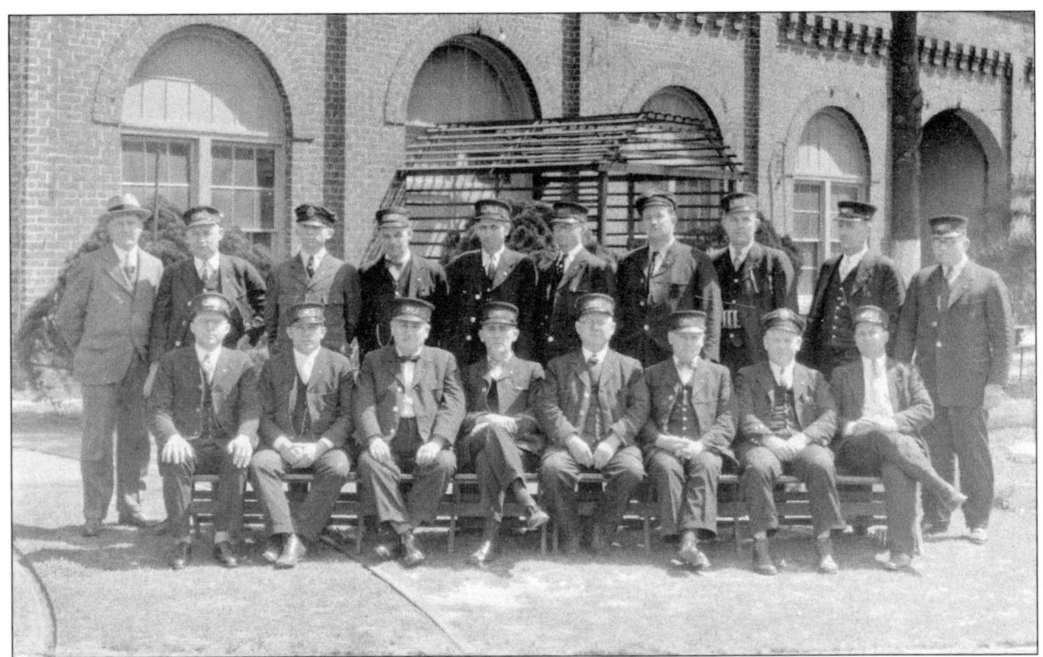

Awards were given to conductors with excellent safety records. A gold star was given for 12 months without an accident, and a silver star was given for 6 months. Most of these conductors are wearing their stars on their lapels.

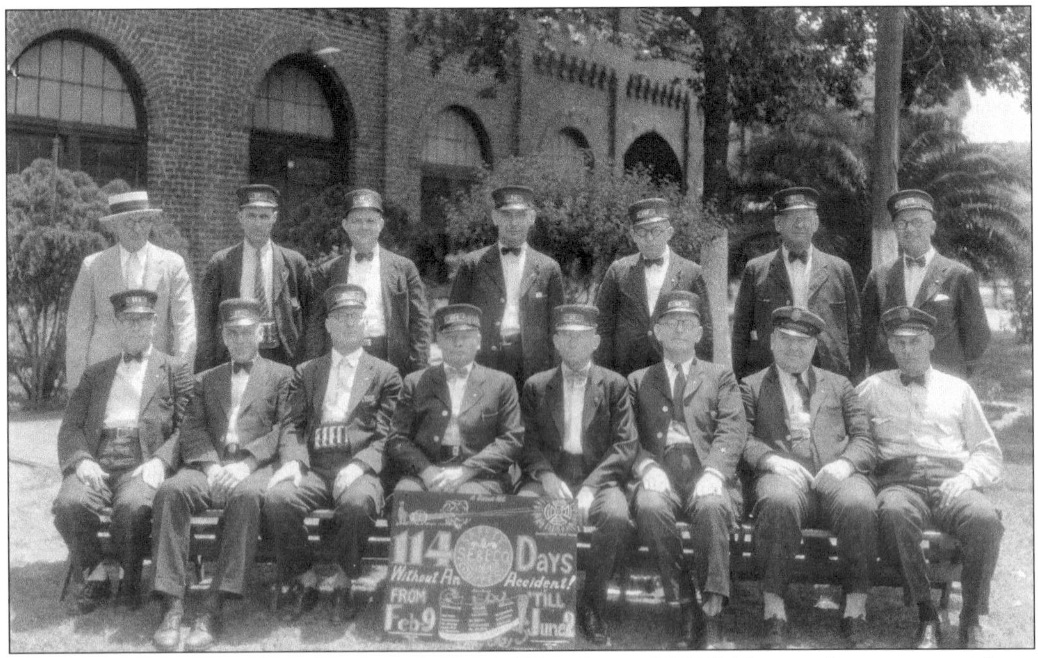

In 1938, SEPCO posted a safety record of 143,381 miles and 12,704 hours of operation without an accident. SEPCO won a nationwide safety award given by the National Safety Council. In 1945, a certificate for honorable mention was given by the American Transit Authority, an organization representing 90% of the industry.

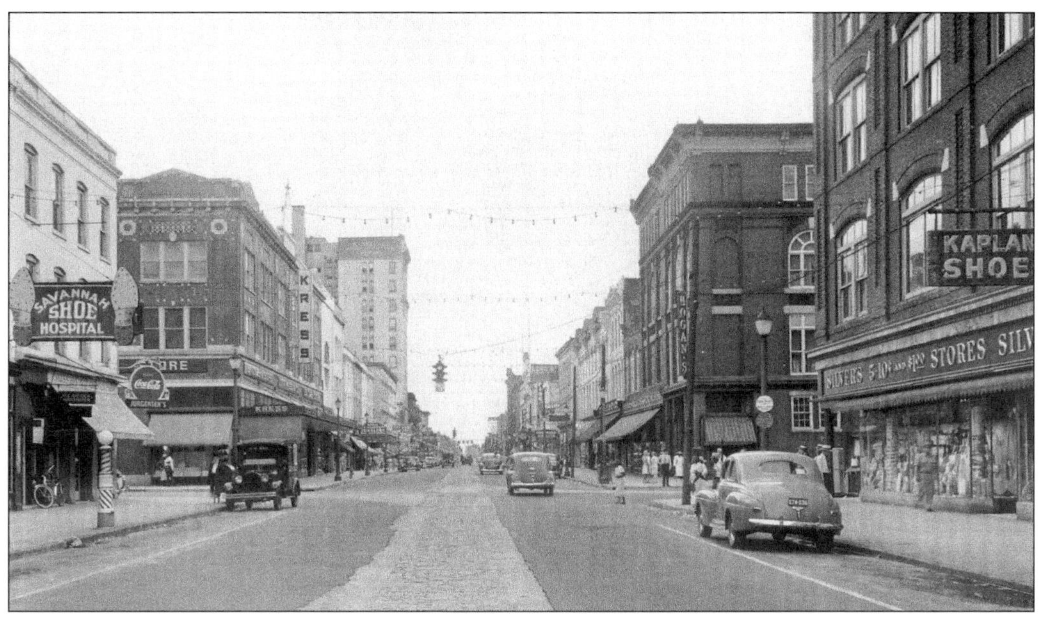

During the Depression, patronage of the streetcars was reduced dramatically, and most of the trolley system was dismantled. By 1945, tracks in the most heavily traveled roads were removed. Nine new buses replaced eight streetcars. Lines removed included the A. & B. Belt Line, the E. & N. Belt Line, Chatham Crescent, Parkside, and steamship terminal.

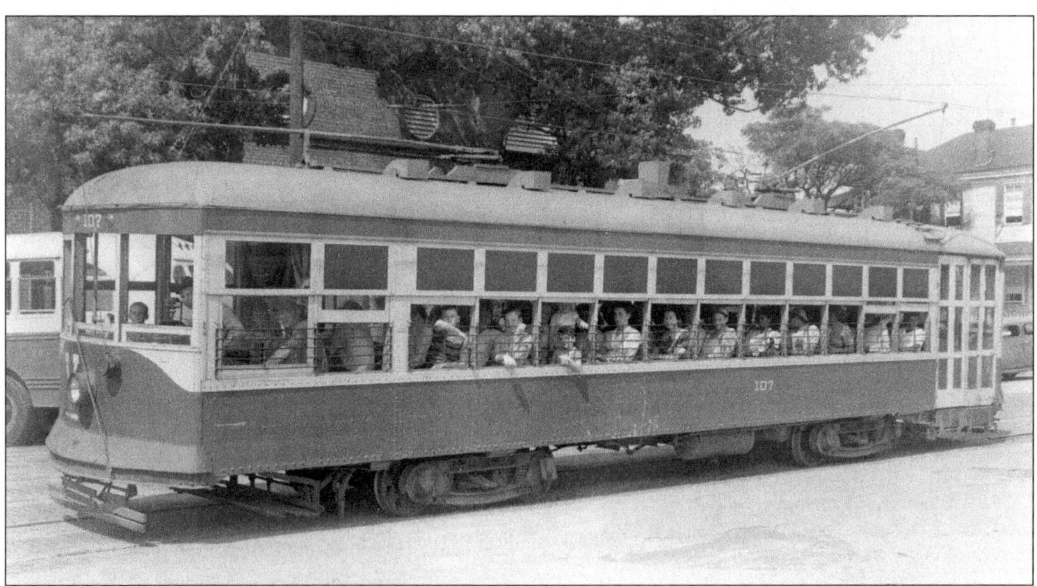

In December of 1945, the transportation division of SEPCO was sold to Savannah Transit Company, a newly formed company that proceeded to phase out streetcars in favor of buses. Of the approximately 85 miles of service, only 20 were run by streetcars.

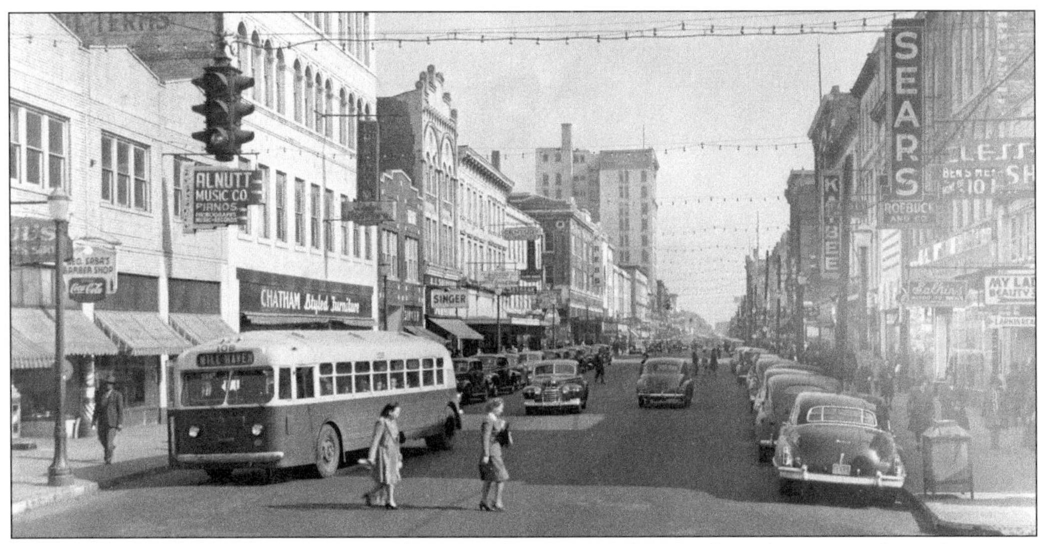

The demise of streetcar service in Chatham County can be attributed to a number of reasons, including the growing popularity and availability of personal automobiles.

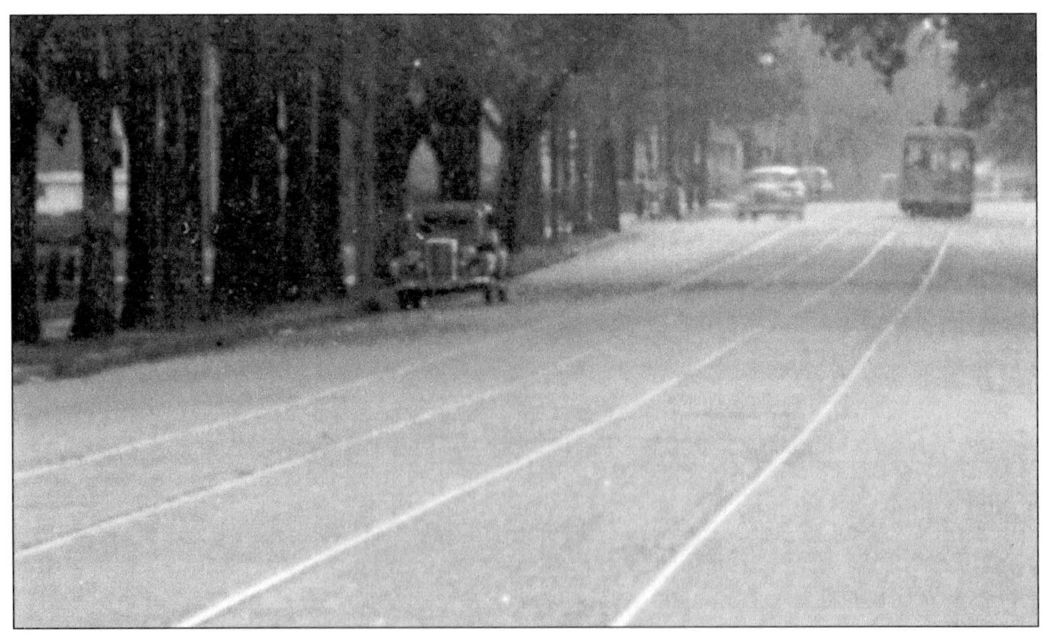

The last streetcar trip to Thunderbolt took place on August 21, 1946. Four days later, at midnight, a Habersham line car left the intersection of Broughton and Abercorn Streets on its last trip. Motorman Luther M. Page, a 35-year veteran, operated the controls. With its return from Fifty-eighth Street, the car made its final run and closed a chapter in Chatham County transportation history.

INDEX

"A.L. Hartridge" Locomotive 26, 57
"Claghorn" Locomotive 57
"Rauers" Locomotive 57
Abrahams, Edmund H. 117
Alexander, A. Leopold 114
Anderson, Edward C. 9
Anderson, George W. 21
Anderson, Jefferson Randolph 63, 81, 114
Ardsley Park 85, 87–88
Atlantic and Gulf Railroad Company 19, 22
Atlantic Coast Line 86
Avondale Rifle Range 35
Baggs, L.H. 114
Baldwin, George J. 112, 114, 115
Bannon Lodge 41
Bannon, Anna M. 41
Barbee Family 49
Barbee, Alexander M. 48
Barbee, William M. 48
Barnard & Anderson Street Railroad 21–25
Beaulieu 7, 10, 15
Belt Line 29, 58, 60, 62, 64, 67, 69, 72
Bethesda Home For Boys 10, 51
Bloodworth, F.D. 67
Blun, H., Jr. 23
Bonaventure Cemetery 10, 17, 20, 35, 36
Brush Electric Light and Power Company 108, 111, 112
Bryan, J.S. 33
Burnside Island 14
Carson, John A.G. 33, 115
Carson, Luke 72
Catholic Cemetery 10, 17, 32
Cedar Hammock 25
Central of Georgia Railroad Company 11, 19, 22, 29, 32, 37, 53, 92
Charlton, Walter G. 63
Chatham Artillery 96–97
Chatham County Traction Company 106–107, 115, 117
Chatham Crescent 85, 87–89 123, 125
Chatham Land and Hotel Company 87
City and Suburban Improvement Company 84
City and Suburban Railway Company 25–26, 30, 47, 52, 53, 57, 59, 60, 70, 72–74, 80, 105, 107, 115
City Market 15, 21, 22, 25, 69, 71, 82
Claghorn, R.S. 70
Coast Line 17, 18, 20, 21, 24, 27–28, 32, 48, 59, 60, 72–73, 83
Collins, Jacob S. 63, 71–72, 81
Collinsville 71, 82
Cooper, William G. 70
Cunningham, C. 33
Cunningham, Henry C. 30, 33
Daffin Park 100–101, 123
Daffin, P.D. 67
Davis, W.V. 114
DeSoto Hotel 26
Dillon, David R. 11
Dixon, M.W. 67
Dorsett, Charles H. 30, 58, 68, 84
Doyle, Capt. Michael J. 41
Edison Electric Company 107, 112
Edison Electric Illuminating Company 113, 115
Electric Railway Company 58, 63, 69, 72–74
Enterprise Railroad 64, 104
Estill, Col. John Holbrook 24, 25, 30, 54, 58, 108
Fall, J.H. 26, 74, 115
Ferrill, Benjamin B. 21
Fetzer, Robert C. 23
Frank Leslie's Illustrated Newspaper 12
Georgia State Industrial College 43
Girard, Edward H. 92
Gordon, Bierne 115
Gordonston 35
Grauel, Albertine 28
Grauel, Lewis 28
Hardee, Maj. Charles S.H. 46
Hardee, N.A. 33
Hartridge, A.L. 25, 70
Hartridge, Julian 21
Haywood, Alfred 16, 21

Hicks, Robert M. 63, 81
Hodgson, William B. 2
Hogg, John B. 18
Isle of Hope 7, 10–11, 13, 15, 21, 25, 37, 43, 46–49, 58, 82
J.W. Fellows and Co. 26
Jasper Spring 66
Johnston, J.H. 72
Jones, Bobby 34
Karow, Edward 33, 67
Kennebunk, Maine 8
Kidder, C.B. 114
Koch, Augustus 79
Laurel Grove Cemetery 19, 21–22, 25, 79, 82, 102, 108
Lester, D.B. 67
Liberty Street Line 25, 26
Lincoln Park 66
Logan, Hugh 63, 81
Mackall, William M., Jr. 63, 114,
Maggioni Shrimp Factory 42
Marshall House 21
Maupas Dairy 29
May, Michael M. 38
McCauley, W.F. 63, 81
Merchants and Mechanics Land Company 58
Mill Haven Line 106
Minis, Abram 114
Montgomery 7, 10–11, 14–15, 19, 21, 25, 39, 52, 57, 67
Morning News 55, 60, 62, 85
Morse, James O. 102
Moses, Cornelius F. 33
Myers, Herman 74, 95
Nugent, Thomas 63, 81
Ocean Steamship Co. 29
Ogeechee Canal 29
Oglethorpe, Gen. James E. 75
Olmstead, Col. Charles H. 14, 68, 70, 84
Olmstead, Florence 14
Page, Luther M. 126
Parsons, George 7, 60, 72–74, 115
Parsons, Henry 72, 115
Paulson, Jacob 81, 115
People's Line 71, 82
Philadelphia 23
Port Wentworth 106, 115
Purse, Daniel Gugel 25, 84, 108
Purse, H.L. 114
Rauers, Jacob 25
Regatta Association of the State of Georgia 39
Reitz, C.A. 67
Rhea, Isaac C. 58, 60
Riesling's Gardens 29
Rogers, O.T. 67
Rose Dhu 58, 67
Rowland, J. 72
Sanberg, Charles E. 23
Sand Fly 10, 59, 80
Saussy, C.S. 33
Savannah, Florida and Western Railroad Company 25, 29, 60, 63, 69, 85
Savannah and Isle of Hope Railroad 58, 67, 85, 107, 115
Savannah & Thunderbolt Railway 15, 53
Savannah and Tybee Railway 53
Savannah Arts Academy 89
Savannah Coliseum 36
Savannah *Daily Herald* 7
Savannah Electric and Power Company 38, 107, 115, 117–118, 121–122, 124–125
Savannah Electric Company 8, 16, 81, 91, 106–107, 114–115, 117
Savannah Golf Club 32
Savannah Lighting Company 107, 117
Savannah *Morning News* 7, 14, 17, 27, 79, 83, 85
Savannah Power Company 115, 117
Savannah Real Estate, Loan and Building Company 81
Savannah, Skidaway & Seaboard Railroad Co. 7, 9, 11, 14–15, 17–19, 21, 24–25, 46–47, 52, 82, 103
Savannah State University 43
Savannah Street and Rural Resort Railroad Company 29, 30, 72
Savannah Street Railroad 72
Savannah Transit Co. 125
Savannah Volunteer Guards 35
Savannah Yacht Club 37, 39, 46
Savannah, Thunderbolt and Isle of Hope Railroad 72, 74, 107, 115
Schley, Dr. J. M. 46
Schley, John 14
Schley, Julian 70
Schuetzen Park 20
Schwarz's Place 29
Screven, Thomas F. 54
Seiler's Concordia Park 29
Shaw, J.C. 30
Smart, Horace P. 30
Southover Land & Improvement Company 68
Southville 29
Springfield Plantation 102
Stone, Charles 112
Stone and Webster 112
Suburban and West End Railway 66, 74
Ten Broeck Race Course 66, 104
Thomas, Edward J. 25, 72, 83
Thomasville 83
Thunderbolt 7, 10, 15, 17, 27, 32, 35, 37–39, 41–44, 58–59, 66–67 104, 126
Tilton, N.O. 54
Twickenham Terrace 35, 104
Tybee Island 26, 53
Tybee Improvement Co. 54
Union Station 92–93
Vernon Park Railway 67
Vernon River 11
Vernonberg 67, 104
Walker, George 108
Warsaw Sound 27
Webster, Edwin 112
Whatley, Joseph L. 68
White Bluff 7, 10–11, 19, 58, 67
Whitefield, Rev. George 51
Whitmarsh Island 17
Wilkinson, W.K. 63, 81
Wilmington Island 17, 39, 66
Wilmington Railroad Co. 17